Navigating Youth, Generating Adulthood
Social Becoming in an African Context

Edited by
Catrine Christiansen, Mats Utas and Henrik E. Vigh

NORDISKA AFRIKAINSTITUTET, UPPSALA 2006

Indexing terms:

Youth
Adolescents
Children
Social environment
Living conditions
Human relations
Social and cultural anthropology
Case studies
Africa

Language checking: Elaine Almén

Cover photo: "Sierra Leonean musician 2 Jay" by Mats Utas

ISBN 91-7106-578-4

Printed in Sweden by Elanders Gotab AB, Stockholm 2006

Contents

Acknowledgements

This book is the result of the *Nordic workshop on researching children and youth in Africa* that we organised at the Nordic Africa Institute in May 2004. The workshop aimed at gathering scholars from the social sciences who are active in the Nordic countries and who carry out research on children and youth in Africa. 25 scholars, symptomatically many of them young and upcoming, presented papers during the three-day workshop in Uppsala and new, fresh, perspectives on children and youth emerged. The conference was funded by the Nordic Africa Institute, and we are in particular grateful to Lennart Wohlgemuth who, when the number of participants exceeded expectations, responded swiftly by allocating additional funding. We also wish to thank Karolina Winbo who administered the event in such an effective and pleasant way.

We would like to dedicate this volume to Björn Lindgren, workshop participant and colleague at the Nordic Africa Institute, who after a short period of illness passed away in November 2004. His warmth and positive attitude will not be forgotten.

Freetown and Copenhagen, March 2006

Mats Utas, Henrik E. Vigh and Catrine Christiansen

YOUTH(E)SCAPES

Navigating Youth, Generating Adulthood

Catrine Christiansen, Mats Utas and Henrik E. Vigh

This book is about contemporary African youth. It is about a generation of people who have been born into social environments in which their possibilities of living decent lives are negligible and in which many have found themselves stuck in positions of inadequate life chances and bleak prospects (Dahrendorf 1979), in 'youthscapes' (cf. Maira and Soep 2004) built on and saturated by prolonged processes of destruction, disease and decline. Since the early 1970s many African youths have aspired to come of age in often volatile and precarious circumstances and have had to shape their lives and strategies accordingly in their attempt to generate meaningful lives for themselves.

One of the primary goals of this book is to present a handful of detailed ethnographic descriptions of these 'youthscapes' in order to further our knowledge of the social possibilities, experiences and fantasies of youth in Africa. Building on extensive fieldwork with children and youth in Africa all the contributions to the book demonstrate how the extended case method is able to illustrate and analyse both young people's daily life and dreams as well as the social, economic and political environments they are set in. However, although in vogue, the pictures that the metaphor of 'scapes' conveys – as a solid surface of enactment – do not always fit the often volatile or fluid political structurations, communities and societies within which we are researching youth on the African continent. The bracketed 'E' in the title of this introductory chapter thus hints at the second primary focus of the book, namely the way that young people move and shape the social environments in which their lives are set. It refers to the way young people in Africa reconfigure "geographies of exclusion and inclusion" (De Boeck and Honwana 2005:1), the way they seek to escape confining structures and navigate economic, social and political turmoil (Vigh 2003; 2006).

Context and constitution

A look back at on this century's last few decades makes it clear that old age was "discovered" only in recent years (…) it certainly demanded some redefinition when an ever-increasing number of old people were found (and found themselves) to represent a mass of elderlies rather than an elite off elders. Before that, however, we had come at last to acknowledge adulthood as a developmental and conflictual phase in its own right, rather than merely the mature end of all development (…) before that (and then only in the sixties, a period of national identity crisis dramatically reflected in the public behaviour of our youth), we had learned to pay full attention to the adolescent identity crisis as central to the developmental dynamics of the life cycle (Erikson 1959). And as pointed out, it had not been before the mid-century that the child's "healthy personality" and all the infantile stages discovered only in this century really became the centre of systematic national attention. (Erikson 1994:9)

Erikson's quote above begs the question: 'What kind of socio-generational category will become dominant next?' Contrary to his intention to describe the revealing of innate psycho-social stages of development the quote directs our attention to the fact that youth – and generational categories in general – are brought to the fore not necessarily only by psychological or biological processes but rather by the specific circumstances that generate and emphasise one generational category over another.

Though all too many anthropological, sociological and psychological studies have granted the concept of youth an *a priori* meaning, seeing it as a developmental or life stage, the transition from childhood to adulthood should not be considered fixed and stable. Generational categories will for most of us – layman and researcher alike – seem self-evident, but rather than being given naturally their meanings and manifestations arise in relation to specific social processes, cultural understandings and historical influences (cf. Mannheim 1952). Youth is differently constituted and configured in different times and places. It may be an influential social category in one context, a marginal one in another and obsolete in a third. Neither its existence nor meaning should be taken for granted (Bucholtz 2002:525–528, Waage, this volume: chapter 2). Rather than pointing our attention to generational categories, such as youth, as cross-cultural universals, the different chapters within this book illuminate that such concepts and categories are dynamic and contested. The chapters show that these concepts are not naturally given but fraught with dificulties.

Being and becoming

Theoretically our point of departure is that we must understand the constitution and dynamics of youth by positioning it within the social contexts and situations that it is actualised in. People are not passively part of a socio-generational category. Though they may be ascribed a generational position, they seek to inhabit, escape or move within this in meaningful ways. In similar vein, this book focuses on the lives and experiences of young people in Africa – on agents who, willingly or unwillingly, see themselves as belonging to the socio-generational category in question, and the ways in which they seek to shape and unfold their lives in a positive manner. Instead of approaching the concept of youth as either a social or cultural entity in itself, or as a rigid developmental life-stage, our view is that we must investigate both how youth position themselves and are positioned within generational categories if we wish to do the topic justice.

In studying young people we must, in other words, see youth as both social *being* and social *becoming*: as a position in movement (Vigh 2003; 2006). Youth is both a social position which is internally and externally shaped and constructed, as well as part of a larger societal and generational process, a state of becoming. We need thus to look at the ways youth are positioned in society and the ways they seek to position themselves in society, to illuminate the ways the category of youth is socio-politically constructed, as well as the ways young people construct counter-positions and definitions. We therefore advocate a *perspectival dualist analysis* of youth, an analysis which sees the social and experiential aspects of youth as inseparable, paying attention to both the meaning that young people create as well as locating them within the social landscape they seek to move.

Power and positions

> My father, if he wants me to do something, he calls me; 'boy' he says 'go get me this… go do that' and I cannot refuse (…) [but] If I need his help he says to me; 'what, you are an adult now' and he will refuse me. (Ignacio, Bissau)

Generational categories, such as childhood, youth and adulthood, are not neutral or natural but rather part of the struggle for influence and authority within almost every society (cf. Bayart 1993). As the above quote, taken from an interview with a young man from Bissau, Guinea Bissau, demonstrates, social and generational age do not necessarily follow biological time or linear chronology but shift according to socio-cultural contexts and configurations of power and positions. The movement from childhood to adulthood is a movement not just between developmental positions but between positions of power, authority and social worth. People are not just young by biological or developmental default. They are positioned and repositioned within generational categories as well as seeking actively to position themselves within these. Within the same day a person can be positioned as child, youth and adult, depending on the situation and the stakes involved in the relationship. When one starts and stops being young is contextually specific and the generational positions we claim or seek are *not* necessarily identical with the ones we are ascribed, our desired social positions do not necessarily correspond with those offered! To call someone a youth is according to Deborah Durham:

> (…) to position him or her in the terms of a variety of social attributes, includ-
> ing not only age but also independence – dependence, authority, rights, abili-
> ties, knowledge, responsibilities, and so on. But in the pragmatic and political
> processes in which such namings take place, the category itself is reconstructed
> and the attributes repositioned among those involved. (2004:593)

Generational positions, such as youth, are, in other words, intricately tied to social processes, and it is only when we move our focus from the realm of chronology or biology to the sphere of social life that we become able to fully realise the complexity of the position and able to illuminate how it is negotiated and unfolds in relation to dynamics of social interaction. Only then can we see, for example, how young Africans seek to make the best of the meagre life chances and navigate their lives towards better positions and possibilities (Vigh 2003, this volume; Utas 2005b, forthcoming a). It is from the duality of being positioned and seeking their own socio-genera-tional position that youth become an important object of investigation, as a category they are positioned in and through which they seek to position themselves in society, which entails that young people have the capacity to function as *social shifters*[1] that "create the social configurations of their utterance but rely on meanings external to the utterance itself" (Durham 2004:593).

---

1. Drawing on the works of Roland Barthes (1983) and Roman Jakobson (1971).

Youth as lived

Since youth does not exist as a monolithic and singular construction we need, as said, to investigate the possibilities and limitations embedded in local understandings and materialisations of the socio-generational position. The book in front of you is therefore committed to detailed illuminations of youth as lived within an array of different African cultures and societies. It focuses on the efforts that youth put into surviving physically and socially, on their attempts at improving their lives, gaining symbolic and social capital and recognition of social worth (Bourdieu 1986, 1992, 1994; cf. Honnert 2003). Yet it does so without losing focus on the way that definitions of youth are constantly negotiated and adapted to the contexts they are actualised and generated within. Looking through this book the reader will thus encounter a myriad of refractions and images of youth across the African continent. One will be led through different descriptions and discussions of youth ranging from ambiguities of modernity, morality, and gender relations in popular music among Luo youth in Kenya (see Prince, chapter 4 this volume), to the lives of young women employed in the textile trade in Lesotho (see Boehm, chapter 5 this volume), to stories of young men trying desperately to escape the position of youth in their attempt to achieve adulthood (see Finnström, chapter 7 this volume; Lovell, chapter 8 this volume; Vigh, chapter 1 this volume, Waage, chapter 2 this volume). The descriptions and discussions of young people's lives thus illuminate such different experiences of youth as one depicting youth as a willingly sought after social position and another depicting youth as a period of life to be over and done with, as it is a time of heightened social marginalisation.

However, instead of being contradictory analyses, the different perspectives reflect the various ways youth is lived. They reflect the fact that youth is inseparably connected to issues of power, authority and, not least, gender, and that there are, of course, negative and positive sides to all social positions – generational or otherwise. Whether youth is strived for as a time of freedom and enjoyment or shunned as a time of dependence and marginalisation, depends not only on cultural factors but equally on the possibilities and life chances open to the youths in question. Descriptions of marginal and impecunious youth in the North are as such reminiscent of many of our descriptions of impoverished youth in the South (Utas 2003), and we should perhaps start paying more attention to levels of affluence and social possibilities as constitutive factors for local construction and valuation of youth. Yet if youth is contextually defined and positioned, dependent on levels of affluence and structurations of power as well as being able to signify positions of very different social worth and possibilities, the question still beckons; what is it exactly we are studying when studying youth?

Life course and life-stage

Within the social and cultural sciences the question has traditionally been answered by a psychologically developmental perspective in which the concept of youth is generally interchanged with the concept of adolescence and defined in relation to increasing hormone levels, physical and psychological maturation (Hall 1905, Erikson 1965). "The adolescent mind is essentially the mind of a *moratorium*, a psychological stage between childhood and adulthood," Erikson says (1965:254, italics in original). According to Erikson youth is a time of life in which one defines and plays with the opportunities and possibilities of social roles in constructing one's adult identity (ibid: chapter 7). Yet, although most of us will agree that the period of adolescence, defined in relation to psycho-somatic terms, is a biological fact, there is no universal physically or psychologically defined threshold over which one passes from one phase to another. In fact, trying to define such a threshold, seems counter-productive as it blinds us to the fact that people move and manipulate the category according to the situation they are in, to the fact that youth is differently defined and lived in different social and cultural contexts (see Mead 1969), and not least to the fact that people can move – and are moved – back and forth between different generational positions.

The common anthropological version of the above definition of youth as a developmental phase in a life course is anchored in the idea of life-stages in which youth is defined in relation to the correspondence between social and physical developmental thresholds (Eisenstadt 1964; Turner 1967; Fortes 1984; Ottenberg 1989). In this perspective young people will classically be seen as young when able to procreate and as adults when actually having procreated and acquired a family (cf. Johnson-Hanks 2002).[2] However, the definition, hinged as it is on a conflation of psychological, physical and social maturation and the idea that lives can be compartmentalised into discrete stages, once again falls short of doing the complexity of youth justice. The developmental or socio-biological understandings of youth are, in themselves, not capable of taking into consideration the man-

---

2. This definition is most often used to describe the social and physical maturation of women rather than men.

ner in which definitions of youth and adulthood are intertwined with issues of power, authority and social worth. They are unable to illuminate the
ways people strive to be included in or escape from the category of youth as
well as the ways they move and are moved within generational categories,
making the movement between generational categories dependent instead
on social, psychological and/or biological maturation. The problem with
the life-stage model is the same as we face when analytically approaching the issue of youth from a developmental, somatic or psychological perspective as we in both cases come to paint a uni-dimensional picture of
our movement within generational categories (ibid). This, however, does
not mean that we should disregard issues of life-stages within the study of
youth (see Barrett 2004). Such ideas are in themselves interesting, as they
have become influential in relation to the life stories and understandings of
the people we research; they have become an emic reality. Yet we should be
careful not to analytically freeze people in categories that they themselves
know or treat as fluid.

Youth culture?

A more recent, and common, perspective has been to focus on youth as
a cultural entity in itself (Hall and Jefferson 1976; Amit-Talai, Wulff et
al. 1995). The last few decades of youth studies within the social sciences
have thus primarily been focussed on *youth culture* (Parsons 1964). That
is, towards researching the ideational systems of meaning and practices
that young people, explicitly or implicitly, create as they interact with other
youth globally and locally. Influenced by the urban sociological studies of
the Chicago School during the first half of the twentieth century, a number
of scholars associated with the Centre for Contemporary Cultural Studies,
also called the Birmingham School, popularised the study of youth as sub-
cultures, thus breaking away from studying youth as a stage in a developmental trajectory and moving towards studying youth in their own right;
as sub-cultures with their own world-views, styles and practices.

The developmental, the life-stage and the sub-cultural perspectives of
youth have all resulted in an array of inspiring work and analytical perspectives. Yet although being influential points of departure within the study
of youth within the social sciences they seem to have divided the waters, as
scholars have engaged themselves in analysing social processes and problems focussing on one or the other. Part of their apparent immutuality
stems from the fact that the approaches paint very different pictures of the

agentive potential and autonomy of youth. The psycho-social and life-stage approaches position youth as an undifferentiated entity locked in a predefined process towards physical, psychological and social maturity, thereby running the risk of portraying youth as necessarily following a 'natural' process of development as their lives are, by their innate psychological and somatic development, being pushed through different life-stages. The consequence of the life-stage perspective is that we gain a picture of youth as having very little agentive capacity to change or move within or between generational categories. The focus on youth culture, on the contrary, can easily paint a picture of youth as an entity, which is socially and culturally detached from the surrounding world. Youth risks, in this perspective, to protrude analytically as an almost autonomous group, capable of constructing worlds of its own and living lives separated from the surrounding society.3

If we look at the two approaches they seem to conjure up a bifurcated view of youth, one perspective – or set of perspectives – emphasising dimensions of power, generations and social processes contra a more semiotic and experience-near focus on community, meaning and discourse. However, making sense of the action of young people entails balancing our analysis between the ways young people see and interpret the world and the ways they are positioned in it as part of families and societies. It entails having an eye towards both the experiential and phenomenological aspect of youth, as well as towards the political and sociological, illuminating how youth are able to move, what they seek to move towards and the ways external forces seek to shape their movements. Rather than seeing these differences as insurmountable, we should see them as apt descriptions of the two different sides of our social existence. Focussing on the intersection between agency and social forces we see how youth actually navigate their lives through social environments. The phenomenological and social perspectives are mutually fundamental in anthropological analysis and we must thus look at not just the ways that youth see their world as topographies of value and recognition, but equally how the surrounding world sees the youth in question and the relationship between the two.

---

3. A perspective most noticeable in the work of James Coleman who argues that there exist distinct teenage societies, as parallel societies in our midst (1961).

Global African childhood and youth

Though the empirical focus of the book is on youth in Africa we nonetheless agree with Sharon Stephens that constructions of youth (as well as childhood) take place in complex processes of globalisation (Stephens 1995). The very concepts are formed and reformed, filled with new meanings and capacities, in relation to other cultures and social complexes worldwide.

During the past two decades young people in Africa have noticeably become a matter of global concern. The last few decades of mediatized focus on the effect of famine, conflict and disease on children and youth, have entailed an increasing research and developmental attentiveness to the social category. In post-war Sierra Leone, for example, youth rapidly emerged as an aid taker category: for instance in 2004 in rural Kono district one survey counted 139 registered groups with a specific focus on youth (Lansana 2004). Furthermore, between 2003 and 2005 UNDP spent 4.2 million USD on youth focused projects in Sierra Leone and it can also be noted that the Sierra Leonean government issued a specific youth policy for Sierra Leone. Similarly, the word youth is employed with increasing frequency in local newspapers, yet with a variety of meanings – most often as local covertly political pressure groups or with references to young ex-combatants of the recent civil war. But this is, of course, not a local phenomenon. The UN Convention of the Rights of the Child (CRC), which since 1989 has been upheld as a global standard of child rearing and child welfare (Boyden 1997; Nieuwenhuys 2001) has provided a framework – the child rights approach – for the United Nations to encourage the establishment of social welfare, compulsory education, child labour legislation and health services throughout the world (Boyden 1997). As Thorsen (this volume) argues, 'adolescent children' in rural Burkina Faso may decide to migrate to town for better work opportunities, which, besides economic gains, may provide desired space of autonomy, new skills, and renegotiations of social positioning. Due to the economic failure of African states to offer such public welfare provision, the framework has provided Western development agencies a basis for implementing universal programmes for children who are thought to be in need of supervision or to be morally and materially neglected as parents are either unable or unwilling to shelter and care for them. Another example is the recent guidelines of the development agency of the Danish Ministry of Foreign Affairs (Danida 2005), where it is the cocktail of HIV/AIDS, poverty, and armed conflicts that is attributed with hindering young Africans from experiencing childhood and youth as safe spaces of socialization and development of skills. Similar to the view on youth within much of cultural studies, the developmental perspective often treats young people as constituting socio-culturally reified and autonomous groups. Youth, as a social category, becomes a parallel stratum that is somehow unattached from the general societal fabric and generational dynamics, and whose calamities can be treated in relative isolation and thus with relative ease.

Intergenerational bargaining

The intertwining of the rampant HIV/AIDS pandemic and the emergence of children and young people as a focal group of international aid in Sub-Saharan Africa has become explicit since the early 1990s, where "the orphan burden" became "a window on the potential for massive social breakdown and dislocation" resulting from the high AIDS-related mortality (see Hunter 1990:681). Taking its point of departure in the CRC framing of childhood and the societal consequences of AIDS, the past decade has witnessed a heavy emphasis on orphans – defined as any person below the age of 18 without one or both parents – in need of primary health care, schooling, and appropriate protection within the family setting (Christiansen et al. 2005). It is notable that this restricted focus on children in certain social situations and guided by particular notions of childhood is reflected in the practical work of development agencies as well as in the upsurge of academic literature feeding public concern and international aid debates (Barnett and Whiteside 2003; Hunter 1990; Heggenhougen et al. 2003; Foster 2000; Ntozi and Ahimbisibwe 1999; Nyambedha et al. 2003).

The importance given to 'the right of the child' to be taken care of by his/her natal parents has raised profound debate in local cultural settings, where the natal parents may give the child for fosterage to a religious instructor or a relative, most often a grandmother (see Goody 1982). As Einarsdóttir (this volume) argues, such acts of fosterage do not reflect parental neglect; on the contrary, such acts are in the West African settings made by parents attending to what they consider to be 'the best interests of the child' (see also Ennew 2002; Stephens 1995). Child fosterage with grandparents has also become a critical issue related to the impact of HIV/AIDS in East and southern Africa, yet the critique has taken a somewhat different turn despite one parent often being alive. While the negative attitude towards the former cultural practice of grandparental fosterage is loaded with ethnocentric ideas about parenthood and child rights (Stephens 1995), the evaluation of the rather similar practice in the context of AIDS is more orientated towards the poverty and physical strain of the grandparents becoming the parents (Hunter and Williamson 2000; Barnett and Whiteside 2003; Nyambedha et al. 2003; Cattell 1994). In this latter perspective, the cultural values of intergenerational living and relations are cherished as appropriate childrearing patterns; the critical points are instead the number of grandchildren and the socio-economic poverty of the grandparents. This points towards changing patterns of generating adulthood in an era when the "intergenerational bargain is becoming progressively harder to maintain" (Barnett and Whiteside 2003:221).

Mobility and morality

When children are classified as youths there is a tendency to shift the conceptualization from victims of HIV/AIDS, conflict or violence to social actors who may contribute to the maintenance or spread of troubles that are burdening their societies. This shift is probably related to the empirical fact that the 15–24 year olds make up the majority of the newly infected (UNAIDS 2004), the militants and agents of organised violence. Yet it is equally due to the theoretical tendency to ascribe more agentive abilities to young people than to children (Utas 2003). Since the HIV prevalence among young females is considerably higher than among their male peers, the sexual behaviour of young girls has become of particular interest to academics and aid agencies (Barnett and Blaikie 1992; Silberschmidt and Rasch 2001). There appear to be two key factors encouraging young females to avoid such risk-taking sexual behaviour: the spread of HIV and religious moralities. In Uganda, for example, these two factors are intertwined, as religious discourses have, from their outset in late 1980s, been part of the prevention campaigns under the slogan 'love faithfully' (Seidel 1990). Yet, the rapid spread of Christian and Muslim reform movements can also be understood as "youthful gestures of self-creation" in public space:

> Religious movements are attractive not only because they offer modes of being and belonging, but also because they construct new imaginations of the community and the individual. (Diouf 2003:7)

In the 'born-again' context, when proclaiming salvation the person is imagined to be empowered with the Holy Spirit and simultaneously breaking the bonds of kinship; a transformation pictured to enhance divine influence and reduce the risk of other people (living and deceased) interfering in the progress of the person's life (Christiansen 2006). While this discourse of certainty and teleology may strongly appeal to the individual young person, the moral discourse of refusal to continue so-called traditional practices empowers youth to depict elders as immoral and influenced by evil forces (van Dijk 1992). While such discursive use is a continuation of that of Christian missionaries and European colonial states, Muslim youth have also been influenced by it both historically and in contemporary integrated reform-minded discourses of morality in their efforts to change the political sphere and enhancing their options of social mobility (Last 1992; Ihle 2003).

Youth(e)scapes

It is not just the participation, appropriation and reconstruction of youth in social and religious institutions that highlights their centrality in contemporary African affairs, but also their appropriation of technological and discursive innovations (see Burgess 2005; Abbink 2005). Globally, youth are especially committed to new techniques of learning, earning and communicating as ways of gaining life chances. Technological inventions such as the mobile phone are examples of such. In Dakar for instance we have noted that sending text messages on mobile phones opens up new corridors of communication between youth, transgressing gender barriers meticulously guarded by parents and other gerontocratic custodians (Utas 2002).

There is an obvious tendency to limit the idea of youth to an assemblage obsessed with surface, where communication is limited to stylishness and where socio-political content is absent or marginal and where youth fashions are directly transferable across social classes, vast geographical areas and widely different cultures (see e.g. Skelton and Valentine 1998). Yet we must acknowledge how different styles are given alternative, if not distinctive, meanings throughout the African continent. As pointed out by Filip De Boeck on youth in the south western diamond mining areas of DRC, through a political economy of elegance, young people refashion the West in their own terms (De Boeck 1999). Similarly, rather than just mimicking the West, we see how young combatants in the Liberian and Sierra Leone Civil Wars fill American action heroes with local meaning. Rather than refashioning local concepts of the hero, they build on their own cultural ideas of heroes in their reading of heroes like Rambo (Carey n.d.; Richards 1994, 1996, 1999; Utas forthcoming a).[4]

---

4. Filip De Boeck has discussed the use of "ninjas" in a similar fashion (De Boeck 2000).

Youth attentiveness to popular culture has in the African setting also motivated local productions and new genres such as 'edu-tainment'. One such example is Soul City, a South African soap opera directed towards a young audience as it focuses on the lives of urban impoverished youth; on uncertainty about future options of making a living in terms of employment, of achieving the status of marriage and reproduction without getting HIV-infected. Yet, as Prince deals with in her chapter (this volume) on local productions of popular music in Kenya, people across age groups listen to the radio marketing of songs addressing the hardship of poverty, the nostalgia of a lost modernity, and the social suffering of HIV/AIDS. While young people may use local and global popular culture to address issues pertinent to their social positioning, popular culture is also a public space of negotiations between people of diverse generations.

So, in relation to peace or conflict, AIDS or abstinence, survival strategies or fashion we need to account for the conflation of the modern and the traditional, as well as the global and local in making sense of the social positions, acts and understandings of youth in Africa. Youth combatants, for example, navigate no simple path of modernity in their contestation of gerontocratic powers. In the Liberian context routes of combatant youth are in part interpreted as traditional and in part modern. In fact modernity itself can be viewed as a traditional pathway travelled by both young fighters and ancestors (Utas forthcoming a). As in De Boeck's works on DRC (De Boeck 2000), young people are frontier characters eking out their living in marginal areas (both geographically and socially) by generating power and wealth from reconstitutions of the social, the cultural, the resourceful and even the apparently barren.

As the different chapters of this book will illuminate young people are thus on the lookout for both social paths and social escapes. They are both social navigators of the present and social generators of individual and collective futures. Being both actors as well as acted upon they are resisting the social death (Hage 2003) of a gerontophallic post-colonial Africa by forcing open societal spaces, navigating both the usual and alternative paths trying to secure decent lives for themselves. At times these efforts lead to religious awakenings, at times to migration and at times to war,[5] but regardless of the chosen trajectories African youth are simultaneously

---

5. Becoming part of what Comaroff and Comaroff have called the 'alien-nation' (1999). Utas has, furthermore, argued that youth warfare and migration rest on the same cultural logic of social upward mobility in the Liberian society (Utas forthcoming b).

generating the future of the continent, turning present day youthscapes into some of tomorrow's core powers.

The structure of the book

The chapters in this volume are based on ethnographic research across the African continent, from Guinea Bissau in the West to Kenya in the East and Lesotho in the South. Common to all the different chapters is that through in-depth analyses of the perceptions, positions, possibilities, and practices of a given group of young people they seek to advance our understanding of contemporary African youth.

The book is divided into three parts each of which is meant to illuminate an important aspect of the social being and becoming of contemporary African youth and which in unison give a detailed picture of the possibilities and difficulties that they face within the difficult politico-economic climate that characterises many current African societies and communities. Since a large part of the contemporary younger generation in Africa is coming of age in societies, which for the last decades have been marked by economic decline and failed governmental systems, the first part, entitled *Navigating Youth*, attends to the ways in which young urban males navigate social relations in their search for life chances and social worth. The first part of the book is thus centred on praxis and Henrik Vigh, Trond Waage and Dorte Thorsen all explore the way young west African males manoeuvre their lives through difficult socio-political environments, taking bearings not just from immediate difficulties or possibilities but also trying to envision possible paths into the future and follow these towards better lives. Vigh and Waage take their point of departure in local idioms used to signify the fluid and adaptive tactical praxis that young urban men make use of in order to ensure their social and physical survival. Exploring the related concepts of *dubriagem* (Guinean Creole) and *se debrouille* (French), they illuminate how young men navigate networks and events. Thorsen's article focuses on how children use migration from rural Burkina Faso to renegotiate their social position and accelerate the transition from childhood to adulthood. She terms the somewhat younger informants 'adolescent children' and argues that the motive is not economic destitution, as it is so often attributed to in the literature on trafficking, but rather that the mobility reflects an active navigation by children in their social becoming. Through anthropological examination of local concepts the three texts illuminate how young people tactically and flexibly navigate the poverty stricken societies their lives are set in bringing us closer to an understanding of the logic behind much youth praxis in the process.

Where the first part of the book carefully explores the modes of action that youth make use of in order to better their existence, the second part of the book, entitled *Gen(d)erating Adulthood*, looks towards some of the positions and goals they are trying to attain. Situated in the garment industry in Lesotho Christian Boehm's chapter illuminates gendered strategies of negotiating new socially and morally accepted female adulthoods. The macro-economic shift in Lesotho from male mining migrants to the current employment of young females in the outsourced garment industry has entailed profound consequences for the processes of household formation and dissociation between marriage and childbearing. Whereas marriage used to mark the female transition from youth to adulthood, young female workers opt for new marital strategies that further enhance their empowered status as wage earners. For the young Luo people in Kenya, maturing into adulthood in the uncertain post-colonial context afflicted by prolonged economic decline and the AIDS epidemic entails generating novel ways of integrating love, death and loss with co-existing moralities and changing gender roles. In popular music these topics are creatively communicated to young males and females experiencing a sense of disconnection (Ferguson 1999) from the imagined modern life, which they navigate towards. Through her presentation of Luo popular music, Ruth Prince argues for an intergenerational 'nostalgia for the lost modernity' in the 1960s–70s in Kenya. The last text in this section deals with young mothers in Guinea-Bissau and their practice of fostering out children. Based on ethnographic fieldwork in the Biombo region, Jonina Einarsdottir illuminates the incompatibility between local notions of the best interests of children and obligations of mothers and the global Convention of the Rights of the Child. While fosterage to the maternal grandmother is locally perceived as a kinship obligation, giving a child to a religious leader or a financially more able caretaker is seen as an appropriate child-raising and networking strategy.

The last section of the book, entitled *In-Exclusion,* contains texts by authors Sverker Finnström and Nadia Lovell. The chapters contain conceptualizations of an "inclusive exclusion" (Hansen and Stepputat 2005:17) of large numbers of young Africans, a faceless throng who experience exclusion from socio-political scenes, citizens' rights, and in some sense even humanity – they embody the *homo sacer* in Agamben' s terminology (Agamben 1998). While Finnström focuses on the geographical marginalization within national boundaries, both are committed to the dialectics of inclusion and exclusion of young people in Africa.

Lovell approaches the political scene in Togo through two apparently divergent life stories of two young students, one turning into a political writer and the other going mad but using madness, and subsequently religion, as a means of criticizing the political sphere. The discussion focuses on the various avenues available to young Togolese on their paths towards adulthood. And Lovell shows that political activism, religion, education, and rebellion all provide diverging yet complementary strategies for expressing political opinions, while simultaneously shaping the identity of the actors themselves. Finnström's text gives an alternative reading of the LRM/A rebels in Northern Uganda. He is able to show discrepancies between the popularized and de-politicized picture of LRM/A and the "on the ground" reading of the movement by young people in the Ugandan North. Strikingly he shows how political claims made by LRM/A make sense to young northerners increasingly excluded by the Ugandan government and, in Finnström's own words, "The more violence the rebels commit against the non-combatant population, the more the government will be blamed by those same exposed people for its failure to protect and provide for its citizens..." (Finnström, chapter 7 this volume). Both Finnström and Lovell present cases where young people "are deprived of a sense of agency in their own predicament" (Lovell, chapter 8 this volume). Both chapters clearly contribute to a larger understanding of how "new forms of political participation and authority exclude and include youth in novel ways, and debates about the nature of citizenship, responsibilities, and the moral, immoral, and amoral nature of social action" (Durham 2000:114).

References

Abbink, J., 2005, "Being young in Africa: The politics of despair and renewal", in J. Abbink and I. van Kessel (eds), *Vanguard or vandals: Youth, politics and conflict in Africa*. Leiden: Brill.

Agamben, G., 1998, *Homo Sacer: sovereign power and bare life*. Stanford, California: Stanford University Press.

Amit-Talai, V. and H. Wulff (eds), 1995, *Youth Cultures: A cross-cultural perspective*. London: Routledge.

Barnett. T. and P. Blaikie, 1992, *AIDS in Africa: Its present and future impact*. London: Belhaven Press.

Barnett, T. and A. Whiteside, 2003, "Dependants: Orphans and the Elderly" in *AIDS in the Twenty-First Century. Disease and Globalization*, pp. 196–221. Palgrave Macmillan: New York:

Barrett, M., 2004, *Paths to adulthood: Freedom, belonging and temporalities in Mbunda biographies from Western Zambia*. Uppsala: Acta Universitatis Upsaliensis.

Barthes, R., 1983, *The fashion system*. New York: Hill and Wang.

Bayart, J.-F., 1993, *The State in Africa: The Politics of the Belly*. London: Longman.

Bourdieu, P., 1986 [1983], "The Forms of Capital", in J.G. Richardson (ed.), *A Handbook of Theory and Research for the Sociology of Education*. Westport: Greenwood Press.

—, 1992 [1977], *Outline of a Theory of Practice*. Cambridge: Cambridge University Press.

—, 1994 [1991], *Language and Symbolic Power*. Cambridge: Polity Press.

Boyden, J., 1997, "Childhood and the Policy Makers: A Comparative Perspective on the Globalization of Childhood", in A. James and A. Prout (eds), *Constructing and Reconstructing Childhood*, pp. 190–230. London: Falmer Press.

Bucholtz, M., 2002, "Youth and cultural practice", *Annual Review of Anthropology*, 31:525–52.

Burgess, T. 2005, "Introduction to youth and citizenship in East Africa", *Africa Today*, 51(3):vii–xxiv.

Cattell, M., 1994, "'Nowadays it isn't easy to advise the young': Grandmothers and granddaughters among Abaluyia of Kenya", *Journal of Cross-Cultural Gerontology*, 9:157–78.

Carey, M., n.d., Unpublished manuscript, *Video and tricksters: Communicating power and shaping image in the Mano River conflict*.

Christiansen, C., 2006, "Conditional Certainties: Ugandan Charismatic Christians Striving for Health and Harmony", Paper presented at the conference "Uncertainty in Contemporary African Lives", Arusha, 9–11 April 2003.

Christiansen, C., M. Daniel and B. Yamba, 2005, "Introduction: Growing up in an Era of AIDS", *African Journal of AIDS Research*, 4(3):135–137.

Coleman, J., 1961, *The Adolescent Society: The social life of the teenager and its impact on education*. New York: The Free Press.

Comaroff, J. and J. Comaroff, 1999, "Alien-Nation: Zombies, immigrants and millenial capitalism", *CODESRIA Bulletin*, (3 and 4 1999):17–28.

Dahrendorf, R., 1979, *Life Chances. Approaches to Social and Political Theory*. London: Weidenfield and Nicolson.

Danida, 2005, *Children and Young People in Danish Development Cooperation*. Guidelines, Danida.

De Boeck, F., 1999, "Domesticating diamonds and dollars: Identity, expenditure and sharing in Southwestern Zaire (1984–1997)", in P. Geschiere and B. Meyer, (eds), *Globalization and identity*. Oxford: Blackwell Publ.

—, 2000, "Borderland breccia: The mutant hero in the historical imagination of a Central-African diamond frontier", *Journal of colonialism and colonial history,* 1(2):1–43.

De Boeck, F. and A. Honwana (eds), 2005, "Children and Youth in Africa: Agency, Identity, and Place", in De Boeck, F. and A. Honwana (eds), *Makers and Breakers: Children and Youth as Emerging Categories in Postcolonial Africa.* Oxford: James Currey.

van Dijk, R., 1992, "Young Puritan Preachers in Post-Independence Malawi", *Africa,* 62(2):159–81.

Diouf, M., 2003, "Engaging Postcolonial Cultures: African Youth and Public Space", *African Studies Review,* 46(1):1–12.

Durham, D., 2000, "Youth and the Social Imagination in Africa: Introduction to Parts 1 and 2", *Anthropological Quarterly,* 73(3):113–20.

—, 2004, "Disappearing youth: Youth as social shifter in Botswana", *American Ethnologist,* 31(4):589–605.

Eisenstadt, S.N., 1964 [1956], *From Generation to Generation: Age groups and social structure.* New York: Free Press.

Ennew, J., 2002, "Future generations and global standards: Children's rights at the start of the millennium." in Jeremy MacClancy (ed.), *Exotic No More. Anthropology on the Front Lines,* pp. 338–58. Chicago: University of Chicago Press.

Erikson, E.H., 1965 [1950], *Childhood and Society.* Hamondsworth: Penguin Books.

—, 1997, *The Life Cycle Completed.* New York: W.W. Norton.

Ferguson, J., 1999, *Expectations of modernity: Myths and meanings of urban life on the Zambian Copperbelt.* Berkeley: University of California Press.

Fortes, M., 1984, "Age, Generation, and Social Structure", in D.E., Kertzer, and J. Kieth (eds), *Age and Anthropological Theory.* London: Ichaca.

Foster, G., 2000, "The capacity of the extended family safety net for orphans in Africa", *Psychology, Health and Medicine,* 5(1):55–62.

Goody, E.N., 1982, *Parenthood and Social Reproduction : Fostering and Occupational Roles in West Africa.* Cambridge: Cambridge University Press.

Hage, G., 2003, "'Comes a Time We Are All Enthusiasm': Understanding Palestinian Suicide Bombers in Times of Exighophobia", *Public Culture,* 15(1):65–89.

Hall, G.S., 1905, Vol. 1 and 2, *Adolescence: Its psychology and its relations to physiology, anthropology, sociology, sex, crime, religion, and education.* New York: Appelton-Century-Crofts.

Hall, S. and T. Jefferson (eds), 1976, *Resistance through Rituals.* London: Hutchinson.

Hansen, T. B. and F. Stepputat (eds), 2005, "On empire and sovereignty", in T.B. Hansen and F. Stepputat (eds), *Sovereign bodies: Citizens, migrants and states in the postcolonial world.* pp. 1–36. Princeton: Princeton University Press.

Heggenhougen, K. et al., 2003, *Situation Analysis of Orphans in Uganda. Orphans and their households: Caring for the future – today.* Kampala: UNAIDS.

Honnert, A., 2003, *Behovet for Anerkendelse: En tekstsamling*, Rasmus Willig ed. København: Hans Reitzels Forlag.

Hunter, S., 1990, "Orphans as a window on the AIDS epidemic in Sub-Saharan Africa: Initial results and implications of a study in Uganda", *Social Science & Medicine*, 31(6):681–90.

Hunter, S. and J. Williamson, 2000, *Children on the Brink: Strategies to support children isolated by HIV/AIDS*. Arlington, VA: USAID.

Ihle, A., 2003, "'It is all about morals': Islam and socila mobility among young and committed Muslims in Tamale, Northern Ghana", Det Humanistiske Fakultet, University of Copenhagen.

Johnson-Hanks, J., 2002, "On the Limits of Life-Stages in Ethnography: Towards a theory of vital conjunctures", *American Anthropologists*, 104(3):865–880.

Jakobson, R., 1971, *Selected writings, vol. 2: Word and language*. The Hague: Mouton.

Lansana, D,N,, 2004, *Baseline survey on youth in Kono* (draft version). Freetown: Network movement for justice and development.

Last, M., 1992, "The Power of Youth, Youth of Power: Notes on the religions of the young in northern Nigeria", in H. d'Almeida-Topo, O. Georg, C Coquery-Vidrovtich and F. Guitart (eds), *Les Jeunes en Afrique. La Politique et la ville,* pp 375–399. Paris: Editions L'Harmattan.

Mannheim, K., 1952, *Essays on the Sociology of Knowledge*. London: Routledge.

Maira, S. and E. Soep (eds), 2004, *Youthscapes: The popular, the national, the global*. Philadelphia: University of Pennsylvania Press.

Mead, M., 1969 [1928], *Coming of Age in Samoa: A study of adolescence and sex in primitive societies*. Harmondsworth: Penguin Books.

Nieuwnhuys, O., 2001, "By the sweat of their brow? 'Street Children', NGOs and Children's Rights in Addis Ababa", *Africa*, 71(4):539–557.

Ntozi, J.P.M. and F.E. Ahimbisibwe, 1999, "Orphan care: The role of the extended family in Northern Uganda", *Health Transition Review*, 8:225–236.

Nyambedha, E.O., S. Wandibba and J. Aagaard-Hansen, 2003, "'Retirement lost' – the newrole of the elderly as caretakers for orphans in Western Kenya", *Journal of Cross-Cultural Gerontology*, 18:33–52.

Ottenberg, S., 1989, *Boyhood rituals in an African society: an interpretation*. Seattle: University of Washington Press.

Parsons, T., 1964, *Essays on Sociological Theory: pure and applied*. New York: The Free Press.

Richards, P., 1994, "Videos and violence on the periphery: Rambo and the war in the forests of the Sierra Leone-Liberia border", *IDS Bulletin,* 25(2):88–93.

—, 1996, *Fighting for the rain forest: war, youth and resources in Sierra Leone*. Oxford: James Currey.

—, 1999, "The social life of war: Rambo, diamonds and young soldiers in Sierra Leone", *Track Two,* 8(1):16–21.

Seidel, G.,1990. "'Thank God I Said No to AIDS': On the changing discourse of AIDS in Uganda", *Discourse & Society,* 1(1):61–84.

Silberschmidt, M. and V. Rasch, 2001, "Adolescent girls, illegal abortions and 'sugar-daddies' in Dar es Salaam: Vulnerable victims and active social agents", *Social Science & Medicine*, 52:1815–26.

Skelton, T. and G. Valentine, 1998, *Cool places: Geographies of youth cultures*. London, New York: Routledge.

Stephens, S., 1995, *Children and the politics of culture*. Princeton NJ: Princeton University Press.

Turner, V., 1967, *The Forest of Symbols: Aspects of Ndembu ritual*. New York: Ithaca.

UNAIDS, 2004, Report on the global AIDS epidemic, 4th global report. UNAIDS.

Utas, M., 2002, "Mobile mania in Dakar – just a modernity mirage?", *LBC Newsletter* no. 2, January 2002:2–3.

—, 2003, *Sweet Battlefields: Youth and the Liberian Civil War*, PhD thesis, Uppsala: Dissertations in Cultural Anthropology (DiCA), Department of Cultural Anthropology and Ethnology, Uppsala University.

—, 2005, "Victimcy, Girlfriending, Soldiering: Tactic Agency in a Young Woman's Social Navigation of the Liberian War Zone", *Anthropological Quarterly*, 78(2):403–30.

—, forthcoming a., "Abject heroes: marginalised youth, modernity and violent pathways of the Liberian Civil War", in J. Hart (ed.), *Years of Conflict: Adolescence, Political Violence and Displacement*. Oxford: Berghahn Books.

—, forthcoming b., "Malignant organisms: Continuities of state-run violence in rural Liberia", in B. Kapferer and B. Bertelsen (eds), *War and the State*. Oxford: Berghahn Books.

Vigh, H., 2003, *Navigating Terrains of War: Youth and Soldiering in Guinea Bissau*, PhD thesis, Department of Anthropology, University of Copenhagen.

—, 2006, *Navigating Terrains of War: Youth and Soldiering in Guinea*. Oxford: Berghahn Books.

NAVIGATING YOUTH

CHAPTER 1

Social Death and Violent Life Chances

Henrik E. Vigh

This chapter discusses the mobilisation of urban youth in West Africa and analyses their engagement in conflict as social navigation. It proposes a view on youth, which sees the generational category as both a social process and position. The chapter illustrates how urban youth navigate the social ties and options that arise in situations of warfare in order to escape the social death that otherwise characterises their situation. Describing how youth is a time of stagnation and truncation of social being for young people in Bissau, Guinea-Bissau, it illuminates how war becomes a terrain of possibility, rather than solely being a space of death. The concept of social navigation thus provides insights into the interplay between objective structures and subjective agency. As an analytical optic it enables us to make sense of the opportunistic, sometimes fatalistic, and tactical ways in which youth struggle to expand the horizons of possibility in a world of conflict, turmoil, and diminishing resources, and allows us to see how conflict engagement becomes a question of balancing social death with violent life chances.

Introduction

Blufo, blufo, bluuufo. The word was being hurled across the street at a local lunatic. A man in his fifties, gone mad during the war and now roaming the streets of inner Bissau competing with the local dogs for leftovers in the city's myriad garbage heaps. Whereas the mentally ill are generally shunned in Europe they seem to attract an abundance of abuse and bantering in Bissau, and verbally blufo was just about the worst anyone could yell at you. Bluuuuufo, Vitór bawled again.

I had earlier learnt that a *blufo* was someone whose penis still had a 'hat'; that is, an un-circumcised person of age; someone who, despite being old enough, had not yet gone to his 'feinadu'.[1] Further exploration revealed that it referred to a man that would never become wise, could never become someone in Guinean society, and could never have a wife. A *blufo* is, as such, a betwixt and between category defined by a discrepancy between chronological and social age. Being a *blufo* means being symbolically stuck in the position of youth without possibilities of gaining the authority and status of adulthood. It is being a social castrato;[2] the nightmare of any young man in Bissau, yet close to being the predicament of a whole generation.

Based on sixteen months of fieldwork with former members of the *Aguentas*, a militia of youth recruited during the civil war in Guinea-Bissau, this chapter seeks to shed light on the mobilisation and engagement in conflict by urban youth in West Africa (cf. Abdulla 1997; Bangura 1997; Utas 2003; Vigh 2003). Rather than the traditional focus on the strategies of influential politicians, warlords or big men the focus is on the socio-political tactics of young soldiers (cf. Clausewitz 1993; cf. de Certeau 1988; Honwana 2000).[3] I will focus on the social *position, possibilities* and *praxis* of youth in Bissau and thereby seek to clarify the relationship between

---

1. The common Creole term for a circumcision ritual, male or female, which is the *rite de passage* into youth, adulthood or seniority, depending on ethnicity and religion.

2. Thanks and acknowledgement are due to the anonymous reviewer for making me aware of the fitting concept of a 'social castrato'.

3. On the traditional relationship between mobilisation, ideology and/or economic incentives see Clausewitz (1993), Collier (2000), Enzensberger (1994), Kaldor (1999). In the same way, the differentiation between *strategy* and *tactics* has its point of departure in Clausewitz' work where tactics designates the plan of action within a given instance of battle and strategy the plan of battle for war. De Certeau uses the distinction to designate different types of social action, where strategy is the act of constructing a space of power and demarcation of will, what I term a *domain*,

youth and warfare as well as contribute to our general understanding of the process of mobilisation. The chapter will illuminate the social position of young men in Bissau and their efforts to move along an expected and desired process of *social becoming*.[4] It will discuss the concept of youth and its social scientific use in situations of war and peace and relay how our various conceptualisations of youth are related to levels of life chances and social possibilities. In conclusion it will demonstrate, via the concept of social navigation, the way in which young urban men through mobilisation, aspire to realise social being and escape the 'social death' that otherwise characterises the lives of many young men in Bissau (cf. Hage 2003).

Youth in war

That youth are particularly closely connected to warfare should come as no surprise. Due to their physical strength and their position in society young men have always constituted the bulk of armies. Yet despite the universality of this connection between youth and violence there is no agreement on how to see the relationship. As such most interpretations and representations (folk as well as professional) emphasise the role of youth in war as being either that of potential victims manipulated into war by powerful seniors, or as being potential perpetrators, non-socialised 'loose molecules' uncontrolled by social and societal constraints (see Seekings 1993; Kaplan in Richards 1996:xv). Young men are, in other words, seen either *as* risk or *at* risk (Bucholtz 2002:532–534; cf. Honwana 2000). They are illuminated as either *mechanically mastered* or *unrestricted agents* and their mobilisation and relation to organised violence seen as either determined by the social or generational order or as completely detached from it (cf. Durham 2000:117; Honwana 2000; Richards 1996:xv; Peters and Richards 1998). A schism noticed by Durham as she states:

---

and tactics the act of moving in and between the domains of others (Clausewitz op. cit., de Certeau op. cit., Vigh 2003).

4. Focusing on the social, I prefer the concept of *becoming* to that of *emergence*. Despite the fact that both refer to a process of constitution, the concept of *becoming* has the advantage of indicating such a process with the entity in question as an active part of its own constitution. More specifically the concept of social becoming designates a movement along an expected and desired life trajectory (cf. Vigh 2003).

Warfare is one of the sites where the agentive nature of young people is most ambiguous (...) are [war engaged] youth victims or perpetrators of violence? (Durham 2000:117)

Twofold youth and a Mannheimian synthesis

However, this difference in perspective is not confined to the study of youth in war. It echoes a more general division within our understanding of the concept of youth as the different views on youth in war, as either radically agentive or determined, coincide with the two primary conceptualisations of youth within the social sciences in general (cf. Olwig 2000, Olwig and Gulløv 2004; Cole 2004). The concept has as such been studied either as an entity in itself; that is a socially and culturally demarcated unit producing a 'sub-culture' (cf. Wulff 1995; Epstein 1998),[5] or as a stage within a larger generational trajectory or life cycle, as a category defined by its position within an inter-generational process of becoming (cf. Fortes 1969, 1984; Meillassoux 1981; Mannheim 1952). Within the first perspective youth constitute a demarcated site of construction of ideas and praxis specific to the group in question, while the second defines youth as a period of liminality, a life stage or status; or more precisely as a transient inter-generational period between childhood and adulthood (cf. Turner 1967; cf. Johnson-Hanks 2002). However, if we want to make sense of the acts of youth we need, I hold, to fuse the two perspectives and see youth in relation to both generational dynamics and the space or position in which agents share similar horizons and points of orientation (Mannheim op. cit.; cf. Schutz and Luckmann 1995:115). We need to analytically approach the concept as both *position* and *process*.

One of the keys to accomplishing this lies in an appropriation of Mannheim's idea of 'generation', in which it becomes possible, both to contextualise youth within a field of forces and to analyse it as an experiential demarcation (Mannheim 1952:289). In a Mannheimian perspective a given group of youth must be seen as bound together by formative experience and interpretative horizons, constituted by their historical becoming as a specific generation growing up in specific circumstances (ibid: 288, 299, 306)[6]

---

5. A perspective, which is most notably related to the so-called 'Birmingham School', i.e. the Birmingham Centre for Contemporary Cultural Studies.

6. Interestingly, the Mannheimian understanding of the phenomenon of generation is also related to warfare as it is born out of his experiences of the First World War

as well as defined by their mutual position in the intergenerational order (Ibid: 290-291). Mannheim's work provides a step towards synthesising the bifurcated view on youth within the social sciences. An appropriation of his focus into the modern social scientific perspective on young people will allow us to illuminate the way youth is lived and constructed as both *position* and *process*; both *being* and *becoming*. Yet if we ask ourselves why the division exists and persists in the first place, the answer seems to be related to a connection between research traditions and the socio-political characteristics of the context we are working within.

Lost generations and existential moratoria

> Contrary to the Western view that youth is the most desirable station in life, adolescent Africans hunger after the age, which will endow them with, an authority currently denied. (Chabal and Daloz 1999:34)

If we look closer at the social scientific work done on youth in general, we see that the portrayals of youth as cultural entities, as the 'owners' and producers of a specific (sub)culture, seem primarily to be focussed on areas of affluence. The perspective is tied to analyses of youth in the North. However, if we move our focus to analyses of youth in areas of poverty and scarcity the movement appears to have the implication that the category no longer designates sub-cultures or socially or culturally demarcated entities, but rather a transient life stage within life cycles and larger generational orders.[7] It would seem, in other words, that the agentive potential and status of 'youth' shrinks as we move from the North to the South and from areas of plenty to areas of scarcity. As will be shown in this chapter, the definition of 'what youth *is*' depends not only on research traditions and the context the category is researched in but on 'what youth are able to do' in the given context. It depends on socio-political factors, on the space of possibilities afforded the specific group of youth in question and on their possibilities of building and maintaining lives for themselves independently of the control of elders or institutions.

In the North, where young people, ideally, have the possibility of building lives for themselves, youth is as the above quote states seen as a posi-

---

and the generational differences in perception and orientation related to it.

7. The move from areas of affluence to areas of poverty entails in other words a move from age to generation as the perceived constitutive factor behind the social position (cf. Fortes 1984).

tive social position; as a demarcated entity. Yet when resources are sparse and tied to political formations or networks, being young often becomes a position of social and political immaturity, drastically changing the status of the social position. "(...) The ultimate meaning of a relative superior status is always a wider range of possible choices", Bauman states (Bauman 1992:27), and the easier it is for young people to gain access to resources and build lives for themselves independently of their elders the more we, as social scientists, see youth as a positively valued social segment in itself. So, despite the Mannheimian possibility of synthesis of the twofold concept, *youth as lived* varies greatly from society to society and from situation to situation, and these variations are, it would seem, directly related to the possibilities of action and life chances of the specific group of young people in question (Dahrendorf 1979).

Chabal and Daloz' earlier comparison between the status of youth in different regions of the world points our attention exactly towards the difference in youth as lived – and, consequentially, the way the concept protrudes from our data – as the wider range of possibilities for youth in the North has imbued the position with high social status and made it a category to aspire to. Whereas adults in the North desire if not to be young then at least to be youthful, youth in the South seem to desire instead the status of adulthood.

In an enlightening introduction to a book on youth culture, Helena Wulff describes how youth, for a diverse group of young people in Manhattan, New York, serves as a *cultural moratorium*. She illuminates the efforts that people in the richer parts of the world put into staying in the social category, "extending their youth by way of experimenting with different roles and thereby delaying adult responsibilities" (Wulff 1995:7; see also Wulff 1994:133). As a cultural moratorium youth is as such a space of freedom, status and amusement. It is the primary space of social and cultural creativity and innovation and perceived as the locus of cultural production.

Yet, if we focus our attention on the South it would seem that the social position somehow loses its positive connotations. Instead of being a sought after social position and identity being young in the South seems to imply being part of a social category that people feel confined to and seek to escape. In Bissau, youth is not as much a space or time of amusement, opportunity or freedom but one of social marginality and liminality. In fact the category of youth in Bissau brings us as far from the idea of a willingly sought after cultural moratorium as we can get, as it designates a social position that people are involuntarily caught in and trying their very best to get out of. This is not to say that Bissauian youth do not appropriate and manipulate the representation of youth being spread through western, global media (see for example Argenti 1998). 'Youth' is globally negotiated and communicated (Stephens 1995) and these global representations have an impact on people in Bissau, yet at a closer look it seems that the fine glaze of style that so many young people spend so much time cultivating is directly related to the fact that this is the sphere of their lives where they actually have a minimum of agentive possibilities. In other words, when looking at the praxis and predicament of the young in relation to social, political and economic factors being young appears not as socially festive but desolate. It protrudes as a predicament of not being able to gain the status and responsibility of adulthood and thus as a social position that people seek to escape as it is characterised by marginality, stagnation and a truncation of social being. It is a *social* moratorium rather than a cultural one.

Social immobility and generational anomie

The difference between the cultural and the social moratorium rests as such on the space of possibility afforded youth. It depends on life chances and opportunities of social becoming. We all live our lives along multiple paths of transition rather than along a single path or a predefined set of stages (cf. Jones and Wallace 1992; Johnson-Hanks 2002),[8] yet the number of possibilities and life chances available to youth varies greatly from place to place and region to region. That the lives of young people in Bissau are more akin to a social than a cultural moratorium is related to economic hardship, decline and a generationally asymmetric control over access to resources that greatly reduces their space of possibilities.

As I commenced my fieldwork none of my informants held a paid job, none had economic possibilities beyond everyday survival, and none had their own household sharing instead rooms with friends or living at the mercy and expense of fathers, mothers, uncles or aunts, or others from the older generations.[9] Furthermore, as resources are needed in order to marry and/or gain independence the combination of uneven distribution and ac-

---

8. It is as important to keep in mind that our processes of social becoming are in the plural and that they do not stop. We do not just aspire to adulthood or specific life stages but to certain versions of adulthood and specific positions and movements within different social ages.

9. Males are ideally expected to supply the resources for the household, yet for the urban population continuous decline has diminished the possibilities of male provision, as urban males are dependent on finding work in order to provide for their

cess to resources and the ongoing period of decline has led to the social dynamics of the generational order being replaced by social inertia (cf. Gable 1995). In other words, as persistent decline makes social networks contract and centre on their key relations an ever-growing group of youth find it increasingly difficult to acquire the resources to fulfil the ritual and social obligations needed to set up a household or in other ways create a space of patronage needed to move along the trajectory of social becoming from youth to adulthood. As those already in control of resources become older and older the group waiting to gain in status and societal position becomes larger and larger. Trapped in the category of youth they await their chance to move on in life and realise their social being (Chabal and Daloz op. cit.). As pointed out by the Comaroffs "the hardening materialities of life" have placed youth in an especially marginal position, and as a result "rather than the more familiar axes of social division – class, race, gender, ethnicity – the dominant line of cleavage here has become one of generation" (Comaroff and Comaroff 1999:284).

Bearing resemblances to the anger noticed in the above quote many young men locate their inability to ensure a future for themselves in the greed of their elders (Ibid: 289). Yet resentment remains simmering as the networks that youth are currently desperately trying to navigate, contract even further. My friend Seku's story provides a good example of the social moratorium of youth, its proximity to social death and of the tension within such generational relationships.

Seku

I was hanging out with Seku. As we had just eaten, we were chatting, leaned back in a couple of chairs with a lazy, digestive ambience settling over the place. Seku shares a *congo* with a couple of his friends – a *congo* being a room, outside of parents' or elders' households, shared as sleeping quarters by a group of youths, which is a common alternative to living under the roof and rules of your father or uncle. Seku's *congo* is an annexe and much like any other such room in Bissau. It is a small, damp, mud brick room with a stamped earthen floor furnished spartanly with a couple of beds, a few chairs (or stools), a hole for a window, and patches of lush green mould for wallpaper. Normally Seku and his roommates, Aliu and Nomé, will spend only their sleeping hours in their *congo* and the rest of

families at the same time as jobs are increasingly difficult to find, consequently changing gender relationships and roles.

the day outside either in their *collegason*, their peer-group, at the stadium playing football or basketball, or running errands. Yet in the rainy season, the place becomes a refuge for their entire *collegason*, as they cram together seeking shelter from the rain turning the small room into a sauna with a malodorous twist.

Seku loves his *congo*, as it grants him the freedom to do as he wishes, to bring girls home, drink, party, and generally live without the condemning interference of his father or other family members. Yet despite not living in his father's house any more and having attained a degree of freedom via his *congo*, Seku is still nearly totally dependent on the goodwill of his family and friends for food and handouts. In other words, despite ideally being expected to be able to take care of himself, and eventually expected to provide for his elders and a family of his own, Seku, at 26 years of age, shares, with the rest of my interlocutors, a common position of dependence.

In Bissau a man has authority over his son if the son is dependent on him,[10] and the period of youth is usually defined by the amount of time it takes the son to free himself of this dependence. For most youth this is said to start when a boy is circumcised or when he begins to *kunsi mindjer*, 'to know women', and he is recognised as having passed into adulthood when he marries, which is possible when one is able to take care of a household (cf. Fortes 1969:205), or in other ways becomes a *patron*. Yet as most urban youth do not inherit land or resources this state of independence is one that they are struggling to reach.[11] And as youth are aggrieved by their lack of ability to achieve autonomy and their inability to move along a trajectory of social becoming generational relations are turning sour.

"Fathers want to be in control of their sons"[12] Seku would complain but being aware that challenging his father's control would probably entail going to bed hungry, he made himself eligible for meals by being subservient; by doing as he was told, doing favours and running errands, whilst all along complaining bitterly at the humiliation of having to act like a *boy* when in fact seeing himself as a *man*. When I asked him what he wanted to do if he could, Seku answered:

---

10. See Meyer Fortes for a wonderfully thorough description of inter-generational relationships and progression among the Tallensi (Fortes 1969 [1949]).

11. In Bissau it is usually the first-born son who inherits the family house and resources.

12. In Creole: *pape misti sedu riba di si fidjus*, literally, "a father wants to be on top of his sons", indicating the level of hierarchy that dominates the relationship.

I want to be the man of my [own] head.[13] I want to be a man of respect, a complete man, complete. You understand? I want to have my own house, children, a wife. I want a job. If you have this then no one can tell you that you are young. You will have your own family, your own job. If you are a complete man then you are the [sole] force of your head.[14]

Seku wants to cross the threshold into adulthood and escape the social moratorium of youth. Neither his situation nor his aspirations are unusual, as young people in Bissau in general live their lives at the margins of power and resource flows. In fact, in the present context, the sentence *"then no one can tell you that you are young"* points our attention exactly to the generally perceived stigma of youth as the category becomes derogatory in use when related to relations of power. The concept frames an interaction within a relationship defined by dominance, and the use of the label 'youth' as belittling in effect shows its presumed distance from authority.[15]

Furthermore, not being *'a man of your own head'* points our attention towards the position of youth as being without the authority and possibility of doing what one wishes, but instead having to follow the wishes of a significant other. 'Being in control of one's head', as the opposite is phrased, involves having the freedom to choose, to make up one's own mind, and follow one's own desire all of which is ideally encompassed in the category of adulthood. In a Guinean perspective Seku is thus not a complete man as he does not control his own life, cannot get a wife nor support a household, but is dependent on the goodwill of his parent.

The relationship between the generational position of youth, social mobility, and access to resources has, in other words, entered into a vicious circle in Bissau. Persistent retrenchment has entailed a decline in resources within family networks as well as a decline in jobs and resources among the urban population, making it impossible to get an adequate income in an attempt to marry,[16] support a family or otherwise create a space of patronage, finally making it impossible to become a man of respect, an adult. It is, as we shall subsequently see in relation to both Bernardhino and Buba, a situation of generational anomie in which it is currently impossible for

---

13. *Misti sedu homi di nja cabeza.*

14. Si *abo i homi completo abo i poder di bu cabeza.*

15. Much like the use of 'boy'.

16. Getting a job – public or private – in Bissau is equally dependent on networks.

youth to attain the role and position, which is prescribed and expected of them (cf. Merton 1968).[17]

Bernardinho

Despite having suffered the ordeal of warfare, of being badly wounded, and of losing rather than winning a war, Bernardinho is one of the more fortunate of the young men I know in Bissau. In fact, having found a job after the war he is currently better off than most other youth. Yet as he is similarly unable to move within the generational order he nonetheless still provides a good example of the precarious situation of youth.

Currently Bernardinho works as a kitchen helper in a local bar and is paid in meals rather than money. Not being paid cash for the work you perform is common in Bissau. As such, many youth do not receive any returns for the odd bits and pieces of work they do, as they are repaid in favours, both past and future. Furthermore, employers are notoriously un-willing to pay what they owe, and being paid in food thus seems to please Bernardinho, as it is at least tangible payment. So despite it being paid *in naturalia* Bernardinho's job is an asset for him, and even though he is poor in economic terms, he is a muscular well-fed man who is unmistakably stronger and in better shape than most of the other young men I know in Bissau.

Bernardinho has had the same girlfriend for the two years I have known him, and our conversation would often drift into the spheres of partners, families and marriage. This particular day, we were standing by the counter of the bar, chatting. Normally, it was used to serve food and drinks, but currently Bernadinho was using it as a chopping board slicing liver for the evening's main (and only) course. Standing there for the time required to chop the best part of three kilos of liver, our conversation drifted from thoughts about the future into the subject of women:

> There are lots of women in Africa, lots. But money... you must have money. If you have a woman but you do not have money she will go and find it where

---

17. There will always be a relative discrepancy between the ideal and the real, the *culturally prescribed* and the *socially possible*. However, there is a difference between having a schism that can be socially and culturally incorporated, and one that is so pervading that it leads to conflict.

she can. If you cannot give her [money] for the market,[18] she will find someone who can.

So she will leave you if you do not have money?

If she needs a thing where will he [her boyfriend] see [get] it? If you do not give her, where will she see it? It is the same with marriage... That is why marriage has nearly stopped in Africa. You can know a woman ten years, but you will never have enough money to marry her. To be a respectable man you need to marry. If you are not married you will not have respect in society. It is the same thing with work. If you have work you can organise your life, you can get married, and afterwards you can start a family... But only someone who knows you... Only someone who knows you will give you a job... These days, young people are frustrated. It is this that makes young people want to leave, so you can have a level of life. You go there [abroad] and then you can send money to your family... But it is sad, because you are far from each other. It is difficult. Africans have difficult lives.

In spite of being lucky, having found a source of regular and generous meals, Bernardinho clearly feels the common sting of the present decline in Guinea-Bissau, as he is socially stuck, locked in the category of youth without possibilities of attaining social mobility. Furthermore, he is acutely aware that his dream of wedlock and social mobility can very easily be played out as a nightmare, since, instead of being able to marry his girlfriend with all the positive consequences it would have, he is faced with the constant possibility of his girlfriend leaving him for someone who can support her. There is, in other words, a massive discrepancy between the desirable and the possible within his prospective orientations.

Not being able to marry leaves Bernardinho without the means of becoming 'a respectable man' and thus locks him in a social moratorium of youth with few options for escape other than leaving the country. Yet migration is, in itself, highly dependent on receiving support from one's networks, not only in order to accumulate sufficient money for the actual journey, but also to get a passport, pay for a visa and establish connections abroad. As the quote shows migration is, despite the difficulties it entails,

---

18. *Dal pa fera.* To give a woman '[money] for the market' is a normal transaction within relationships before or after sexual encounters. *Dal pa fera* should, however, not be mistaken for actual payment, which is referred to as X [*schish*] (i.e. x-amount of money) and which entails a degree of prostitution. The payment of X *terminates* a relationship whereas the payment of 'money for the market' *consolidates* it. Although the amounts in question might be identical they are very different forms of transaction, with very different symbolic values and consequences.

seen by many people in Bissau as one of the only means – together with sol-diering – of having a tolerable life, indicating that a locally generated way out of the social moratorium is currently not deemed possible. Or as my friend Amadu said, showing me the newly received EU visa in his passport: "Look, is it not beautiful? I am so afraid that I will lose it... You know, [if I lose it and] if someone finds it, it is like a dead who sees life."

Buba

Buba was, to a large degree, in the same situation as Bernardinho though he had no job, and no prospect of receiving regular meals as he relied for support on the goodwill and already strained finances of his uncle. Buba's reasons for joining the Aguentas were directly related to his family net-work. His uncle had been an officer, 'loyal' to the former President, and had encouraged Buba to enlist; this, combined with the fact that most of his friends were also going, had been sufficient motivation for Buba to join. However, as the *Governo* had lost the war Buba's uncle had lost his privileges, had his house and property taken away from him and was left with a bare minimum, of which there was no longer enough to see to Buba's needs.

The first time I met Buba he was in a bit of a state. Having faced a traumatic period at the end of the war, he was a nervous and extremely vigilant person who in many ways gave the impression of being trapped or cornered. He was terrified of possible persecution and constantly afraid of being caught by the *Junta Militar*. Even though he agreed to participate in interviews, our first few attempts were unsuccessful because he began to whisper as soon as I took out my pen and notebook let alone started the tape recorder. It should be said, however, that Buba really was in a specially difficult position since he had been one of the few Muslims from Bissau to have joined the Aguentas, and in this way was somehow seen to have been fighting against his own as a high proportion of the *Junta* officers were Muslims.

However, despite Buba being Fula on his father's side, he is Papel on his mother's side and maintains a close relationship to his mother's eldest brother, the *Governo* officer,[19] who, the Papel being matrilineal and avun-culo-local, is traditionally the most important male figure in a Papel per-

---

19. The Papels constitute the fifth largest ethnic group in Guinea-Bissau and tradi-tionally occupy the land around the country's capital. As urban youth the majority of the Aguentas were Papel.

spective. Moreover, his girlfriend, with whom he has a child, and most of his friends are Papels. Whenever I met Buba he was thus in the company of Papels, both when it came to friendship and romance. "You are fucking my kin", Vitór, his best friend, and both Papel and Aguenta, would tease him. Yet not being a practising Muslim, Buba sometimes seemed as much of a Papel as many of my other informants.

When I came back to Bissau after a year, I went to see Buba again. When I had left, he was living by himself in a small windowless annexe built of *dubi*, mud bricks, with a corrugated-iron roof. The room had been provided for him by his uncle and can at best be said to be better than nothing. However he was planning to move into something better when circumstances allowed, evidently thinking that better times were looming somewhere around the corner; his main concern was with his girlfriend and baby. "When I get work, I will get my child and girlfriend", he had said in our last interview and I had left Bissau with a hope of Buba improving his life and life chances, of finding better accommodation and being able to establish a household so he could be with his family. Returning in March 2002 I was therefore eager to see how he had got on. But not much had changed for the better. Buba was still living alone in his annexe, and the possibility of life improvements coming his way had not materialised but rather deteriorated. He had become noticeably skinnier, diminished in fervour and physique, and I found it hard not to show my alarm at the sight of his weakening. "Now things have gotten even worse", he said. "Before we had enough for one shot a day [one meal a day],[20] but now, not even that", continuing:

> Young people are tired here. If you do not have work, and your father does not have, then it is a great tiredness (*kansera*) for you. If you do not work, if you do not have money, you cannot get married. My son is there (he points towards the neighbourhood of Pilun). I cannot take him... Because, I do not have a job, so I have to leave them there. I cannot go and look for them... You know... women cannot suffer like men. They cannot sit [for] one day, two days without eating. They cannot! So I have to leave them there [with his wife's family].

Buba's circumstances are a good example of the unpleasantness of the social moratorium as lived. "Women cannot suffer like men" is his way of explaining why he cannot live with his wife. As he is incapable of finding the resources needed to grant himself a meal a day, he is aware that he can-

---

20. *Um tiro kada dia*, meaning 'one meal a day' (see also Lourenço-Lindell 2002:71).

not tend to the primary needs of his wife and baby, and is therefore unable to fulfil his emotional desire, social ambition and obligation. Not having money to pay for the wedding ritual and host a marriage celebration, and to thus publicly mark the transition from youth to adulthood is one thing. However, even without this Buba is not capable of taking care of his child and girlfriend. The social moratorium as lived is in other words more than just generational anomie. It is a state of massive marginalisation, abject poverty, impairment of social being, and *um tiro kada dia,* one shot of food a day – if lucky.

Social death

Yet, like most young people Buba is not dying of starvation. His imminent death is not physical but social. Despite the disastrous combination of lo-cal, regional and global economic and political processes, which are the cause of the sad, current state of affairs, Buba is still able to feed off his fam-ily and friendship networks in order to cover most of his daily needs. He is, however, unable to attend to his social needs and fulfil a process of social becoming. A key social feature of youth in Bissau is, as such, *social death*; that is, an "absence of the possibility of a worthy life" (Hage 2003:132).

The underlying reason behind this drastic lack possibilities and re-sources on the ground is to be located in a combination of thirty years of disastrous local politics and international inequality producing structures. Yet, whatever the cause, the consequence of the dire state of affairs for the lives of urban youth is that the possibility of progressing meaningfully in life has become close to no existent. *Bissau murri'dja*, Bissau has already died, people say, indicating that generalised stagnation and retrenchment are seen to have frozen the city in a futureless state of decline and hardship; of crisis, conflict and warfare (see also Gable 1995:243; Ferguson 1999) and the process of decline and crisis seems especially severe in relation to young, urban males.

Both Meyer Fortes (1984) and Claude Meillassoux (1981) have illumi-nated the way in which young men in Africa struggle to fulfil themselves socially by attaining marriage. They show how the social award of marriage functions as a gerontocratic element of control; as a tool in the hands of the powerful elders controlling access to land, wealth and, not least, social worth and recognition. Young men have, as such, traditionally had to forge liaisons, run errands and be subservient to important elders in the hope of future reciprocal returns that will enable them to achieve social status and recognition, be it through marriage or otherwise. There is, in other words, nothing new about the fact that elites profit from the services of young men, but there is, however, a change in affairs from the traditional patrimonial workings of power, described by Fortes and Meillasoux, to the current patrimionial structurations of power in contemporary West Africa (cf. Eisenstadt 1973; Bayart 1993; Richards 1996; Bangura 1997). The current economic state of affairs in Bissau is so severe that only very few elders have the option of passing on land or possibilities of revenue as the political landscape in Bissau is in a situation where reciprocal returns have diminished drastically to the point of being mere distant possibilities. In other words, as urban youth do not inherit land to cultivate and settle on, or benefit from the services of a diminished state, their lives become characterised by an acute lack of social options (Ferguson 1999; Utas 2003).

Not being able to gain access to the resources (symbolic and material) required to be a *homi completto*, a complete man, the vast majority of young men in Bissau thus conform to what has been termed the 'lost generation', a group of "young people [who] have finished their schooling, are without employment in the formal sector, yet are not in a position to set up an independent household" (O'Brien 1996:57; cf. Seekings 1996). As decline has halted the flow of resources between generations and crippled the state's ability to provide routes to social mobility, urban males have become locked in the social position of youth without the possibility of achieving adulthood.[21] They are unable to attain the momentum and progress of life that is socially and culturally desired and expected, resulting in (temporary) social death – in a social moratorium.

From patrimonialism to the economy of affection

What we have seen thus far is that the social position of youth in Bissau is characterised by social confinement, a lack of inter-generational mobility and life chances and, not least, an impossibility for social becoming. The lives of most of the young men I spoke to in Bissau resemble as such the problematic social position of the *blufo* described in the introductory paragraph of the chapter as they bear the burden and stigma of inter-generational immobility and social stagnation: that is, of being confined to a social and generational position that they ideally ought to transcend.

---

21. Thanks to Karen Tranberg Hansen for the notion of 'achieving adulthood' (personal communication, Autumn 2002).

Yet, if we wish to avoid the pitfall of seeing young people as either radically determined or agentive we need to go further than merely highlighting the troublesome situation of young men in Bissau. Young people obviously do not embrace their marginality and having shed light on the social position of youth in Bissau I will now look towards the ways youth seek to escape the social moratorium of youth and seek to bring about a realisation of being. I will focus my attention on social *possibilities* and *praxis* and illuminate the social relationships and networks that young people navigate in order to gain a positive social existence.

Focussing on the navigational possibilities within the political space – or non-space – of youth in Bissau there are ideally three more or less available (and often interconnected) options for young men if they wish to tend to their material and social needs, namely *migration*, the *economy of affection* or *patrimonialism*. Of these, migration stands out as the most desirable yet the most difficult to attain, as it demands considerable resources, not only to pay for the journey, but also to grease the entire system that provides you with the passport and visa. However, migration makes it possible to rapidly become someone, *un algin*. In other words, by becoming migrants youths hope that they will be able to gain an adequate income to create a space of patronage (a domain within the social terrain) and support a household and extended family in Guinea-Bissau. Yet ironically the prize for gaining rapid status at home is often to endure minimal contact with the household one supports as well as being placed at the lowest status level in the host country in the North.

From the economy of affection to patrimonialism

An agent can also tend to his needs through the economy of affection (and obligation) (Hydén 1983; Lourenço-Lindell 1996), relying on the fact that family, friends, religious and ethnic networks will feed him when in need and that he –if lucky – will gain an inheritance of worth. Yet as we have seen, due to the prolonged decline, youth are increasingly being marginalised within this economy of affection, as they are last in the line of obligation, that is, the ones that nuclear families and networks are least obliged to feed or help financially. Many youths do survive via the economy of affection, but it is important to note that family relations are used to cover one's immediate needs rather than offering a way out of the social moratorium. In fact, only very few are able to acquire sufficient resources from family networks to secure themselves a future. *Si bu familia ka tene...*, "if your family does not have...", people say, not needing to finish the sentence as the resulting hardship is evident.

Patrimonial (im)possibilities

'If your family does not have' thus means that escaping the social moratorium is going to be tough seeing that the few resources there are, are in the hands of a few patrons, *homi garandis*, who control the access to and flow of resources and their flow through Guinean society.[22] As youth are normally not able to access the amount of resources needed to maintain a household through family networks, one of the only possibilities left is to find the backing of a wealthy patron, thus entering a patrimonial network. Patrimonialism has been defined by Bangura as

> a system of resource distribution that ties recipients or clients to the strategic goals of benefactors or patrons. In the distribution of 'patrimony', or public resources, both patrons and clients attach more importance to personal loyalties than to the bureaucratic rules that should otherwise govern the allocation of such resources. (Bangura 1997:130)

There is, however, a navigational continuum from relations of affection and close network obligation to patron-client relationships to actual patrimonial networks as socio-political structures that distribute public resources on the basis of personal relations. Youths seeking to enter political factions do so by trying to gain a reciprocal relationship to a patron, at any point in the patrimonial network, and they are aware that they will have to bow and scrape their way through such networks before gaining a possibility to actually prosper from them. Most of my informants were, in other words, living off the economy of affection and obligation while simultaneously looking for ways of forging patrimonial ties and thereby gaining a possibility to tend both to their material and social needs, their immediate and future situation. Yet because the shortage of resources make both the economy of affection as well as patrimonial networks increasingly difficult to access, as they centre upon themselves in times of crisis (Douglas 1987:123), being exploited by a patron through an unequal exchange of resources, favours

---

22. Mitchell differentiates between action sets and personal networks. An action set is, in this perspective, an instrumentally defined network actualised in relation to a short-term period of time. A personal network, in contrast, exists simultaneously on the basis of different interests and persists beyond the duration of a particular transaction (Mitchell 1969:38).

and obligations is currently the best many youth can hope for (cf. Hinkela-mmert 1993), as even negative reciprocity induces a social relationship with – at least – the possibility of reciprocation (cf. Sahlins 1974) granting youth affiliation with a patrimonial network, an opportunity for bettering their lives in the future and acquiring social capital (cf. Bourdieu 1986). Beyond being exploitative the relationship encloses, in other words, a possibility.[23]

As resources decrease, young men are thus increasingly dependent on finding an entry into patrimonial networks in order to secure themselves a way out of the social moratorium. While family networks may sustain one's existence they do not and cannot normally support an agent in his efforts to become *homi completto*, a complete man, as it is called in Creole. For this the youth must turn towards the patrimonial networks that it is possible to navigate in trying to improve one's life situation and enhance one's life chances.[24]

From patrimonialism to warlordism

Navigating networks, from the economy of affection (and obligation) through to patrimonialism, is, in other words, currently not just the primary way of gaining access to resources, ranging from a ticket to Europe to a daily meal, but the *only* way. Yet, focussing on how young men plan their life trajectories and tend to both immediate and future needs reveals that it is not the specific patrimonial network that takes centre stage but rather the prospect of social mobility. Attention to the latter illuminates the extent to which my informants navigate the possibilities opened up by factionalist politics while not being bound by factional loyalties.[25] The turbulence of factional politics provides, in a Dahrendorfian idiom, the social options

23. Patrimonialism is obviously not exploitive as a straightforward exchange of favours and obligations. However the interaction on which patron-client relationships are based is between the holder of capital and positions (symbolic, political or economic), and a person seeking the particular resource. The deeper the crisis or decline the more the holder is able to define the terms of exchange in relation to the demand on the resource(s) s/he controls (cf. Eisenstadt and Roninger 1981). Currently in Bissau, the terms of exchange are extremely unfavourable for those seeking patronage and we are thus seeing youth running errands and showing servility for the mere possibility of reciprocal obligation.

24. The relation between the economy of affection, patrimonialism and state is thus one of graduation rather than division.

25. The reference to factions makes further sense in the present context as there are currently no revolutionary parties in Guinea-Bissau with alternative political views on the organisation of state affairs and the current societal order in general.

that open up social ties and networks for the navigational efforts of youth (Dahrendorf 1979),[26] and the focus of my informants is not on charismatic leaders or ideology but on the social possibilities and life chances opened up by network competition. It is 'political' movement, which counters our 'normal', hierarchical understanding of state, and our normal idea of the movement within political structures as ideologically motivated and differentiated.

Seen from 'below' or 'within' there is no singular political order or state in Bissau, but rhizomatic networks and possibilities of movements crosscutting ideological boundaries, state demarcations and national boundaries. The state in Africa is "a plural space of interaction and enunciation [that] does not exist beyond the uses made of it by all social groups, including the most subordinated", that is "a state of variable polarisation" (Bayart 1993:252), with people trying to navigate these states of variable polarisation, imagining new political trajectories and moving between interconnected networks, as they are engaged in the politics of survival and the quest for social becoming. The political space of youth in Bissau is factionally and patrimonially defined, as they constitute the only available options for escaping the social moratorium and seeking to build a *domain* within the social *terrain* (Vigh 2003). The tragic irony is that in this perspective youth are locked in a social position within a socio-politically very turbulent society. Yet as we shall see, there is a situation, which shakes loose hardened configurations and opens enclosed networks, namely that of warfare or heightened conflict. Regardless of their contraction in the crises normally leading up to them political factions and their patrimonial structures will normally open themselves up to young people in such situations, as young men go from being secondary to their existence to being prime agents in defence of their access to resources and positions of redistribution. Because the militarisation of patrimonial politics turns it into warlord politics this entails that the networks in question begin to offer patronage in exchange for defence,[27] providing possible routes out of the social moratorium of youth.

What we have seen so far is thus how youth has become a space of confinement, as continuing economic decline has made it difficult for them

---

26. That is not to say that conflict and warfare are the only social options open to youth (in which case the percentage of mobilisation would have been far greater) but that they are among the few.

27. On warlord politics see, for example, Duffield (1998), Reno (1998, 2000), Richards (2006).

to set their lives along prescribed and desired life trajectories. Yet, be it in terms of symbolic, cultural or economic capital, agents will always try to secure an acceptable standard of life, and so we may broaden our current investigation by looking at how youth seek to survive when networks have contracted to a bare minimum and resources are barricaded out of reach; when stuck in a social moratorium with very few possibilities of getting out of it. In Creole the answer is given via a term which is at the same time a cultural institution, a self-identity as well as a praxis. The answer is *dubriagem.*

Dubriagem and social navigation

I first encountered the word *dubriagem*[28] when talking to Pedro and Justino about their life chances (Dahrendorf 1979) in the light of Bissau's disastrous deterioration, and the dismal predictability of further trouble. As they were weaving a picture of the hardships that characterised their situation as urban youths – of unemployment, conflict and retrenchment – a word surfaced which was immediately transmuted into a listing of acts and relationships that could help you get a job, a meal, or just get by. As I asked about the unfamiliar word, Pedro and Justino responded in unison: "*dubria, dubria*". Pedro continued: "you *dubria...* it's movement, dynamism, *dynamismo*", he said.

Their attempts at verbally explaining the concept for me were, however, far surpassed by their bodily movement. As they were talking Pedro had started moving his upper body in a disjointed yet rhythmical sway. Looking somewhat as if he was shadow-boxing he wove and bobbed his torso back and forth as though dodging invisible pulls and pushes. Only later did it dawn on me that what he was in fact dodging were the pushes and

---

28. At first I thought the words *dubria* or *dubriagem* were Creole, as the term apparently does not exist in Portuguese, or at least no longer exists, but is translated instead as *disenrascar* 'to disentangle or to free from difficulty' (*Portuguese-English Dictionary* 1963, George G. Harrap & Co., London). However, I discovered that the term is used in neighbouring Francophone African countries, as it has a parallel in the French verb *se debrouiller*, 'to get by, get the best out of a situation' (Reed-Danahay 1996:63–4), which is related to *debrouillardise*, 'the ability to get by'. Etymologically the word is related to *brouillard*, 'fog', and interestingly the word has a maritime use, meaning 'to clear up as cloud or fog drifts away' (ibid, *Fransk-Dansk Ordbog*, H. Hagerup, København 1964). In the current context, the relationship between *dubriagem*, haze and fog aptly describes the social conditions in which my informants seek to live their lives and relates the vernacular concept directly to the analytical concept of *social navigation*.

pulls of social forces. His metaphorical shadow-boxing was an embodied description of how one moves through a social environment in motion.

Dubriagem is, in Pedro's words, *dynamismo*; a dynamic quality of attentiveness and ability to act in relation to the movement of the social terrain one's life is set in (see also Waage, this volume, chapter 2). It is motion within motion requiring both an assessment of *immediate* dangers and possibilities as well as an ability to envision the unfolding of the social terrain and to plot and actualise one's movement from the present into the *imagined* future. It is, in this perspective, both emplotment and actualisation; simultaneously an act of analysing possibilities within a social environment, drawing trajectories through it and actualising these in praxis. As such, it designates both the action enabling one to survive in the here and now as well as moving into the imagined future towards possibilities and life chances.

Dubriagem thus refers to the praxis of immediate survival as well as to gaining a perspective on changing social possibilities and possible trajectories. It is both the praxis of navigating a road through shifting or opaque socio-political circumstances as well as the process of plotting it, and though mobilisation might appear to be a direct road to physical destruction it can in fact be a roundabout route to the construction of future social being.

> *You said you joined the Aguentas to see your life.*[29] *What is this?*
>
> If you are born here [in Bissau] and you do not have, if your family does not have, [then] you have to look for your life. You must *dubria*. If you do not *dubria* with life you will not see it.
>
> *See what?*
>
> [Annoyed] Your life! Me… If I do not *dubria*, I will not have… I will stay like this without money, a family, not even anything. (Carlos)

The above quote directs our attention towards the relationship between *dubriagem*, social becoming and the escape from the social moratorium. To 'look for one's life' and to have to *dubria* in order to 'see it' underlines that Carlos has to construe and navigate a clear passage through an opaque and changeable environment. His words illustrate how he is engaged in both a process of disentanglement from confining structures and relations as well as in a drawing of a line of flight into an envisioned future. *Dubriagem*, then, is to simultaneously keep oneself free of immediate social dangers and direct one's life, through a shifting and uncertain social environment,

---

29. *Busca nha vida.*

towards better possible futures and improved life chances. In Adilson's words:

> *Why did you go to the Aguentas?*
>
> Because I understood that they [the Government forces] would be able to send me my day of change [*dia di seku*]...[30] After... After the war, if all went well and we won, there was something (...) If you had a good level you would get money to put in your pocket, or they would find you work.
>
> *Did they say what work, or just work?*
>
> Just work, abroad, in a place outside.
>
> *Okay, in other states. Where did you want to go?*
>
> Whatever country they would send me to.
>
> *In Africa or Europe?*
>
> No, in Europe. (Adilson)

Mobilisation offered – and offers – Adilson a road out of his present stalemate. At 34, he is one of the oldest Aguentas I know, yet being without a household of his own, a job, a wife, or even the ability to take care of himself he is bitterly trapped in the category of youth. By gaining access to a patrimonial network via mobilisation Adilson saw a chance of changing his life and increasing his life chances. He saw a chance to reposition himself socially, to embark on a process of social becoming by gaining that, which is most treasured in Bissau, absence: the empty space left by migration (Pink 2001:103; cf. Gable 1995).

Rather than being tied to greed or immediate economic gratification, or being examples of the radically agentive or determined nature of the youth in question, mobilisation is, in other words, tied to a possible realisation of social being, a fact that becomes even clearer in the following quote by Paulo:

> When the war started we were in Prabis... Many people went to Prabis; many people went there... Like we sat there [and] we could hear how they shot at each other, we could hear how there was war. Since we sat there we thought like, "We are clever, we can go and join the troops. We can quickly become someone big, quickly."

---

30. *They,* refers both to the 'big men' on the Government side, as well as to Government recruitment officers who were sent to Papel bairros, neighbourhoods, and other areas to convince able-bodied males to join the Aguentas.

The above quote illuminates the tactical evaluation of present and future possibilities embedded in the act of mobilisation. Entering the army in order to 'see one's life', i.e. to gain clarity about one's possibility of movement and possible trajectories, was a common description of the motivating factor behind joining the Aguentas. However, Paulo's mobilisation should not be seen a sign of him being a 'loose molecule' (cf. Kaplan in Richards 1986), but rather as an example of the way youth take bearing of the movement of social forces and tactically navigate the space opened by others' strategy of warfare, which in Guinea-Bissau is literally 'to *dubria* with one's life'.[31]

No kai na dubria, 'we [the Aguentas] fell trying to dubria', Paulo said when I revisited him in autumn 2003, as half of the youths that were recruited into the Aguentas had fallen on the battlefield. Yet despite the fact that Paulo's tactics failed ungracefully his story offers a good description of how he as an urban youth sought to navigate war as a vital conjuncture (cf. Johnson-Hanks 2002). It shows us that mobilisation is directed both towards the *immediate* and the *imagined*, towards escaping social death and the social moratorium of youth, increasing one's life chances and gaining momentum in one's process of social becoming.

Navigation is thus centred on both the near and the far, a here and a there (de Certeau 1988:99). When navigating we imagine and actualise a path through unstable social terrains, simultaneously moving across the next obstacle or wave and negotiating the many more to come on one's way along an envisioned course.[32] In the same way, the mobilisation of youths into war becomes less puzzling if we see it not only in relation to immediate gratifications but place it instead within an evaluation of immediate and future needs and possibilities in relation to a shifting and unstable terrain. Social navigation allows us, in this manner, to see the way we move within moving social environments. It represents the phenomenon of engaging in a terrain, which at the same time engages you, or, in a more kinetic per-

---

31. *Dubria ku vida.*

32. Certain other perspectives on praxis have also emphasised this orientation towards the yet to come. Schutz' idea of horizon refers, among other things, to a future province of action (Schutz and Luckmann 1995), while the idea of project and prospect as protention (Husserl 1964:76) is similar to the prospective aspects of the social imaginary. Bourdieu's notion of illusio as "a feel for the game" is equally related to 'a future in the making', as it entails that "one positions oneself not where the ball is but where it will be [and that] one invests oneself not where the profit is, but where it will be" (Bourdieu 1998:79).

spective, moving within an element, which simultaneously moves you.[33] As such the concept is especially apt at illuminating praxis in situations of change and turmoil as it distances us from the faulty image of plotting and action as being different sequences along a line of movement within stable fields (cf. Ingold 2000:229).[34]

In order to make sense of the mobilisation of the Aguentas we need in other words to relate their engagement in war to the space of minimal life chances they are confined to, the shifting social terrain they inhabit and – as the focus on social becoming has revealed – the future realisation of social being they seek to bring about. And as an imagined and immediate stratagem for moving toward a goal while at the same time being moved by the social terrain the concept of social navigation provides insights into exactly this interplay between objective structures and subjective agency. It enables us to make sense of the opportunistic, sometimes fatalistic, and tactical ways in which youth struggle to expand the horizons of possibility in a world of conflict, turmoil, and diminishing resources; to make sense of the way that they seek to navigate networks and events as the social terrain their lives are embedded in oscillates between peace, conflict and (at times) warfare.

---

33. Generally, the concept of navigation seems to occur in relation to descriptions of praxis in unstable places. As such, Honwana (2000:77), Johnson-Hanks (2002:878) and Mertz (2002:265) all refer to navigation in relation to contexts of social change – though unfortunately without elaborating on the concept. Such an elaboration can, however, as I have shown through the concept of *dubriagem*, be found ethnographically. Furthermore, Trond Waage's description of how youth *se debrouille* in Ngaoundéré, Cameroun, explains in detail how, through improvisation, they seek to survive and gain the foundations for their existence in an opaque and uncertain context (Waage 2002). Similarly, both the concepts of *dubriagem* and *se debrouille* bear resemblance to the Brazilian praxis of *Jeitinho* as "a way of achieving one's goal (...) by using (...) ones informal social and personal resources" (Barbosa 1995:36).

34. Navigation is, in my usage, defined as motion within motion rather than being dependent on the use of maps (Ingold 2000). If we exchange 'map' for 'social imaginary', navigation as process thus combines map-making and way-finding, as we simultaneously navigate the immediate and the imagined, i.e. the next hurdle, as well as the many imagined ones to come, in our movement towards a distant goal. The fact that Ingold needs to add the adjective 'terrestrial' when talking about navigation on land further indicates the problems inherent in his definition.

Conclusion

We all navigate our lives along multiple trajectories of social becoming related to culturally defined and socially prescribed and/or desired ideas of personhood. What the focus on the Aguentas and young men in Bissau shows is that many of these are deeply embedded in generational dynamics. Social becoming in Bissau is directly related to generation and the concept of youth must, in this context, be seen in a generational perspective both in relation to how youth are defined by others and to how they define themselves. Youth is generationally not chronologically defined and though we should not regress to a static and compartmentalised idea of life stages the focus on generational dynamics enables us to see how youth envision and plot their life trajectories striving to attain adulthood and realise social being. They navigate their lives towards social, symbolic and economic capital in order to escape the social moratorium of youth.

What we have seen, when focussing on the Aguentas, and Bissauian youth in general, is thus a group of agents whose possibilities and life chances are limited in the extreme, yet who are constantly attempting to navigate the social terrain they are positioned in by relating the movement of their socio-political environment to shifting social possibilities and ties. What happens in situations of conflict and war in Bissau is that as they become militarised patrimonial networks start to mobilise young people to defend their interests. The networks that were formerly retrenched and inaccessible to most youths begin to offer patronage in return for defence. And patronage offers, in turn, futures. It enables youth to begin to 'see their lives' and to avoid social death, making mobilisation a possible 'day of change', a *dia di seku* that provides prospects and an escape from the social moratorium a youth. The mobilisation of the Aguentas is an example of how being a young, urban male in Bissau entails having to balance between social death and violent life chances.

References

Abdullah, I., 1997, "Bush Path to Destruction: The Origin and Character of the Revolutionary United Front (RUF/SL)", *Africa Development*, vol. 22, nos. 3–4:45–76.

Argenti, N., 1998, "Air Youth: Performance, Violence and the State in Cameroon", *Journal of the Royal Anthropological Institute*, 4(4):753–782.

Bangura, Y., 1997, "Understanding the Political and Cultural Dynamics of the Sierra Leone War: A Critique of Paul Richards's Fighting for the Rain Forest", *Africa Development*, vol. 22, nos. 3–4:117–148.

Barbosa, L.N. de H., 1995, "The Brazilian Jeitinho: An exercise in national identity", in D.J. Hess and R. A. DaMatta (eds), *The Brazilian Puzzle: Culture on the borderland of the western world*. New York: Columbia University Press.

Bauman, Z., 1992, "Survival as a Social Construct", *Theory, Culture and Society* vol. 9, no. 1:1–36.

Bayart, J.-F., 1993, *The State in Africa: The Politics of the Belly*. London: Longman.

Bourdieu, P., 1986, [1983], The Forms of Capital in J. G. Richardson (ed.), *A Handbook of Theory and Research for the Sociology of Education*. Westport: Greenwood Press.

—, 1998, *Practical Reason: On the theory of action*. Cambridge: Polity Press.

Bucholtz, M., 2002, "Youth and Cultural Practice", *Annual Review of Anthropology*, 31:525–52.

de Certeau, M., 1988, [1984], *The Practice of Everyday Life*. Berkeley: University of California Press.

Chabal, P. and J.-P. Daloz, 1999, *Africa Works: Disorder as Political Instrument*. Oxford: James Currey.

Clausewitz, C.M. von., 1997 [1976], *On War*. Ware: Wordsworth.

Cole, J., 2004., "Fresh Contact in Tamatave, Madagascar: Sex, Money, and Intergenerational Transformation", *American Ethnologist*, 31(4):573–88.

Collier, P., 2000, "Doing Well out of War: an economic perspective", in M. Berdal, and D. Malone (eds), *Greed and Grievance: economic agendas in civil wars*. Boulder, CO: Lynne Rienner Publishers.

Comaroff, J.L. and J. Comaroff, 1999, "Occult Economies and the Violence of Abstraction: Notes from the South African Postcolony", *American Ethnologist*, 26(2):279–303.

Dahrendorf, R., 1979, *Life Chances: Approaches to Social and Political Theory*. Chicago: University of Chicago Press.

De Boeck, F. and A. Honwana, 2005, "Children and Youth in Africa: Agency, Identity, and Place", in F. De Boeck and A. Honwana (eds), *Makers and Breakers: Children and Youth as Emerging Categories in Postcolonial Africa*. Oxford: James Currey.

Douglas, M., 1987, *How Institutions Think*. London: Routledge.

Duffield, M., 1998, "Post-Modern Conflict: warlords, post-adjustment states and private protection", *Civil Wars*, 1(1):65-102.

Durham, D., 2000, "Youth and the Social Imagination in Africa: Introduction to Parts 1 and 2", *Anthropological Quarterly,* 73(3):113–20.

Eisenstadt, S.N., 1964 [1956], *From Generation to Generation: age groups and social structure.* New York: Free Press.

Eisenstadt, S.N. and L. Roniger, 1981, "The Study of Patron–Client Relations and Recent Development in Sociological Theory", in S.N. Eisenstadt and R. Lemarchand (eds), *Political Clientelism, Patronage and Development.* London: Sage.

Enzensberger, H.M., 1994, *Civil War.* London: Granada Books.

Epstein, J.S. (ed.), 1998, Y*outh Culture: identity in a post modern world.* Malden, MA.: Blackwell.

Ferguson, J., 1999, *Expectations of Modernity: Myths and Meanings of Urban Life on the Zambian Copperbelt.* Berkley: University of California Press.

Fortes, M., 1969, [1949], *The Web of Kinship among the Tellensi: The Second Part of an Analysis of the Social Structure of a Trans Volta Tribe.* London: Oxford University Press.

—, 1984, "Age, Generation, and Social Structure", in D.E. Kertzer and J. Kieth (eds), *Age and Anthropological Theory.* London: Ichaca.

Gable, E., 1995, "The Decolonization of Consciousness: Local Sceptics and the 'Will to be Modern' in a West-African Village", *American Ethnologist,* 22(2):242–57.

Hage, G., 2003, "'Comes a Time We Are All Enthusiasm': Understanding Palestinian Suicide Bombers in Times of Exighophobia", *Public Culture,* 15(1): 65–89.

Hinkelammert, F.J., 1993, "The Crisis of Socialism and the Third World", *Monthly Review: an Independent Socialist Magazine,* 45(3):105–14.

Honwana, A., 2000, "Innocents ou Coupables? Les Enfants-Soldats comme Acteurs Tactiques", *Politique Africaine,* vol. 80:58–79.

Husserl, E., 1964, *Phenomenology of Internal Time-consciousness.* Bloomington: Indiana University Press.

Hydén, G., 1983, *No Shortcuts to Progress.* London: Heinemann Educational.

Ingold, T., 2000, "To Journey Along a Way of Life: Maps, Wayfinding and Navigation", in T. Ingold *The Perception of the Environment: Essays in Livelihood, Dwelling and Skill.* London: Routledge.

Johnson-Hanks, J., 2002, "On the Limits of Life-Stages in Ethnography: Towards a Theory of Vital Conjuctures", *American Anthropologists,* vol. 104, no. 3:865–880.

Jones, G. and C. Wallace, 1992, *Youth, Family and Citizenship.* Buckingham: Open University Press.

Kaldor, M., 1999, *New & Old Wars: Organised violence in a global era.* Cambridge: Polity Press.

Lourenço-Lindell, I., 1996, "How Do the Urban Poor Stay Alive? Modes of Food Provisioning in a Squatter Settlement in Bissau", *African Urban Quarterly,* 11(2):163–68.

—, 2002, *Walking the Tight Rope: Informal Livelihoods and Social Network in a West African City*. Stockholm Studies in Human Geography, no. 9:71. Stockholm University.

Mannheim, K., 1952, *Essays on the Sociology of Knowledge*. London: Routledge.

Meillassoux, C., 1981, [1978], *Maidens, Meal and Money: Capitalism and the Domestic Community*. Cambridge: Cambridge University Press.

Merton, R.K., 1968, [1949], *Social Theory and Social Structure*. New York: Free Press.

Mertz, E., 2002, "The Perfidy of the Gaze and the Pain of Uncertainty", in C. J. Greenhouse, E. Mertz, and K.B. Warren (eds), *Ethnography in Unstable Places: Everyday lives in the context of dramatic social change*. Durham: Duke University Press.

Mitchell, C.J., 1969, "The Concept and Use of Social Networks", in J.C. Mitchell (ed.), *Social Networks in Urban Situations: analyses of personal relationships in central African towns*. Manchester: Manchester University Press.

O'Brien, D.B.C., 1996, "A Lost Generation? Youth, Identity and State Decay in West Africa", in R.P. Werbner and T. Ranger (eds), *Postcolonial Identities in Africa*. London: Zed Books.

Olwig, K.F., 2000, "Generations in the Making: The role of children." Paper presented at the 6th Biennial EASA Conference, Krakow.

Olwig, K.F. and E. Gulløv, 2004, "Towards an Anthropology of Children and Place", in K.F. Olwig and E. Gulløv (eds), *Children's Places: Cross-Cultural Perspectives*. London: Routledge.

Pink, S., 2001, "Sunglasses, Suitcases, and Other Symbols: Creativity and Indirect Communication in Festive and Everyday Performance", in J. Hendry and C.W. Watson (eds), *An Anthropology of Indirect Communication*. London: Routledge.

Peters, K. and P. Richards, 1998, "'Why We Fight': Voices of Youth Combatants in Sierra Leone", *Africa*, 68(2):183–210.

Reed-Danahay, D., 1996, *Education and Identity in Rural France*. Cambridge: Cambridge University Press.

Reno, W., 1998, *Warlord Politics and African States*. Boulder, CO.: Lynne Rienner.

—, 2000, "Clandestine Economies, Violence and States in Africa", *Journal of International Affairs*, 53(2):433-451.

Richards, P., 1996, *Fighting for the Rain Forest: War, Youth & Resources in Sierra Leone*. Portsmouth, NH: Heinemann.

Sahlins, M., 1974, *Stone Age Economies*. London: Tavistock Publications.

Schutz, A. and T. Luckmann, 1995, [1989], *The Structures of the Life-World*. Evanston: Northwestern University Press.

Seekings, J., 1993, *Heroes of Villains? : Youth politics in the 1980s*. Johannesburg: Raven Press.

—, 1996, "The Lost Generation: South Africa's Youth Problem in the Early 1990s", *Transformations*, 29:103–125.

Stephens, S., 1995, "Children and the politics of culture in 'Late Capitalism'", in S. Stephens (ed.), *Children and the Poitics of Culture*. Princeton: Princeton University Press.

Turner, V., 1967, *The Forest of Symbols: Aspects of Ndembu Ritual.* New York: Ithaca.

Utas, M., 2003, *Sweet Battlefields: Youth and the Liberian Civil War,* PhD thesis. Uppsala: Dissertations in Cultural Anthropology (DiCA), Department of Cultural Anthropology and Ethnology, Uppsala University.

Vigh, H.E., 2003, *Navigating Terrains of War: Youth and Soldiering in Bissau,* PhD thesis, Department of Anthropology, University of Copenhagen.

Waage, T., 2002, "*Chez Nous On Se Debrouille.*" *Om å håndtere uforutsigtbarhet: Fortellinger fra syv ungdomsmiljøer i den polyetniske byen Ngaoundéré i Nord-Kamerun.* PhD dissertation, *Visual Anthropology,* University of Tromsø, Norway.

Wulff, H., 1994, Ungdomskultur i Sverige, *FUS-rapport,* nr. 6:127–141. Stokholm: Brutus Östlings Bokförlag Symposion.

—, 1995, "Introduction, Introducing Youth Culture in Its Own Right: The State of the Art and New Possibilities", in V. Amit-Talai and H. Wulff (ed.), *Youth Cultures: A cross-cultural perspective.* London: Routledge.

CHAPTER 2

Coping with Unpredictability
'Preparing for life' in Ngaoundéré, Cameroon

Trond Waage

Like many other fast-growing African cities, Ngaoundéré in
Northern Cameroon, can be seen both as a harsh and stressful
environment for young people, and as a place for new opportunities. The everyday expression, *'Je me debrouille'* (I'm coping) signifies a shared way of interpreting challenging everyday
survival situations in a culturally, ethnically and religiously
heterogeneous society. It is also a sign of common strategies negotiating their way through the social landscape. Through the
description of everyday life challenges to motorcycle taxi-drivers,
water carriers, students, porters and doughnut-bakers, who are
Christians and Muslims, males and females of different ethnic
origin, the chapter contributes to the analysis of the flexibility
needed for succeeding in an urban milieu. What young people
in Ngaoundéré have in common is how they are forced to negotiate their access into different and for them often unknown
social fields. In the process of getting access to these fields they
acquire new knowledge. These young people's main challenge
for succeeding in their personal project is to find ways to act
out new knowledge and new roles in ways that are accepted
within the framework of local ideals for respectable identities.

Introduction[1]

A man goes to a police station to apply for an identity card. On the application form, he states his occupation as 'je me debrouille'.[2] When the police officer asks him to specify what he does for a living, he retorts:

Je me débrouille.
N'est-ce pas, je fais ce que je vois,
et ce que je ne vois pas, je ne fais pas.[3]

'Je me débrouille' is a stock phrase commonly used by young people in Ngaoundéré, and in the rest of Cameroon when they explain how they cope with unforeseen everyday life situations and challenges in the urban social environment. Young people usually voice the expression with a smile, which highlights the significance to young adults in contemporary Cameroon of the qualities of resilience, flexibility, creativity and sociability as essential for coping with these challenging demands. *'Je me débrouille'* similarly indicates a speaker's openness to new suggestions and possibilities for employment or earning a living in his/her urban setting. Jean Miché Kankan's anecdote illustrates the difficulty Cameroonians face in expressing through a received colonial language, the complex everyday post-colonial exigencies for social mobility.

In the book *The Criminalization of the State in Africa* (1999), Bayart, Ellis and Hibou write about cultural repertoires for social mobility, which are linked to myths and folktales on societies' founding fathers. These founding fathers are presented as heroes who emerge from the wild bush to take control of kingdoms by virtue of their personal powers of performance in the domains of war, hunting, magic and love. The same is true of the existence of modern states where one finds social practices that highlight trickery and deception as important social values. The *Trickster*, (which in for instance Kinshasa is given the local name *débrouillardise*) is a common character associated with "the greasy pole of politics". The Trickster has a stock of tricks, changes alliances and demonstrates a high frequency of

---

1. Thanks to the editors, to Marianne Gullestad, Lisbet Holtedahl, Anniken Førde, Ismael Chibikom, Hamadou, Mahmoudou Djingui, Bente Sundsvold, Bjørn Arntsen, Esperance Kashala, and an anonymous referee for comments at different stages in the work with this article.

2. French: "I'm fending myself" or "I'm coping with this complicated situation"

3. French: "I'm fending myself. Doing what I "see" and what I don't "see", I don't do". Quotation from the renowned Cameroonian comedian Jean Miché Kankan's sketch titled *'La carte d'identité'*.

social redistribution in his cultural repertoire (1999:34–9). He utilizes all kinds of ambiguities, which lie at the heart of recurrent social phenomena found in contemporary Africa, among which are the wholesale looting of cities, banditry, prostitution, and other social ills (1999:15). It is in this light that Bayart et al. (1999:35) posit that by gathering biographical data on the founding fathers of modern Africa, most of whom started out from obscure origins before climbing to the top positions in politics, one could understand the recent development of the African state.

Inspired by this statement this article stresses the importance of empirically describing specific social situations and life experiences through the biographies of differently positioned young people, in order to understand what it means to be young in cities like Ngaoundéré. In so doing, I will identify strategies that motorcycle taxi-drivers, students, water carriers, doughnut-bakers, porters, unemployed Muslims and Christians, females and males of different ethnic origins employ in their everyday struggles to climb towards new and better positions. These strategies may appear to be flexible, creative, traditional, limited by ideals of respectability and characterized by trickery.

Youths in Africa have lately been characterized in negative and highly generalized terms as a problem: they are marginalized, disempowered, and reduced to the status of an underclass; in fact, they are a lost generation (Kaplan 1994; Richards 1995, Abdullah and Bangura 1997).

I will in this article use an actor oriented point of view where I set out to examine the problems and challenges young people in Ngaoundéré face in their everyday lives: what they 'see' and how they express their lives' circumstances. I will enquire into how they organize and make sense of their daily lives within a stressful environment. My perception is that what young people 'see' has changed in Ngaoundéré over time. Due to the continuous process of economic and social change, each generation has somewhat different experiences from those before it. Like Bayart et al. (op. cit.) I will use folktales, here as local elders' representations of their 'idealized' past, to discover continuity and change when it comes to young people's strategies and opportunities in Ngaoundéré. The experiences of the youths in question are open-ended. This chapter argues that the lives and the future of young people in Ngaoundéré are characterized, in contrast to their grandparents, by a high degree of insecurity and unpredictability. They rarely attain the goals they set out to reach.

The chapter present specific descriptions of some young people's everyday lives in Ngaoundéré, through a combination of life-stories and situation analysis to explain how young people circulate between social fields (Grønhaug 1978). This approach will help me in analysing role and identity negotiations and through these understanding proper dynamics within different social fields in this fast changing city. Thus I will have the empirical material and analytical tool to identity the different barriers, challenges and options for getting access to new social positions in the city. Finally this debate leads me to question the fruitfulness of using 'youth' as a concept in analysing processes of social change in urban Cameroon.

Youth in Ngaoundéré

'Youth is just a word.'
Pierre Bourdieu

The town of Ngaoundéré is situated in northern Cameroon, where the rainforest meets the savannah, where Christianity meets Islam, and where 'cattle herders' meet 'cultivators'. It is a culturally, ethnically and religiously heterogeneous society, and like many other fast-growing African cities, it is a harsh and stressful environment for young people, and one in which they find a critical need to be inventive and to demonstrate qualities of endurance as they strive to realize their particular conception of 'the good life'.

The town has experienced an enormous growth, from about 30,000 inhabitants to approximately 300,000 in less than 40 years.[4] It has become a crossroads for people coming from neighbouring villages, from all over Cameroon and from poorer neighbour states such as Chad, The Central African Republic (CAR), Niger, Mali and also from Nigeria. In 1950 two-thirds of the population in Ngaoundéré were subjected to various Muslim groups[5] (Frölich 1954). The town had and still has an ethnically organized structure (Burnham 1996).[6] It has since evolved from a subsistent feudal and cattle economy into the administrative centre of the province. Ngaoundéré is also a communication centre with an airport, a bus station and is the northernmost point of the national railway line, which distributes goods and imports northward to Chad and the CAR and cotton, maize and meat southward to the rest of the country. One of the

---

4. Frølich 1954 and unpublished report from The American Peace Corps 2000.

5. Muslims then belonged to the ethnic groups Fulani, Hausa and Kanuri.

6. Cameroon has about 14 million people and some 279 ethnic groups with different languages.

major changes that have occurred in Ngaoundéré is the recent importance given to formal education, which has superseded the weekly trade in cattle that still attracts most people from the neighbouring areas into town. Since the 1990s, Ngaoundéré has along with other higher institutions of learning been endowed with a university, and these enrol thousands of young people from all over the country. Most come to these institutions armed with dreams of obtaining future and fixed positions as civil servants. The growing impact of Western education has transformed economic careers and the access to social positions (Waage 2002).

Since the mid-eighties, Cameroon has undergone a severe economic crisis resulting from a fall in the world prices of raw materials such as coffee, cocoa, sugar and plant oil, in addition to a rise in the value of the dollar. In 1993 and 1994 the salaries of civil servants were slashed by 50–60 per cent while the Franc CFA was devalued by 50 per cent. In 1994 the paycheque of civil servants was only 17. 5 per cent of what they had as income the year before. At the same time prices for imported goods rose and school and university fees were introduced. The economic situation made it difficult for young people to access higher education and obtain jobs with the state. The more predictable way to be recruited into public professional schools has been through patronage coupled with graft. Most of the population that comes to Ngaoundéré is youthful and in search of employment or further education. Several authors have pointed out this phenomenon as occurring all over Africa though De Boeck and Honwana (2005) also note that remarkably little is known about this process.

Despite the above facts, it would be difficult to justify a research project on the 'youth' from an emic perspective. The concept of 'youth' or 'being young' does not seem to have an exact equivalence in the many local languages used in Ngaoundéré (as is the case with many African languages).[7] Elders in Ngaoundéré often asked me about my work because they knew that I was affiliated to the University of Ngaoundéré and to the locally well-known Anthropos project.[8] In trying to explain my project to them,

---

7. It must be remembered that youth is also a relatively new concept in the European context as well.

8. The Anthropos project is a university collaboration between the University of Ngaoundéré and the University of Tromsø, Norway that has been running since 1992. The main purpose of the project, which is a collaboration between two peripheral universities, has been to establish research knowledge together, and to promote the development of research in Northern-Cameroon.

I used the following French expressions: '*la situation actuelle des jeunes*'[9] or '*la culture des jeunes*'[10]. Malam Baba Hayatou who is in his seventies and lives in one of the chiefly Muslim neighbourhoods responded to my explanation by saying: "Here in Ngaoundéré we don't know this word 'youth'". The concepts used to establish the difference between a child and an adult in Fulani[11] are: '*buduruwa*' and '*derkeedjo*', which translate respectively as unmarried girl and unmarried boy.

Baba Hayathou recalls that in the past, one's marital status in Ngaoundéré had fixed concrete social implications. These meanings differed depending on one's ethnic background, one's group's ecological/economic adaptation and religious affiliation. A Muslim Fulani marriage meant that one had gone through Islamic training with its different constitutive rituals spanning from birth to marriage upon which the young were given cattle, livestock and the necessary requirements for marriage. One was ready for marriage when one had 'learned the Koran'. Marriage was a result of negotiation between families. At this stage '*buduruwa*' and '*derkeedjo*' were socially and economically ready to start a new life. While the young man possessed the religious training needed to participate in political and religious life, the young woman was ready to run a household. The young couple was provided with enough livestock to cater for a small family.

Malam Baba Hayathou claims that the just-marrieds were 'ready for life', a start that was made possible in the first place through moral training provided by the Koran school, which in turn was made socially significant through public rituals. Secondly, this start was initiated within the framework of two different family networks that offered mutual support to the young couple. Just-married couples possessed a role repertoire that positioned them within an existing social structure where ethnic groups functioned as corporate groups.

Among other groups, such as Christians and animists,[12] who lived mostly through land cultivation, marriage also occupied a status of similar importance for the young and the preparations were comparable. At a certain point, when a young man was ready to take care of himself as an

---

9. French: The actual situation for young people.

10. French: Youth culture.

11. Fulani is the lingua franca in most of Northern Cameroon. And the Fulani have, since the Jiihad in 1804, been the most powerful ethnic group in Northern Cameroon, at least up to the end of president Ahidjo's era.

12. These groups are mostly called pagans in the literature from this region (Burnham 1980, 1996; Schultz 1984; Eldridge 1981 etc).

individual and to look after a partner, he was quickly wedded to a wife. Among the Gbaya for example, a young man was ready to marry when he had built a house for himself, cleared sufficient land for cultivation, and demonstrated that he was capable of obtaining a good harvest from the land. The size of the harvest enabled him to choose the 'best' among the girls meaning, one that was beautiful and hardworking.

These elders of different ethnic stock are seen to recall a "utopian past" while presenting their ethnicity as the one important framework in explaining youth integration into adult society. This assertion has had great influence in the ethnography of the region where the processes of socialisation (explicit or implicit), have been described as dependent on social relations within an ethnic group (Frølich 1954; Stenning 1962; Burnham 1980, 1996; Mahmoudou 2000). Ninga Songo sums up the how the socialisation process has changed within the Gabya community (1993:186. My translation) as follows:

Socialization into the society of necessity was effected through rites de passage within the ethnic group. Initiation rites imbued the young with general rules for moral and social behaviour. Today the socialization process is fragmented between the family, the school and one of the world religions, and consists of a variation of values.

Both Muslim and Christian elders in Ngaoundéré are concerned about unmarried girls and boys who have passed the expected wedding age as well as their lack of the material means to start up a responsible adult life. Traditional rites of initiation have either lost their former significance or are postponed. Many youths live in their parents' homes far beyond the traditional marital age and others stick to formal education while many migrate to town where they basically live at subsistence level. In some instances young people move in to live temporarily with kinsmen or acquaintances.

The 'young' confirm this feeling of not getting started in adult life: *'Je fais tout pour me fixer'*[13]. In contradiction to the elders' description, the youth's social landscape depicts a frenetic individualism as they themselves state: *'Chacun pour soi'*,[14] *'Il n'y a pas de méthode pour trouver une place.'*[15] The relevance of family and ethnic group has diminished since Baba Hayathou was 'young'.

---

13. French: I do everything for finding myself a fixed position. See Munkejord 2002.

14. French: Each and everyone for him/herself.

15. French: There are no given methods for finding a place.

This work arises then from the need to use young people as an empirical focus for discovering the relevance of age, ethnicity, religion and "criminality" in concrete social processes, particularly in fast growing cities on the African continent. This is because it is reasonable to expect an ongoing negotiation on what are relevant social categories and ways of behaving in cities characterized by a high degree of immigration, as described in the early urban studies in Africa (Mitchell 1956; Cohen 1969). 'Youth' will here be understood as a relatively 'new' phase, where the *'buduruwa'* and *'derkeedjo'* seek to chart their life courses or to find clarified positions in life. These processes are characterized by liminality, where young men and women often find themselves 'betwixt' and 'between' (Turner 1964). The difference between Turner's well-known examples and the situation of youth in Ngaoundéré today is that in the latter case, *rites de passage* have to a large extent lost their practical functions (such as the economic aspect). Attaining marital status in Ngaoundéré today is not a guarantee for a predictable life.

Continuity and change in identity management

The change in development that has taken place in the town of Ngaoundéré over the years has also led to increased complexity in the social construction of persons (see Barth 1981). Paradoxically, there appears to be a high degree of continuity when it comes to what kinds of identity are of social relevance in the town. Particularly striking is the relevance of ethnic identities. A closer look indicates much unpredictability in the social relevance of established identities: they do not allow for the flexible role adaptations needed to cope with new socio-economic contingencies.

Rudie (1994) states that to study the process of individualization within the context of recent global changes, one of necessity has to secure emic ideas about what a person is and those skills and experiences they bear. She recommends the division between roles and identity negotiations in any analysis. It is through emphasizing the dynamism of the negotiations between these levels that transformations can be identified, and the relation between individualization and modernization can be analytically captured. Role-negotiation brings about moments of interaction where cultural and social agreements are continuously being negotiated and re-negotiated. The socialization process as understood within this perspective is about testing out new skills through role-negotiations. Through role-practice, the temporary and imperfect become visible. Roles are continuously negotiated if there is disagreement between two or more understandings of a situation. Rudie uses the concept of identity to point out the skills behind role-practice. Identity here refers to the contrast with 'the meaningful other' and to exclusion. From her perspective, roles are fleeting and always changing. New experiences are added just as new rules for action are laid down. However, in spite of the transformation of roles and the appropriation of new roles, identities and identity-contrasts can be seen as consistent over time.

One example is that of female Muslim students at the University of Ngaoundéré who face significant difficulties in managing their identities as students. Male motorcycle taxi-drivers in Ngaoundéré experience similar problems: they see themselves as serious drivers, though unfortunately they are also associated with increased criminality in the urban centre. From their social behaviour, female students and male motorcycle taxi-drivers are judged following moral standards, which they do not perceive as relevant to their roles. This constitutes a real life dilemma for young people as well as an analytical dilemma for researchers.

Thus, the relation between the position/role available for an actor and his/her different identities is complicated. It is useful to establish a distinction between roles and statuses that define the situation and other roles, statuses and identities that are a part of the same relationship. Several roles and identities might be relevant in one situation but they do not need to be connected (Gullestad 1984:22). For a motorcycle taxi-driver in Ngaoundéré, being a good chauffeur and a skilled technician are roles which are highly respected by colleagues. The same applies to the *'clando'* or 'clandestine' identity of most adults in the population. Being a good and respected Muslim in Ngaoundéré is an important identity trait that increases one's chances of success in different economic and social fields.

Markers such as clothing, Islam and particular ways of behaving that are connected to a Fulani identity (Ver Eecke 1989:4) express identity contrasts in Ngaoundéré. While there is continuity in the sign repertoire, the role repertoires of the Fulani and other groups change dramatically. These changes make young people from the different ethnic and religious groups similar in various dimensions. Firstly, the identity contrasts between Fulani and Gbaya, that is, between men and women, and between the respected and disrespected is redefined. Secondly, there is a repertoire of cultural material which is not referred to in identity negotiations and which is being transferred. The continuity in some aspects of identity negotiations makes it important to be aware of the methodological challenges in studying transformation processes among 'youth' in an African urban setting (see Devisch 1995).

Young people in Ngaoundéré search for roles and identifications outside the local field. Muslims, for instance, identify strongly with both Western and Arabic ideals. Despite this tendency, Fulani identity has continued as 'the meaningful other' for many young people in Ngaoundéré. At the same time the roles, knowledge and experiences of persons who strive to achieve a Fulani identity have changed. This is why we have to examine the relevance of established identity-contrasts for group dynamics and the consequences of the changed and expanded role and knowledge repertoires.

The town of Ngaoundéré can be analysed in terms of its inventory of roles which has increased enormously, from relatively few ethnic groups with a limited set of economic adaptations to an enormous variation of knowledge systems and economic/ecological adaptations. To a great extent, unlike thirty to forty years ago, Christian and Muslim women and men now have to take into account both the value and the potential risks of new knowledge (Holtedahl 1993). We can assume, with Bourdieu (1998), that the future is uncertain for young people.

In the following passage I will present six young persons that are differently positioned in the social web in Ngaoundéré and describe their opportunity situations to exemplify some of the challenges they face in their everyday life. What these young people have in common is that they are forced to negotiate access into different and often unknown social fields, which shape their identity and in the same way contribute to shaping them as persons. In the long term this will lead to the development of social forms within the urban space. This presentation focuses on aspects of life careers, with an emphasis on processes of negotiation. These young people are seen as faced with a dilemma between new opportunities and traditional cultural values, and many of them live with a high degree of unpredictability. I have been doing fieldwork in Ngaoundéré on and off for the last ten years, and I have followed the development of the town. In my work I try to understand their lives through different actors' definitions of social situations over time (Waage 2002a). Coming from a very different cultural context (northern Norway) this has been a challenging discovery process for me. Using both video rushes and still photographs has been crucial for me in finding a useful place for myself in the field, establishing dialogue and subsequently interpreting what my informants and I 'see' in different situations. The dialogue between my collaborators and me has to a large extent been based on visual material we have produced together. Several films are the result of this work (Waage 2002b, 2003).

Zeinabou: First generation of female students

Female students at the University of Ngaoundéré represent a new category of social persons in Northern Cameroon. In general, women are classified as unmarried, married, widowed or divorced. The first three categories constitute women under the titular control of a man who is either the father or husband. Women who are separated or divorced live as *'femmes libres'* (French: free women, a derogatory term). This category of women survives largely through trading and through the gifts they receive from their lovers (Holtedahl 1993). Female students are in a sense, *'libres'* before they get married. Young women who are currently finalizing their Master's degrees at the university are the first generation of university-educated women in Northern Cameroon.

Zeinabou is of Kotoko origin from the Far-North Province. Her father holds an important job at the Ngaoundéré city council. She has three close friends whom she met during her first years at university. She became acquainted with them when female students organized themselves in response to vicious rumours that were spread about them on campus and in town. Zeinabou's father had received several letters from male Muslim students who complained about Zeinabou's social behaviour: she wore jeans instead of the traditional Muslim dress and she discussed freely with boys as well as took part in social activities that they found culturally unbecoming. Zeinabou's father was forced to stop funding her studies and she found it difficult to convince him about her resolve to stay in school. Luckily, she met a boyfriend and they became engaged. This was a significant change in status, which mollified her father. However, since her fiancé was also a student and consequently a dependant, he could not take care of her financial needs, as is the custom. Her next challenge then was to convince her father to resume sponsoring her studies. Zeinabou's fiancé finally got a grant to study in France and they planned to marry on his return. Unfortunately, things did not turn out that way. Her fiancé's mother refused to let him marry Zeinabou because of her educated status. Zeinabou later heard that his mother threatened him with sorcery if he married her. She forced him to marry a young girl that she herself found for him.

Later on, she heard that life was not easy for her former fiancé and that he still nursed the desire to marry her. Since she wanted a monogamous marriage based on love becoming a second, third or fourth wife in the former fiancé's household was out of question. But then as time went on, she discovered that it was impossible to find the 'right' man. By this, she meant a man whose parents were ready to accept an 'old' and educated woman like her (she is above 25 while the normal marrying age is much lower). Her father found her situation difficult so that after she obtained her Bachelor's degree, he refused to provide the necessary finances for her to further her studies. He informed her about a friend of his who had hinted that he liked her. Zeinabou became very upset with him since she could only marry a man she loved. Beside this, she felt hurt that her father was unable to pay for her tuition at university although he could afford to marry a third wife (which requires a lot of money). Zeinabou was forced to move to a cousin's house and to look for other sources of income to continue her schooling.

Zeinabou found herself in a frustrating predicament. She remembers her early years at university as a rich time when students often discussed the Koran from a feminist perspective. They would question if a man has the right to marry several wives and what the woman's actual position in society was. As young women, they often met to encourage one another on the need to continue their studies. They came to realize that attending university enlightened them but closed the possibilities of them getting married. When Aishathou, a close friend of hers married her student-boyfriend, Zeinabou cried with happiness. Zeinabou moved to her mother's village where she made pottery for a living and from where she applied for a scholarship to study in Europe.

David: From 'big' to 'little' brother

David is one of the many young men who leave the rural areas for town in order to find employment. He is a native Pere, an ethnic group formerly enslaved by the Muslim Fulani – the ethnic group that occupies the most powerful positions in Ngaoundéré (Djedda 1998). Norwegian missionaries have worked among the Pere since the 1950s. Their initial motivation was to free them from Fulani domination and to baptize them (Lode 1990). David is one of a small number from his ethnic group that have been Christianised, acquired primary education and continued to high school. He was motivated by the missionaries to move to town where they paid for his school fees.

In town, he moved in with his cousin Soumo who worked as a journalist for the national radio (CRTV). Soumo ran programmes on the Pere people over the local radio station. Subsequently David and Soumo were instrumental in founding an association for the Pere. For some years now, this organization (called MOLNIM) has been highly instrumental in revitalizing Pere identity, particularly among the urbanized (Waage 2002).

David's dream is to obtain a job as a civil servant. While waiting for this opportunity, he was admitted to some watchman courses organized by the army. This enabled him to find a job as a night watchman at a project office of the Norwegian mission station, and another as a luggage porter at the local railway terminal.

At present, David earns a regular income. In the household, which he heads with Soumo the journalist, they let other *'frères'*[16] from their village or home area to live with them. David claims that it is an obligation for all Pere to take care of other *'frères'* who come to town. To come to town you need someone willing to receive you. The younger boys and girls who live with David and Soumo call them *'grand-frères'* (elder brothers). One differentiating aspect between the *'grand-frères'* and the others in the household is that when visitors come by and the household assembles, only the *'grand-frères'* are allowed to talk with them. Deferring to them is a mark of respect.

David sent a young woman who lived with him in the household to their Pere homeland to propose marriage to a number of girls on a ranked list. The family of the second girl on the list accepted his proposal and she arrived to be his bride some time later. After his wedding, he went back to his village for a few weeks to present his wife to his family. During this period the Cameroonian railway was sold to a South African company. When he came back, it turned out that only those who were working during the period that the railway changed ownership had kept their jobs.

David's wife was by now pregnant. When the baby was born, the mother left to have arest with her parents. After she left, the office he watched at night closed down (due to the lack of international funding). He subsequently lost his job. His wife did not come back after six months as foreseen. David heard that her parents were not satisfied with how their daughter was provided for. He thus became dependent on his *'frère'* Soumo who allowed him to stay on in the household.

David thus joined the silent ones in the household, who do not respond to visitors' questions or initiatives when Soumo is around. He has lost his position as a *'grand-frère'*. Now he works occasionally with a handcart

---

16. That is, "brothers", kinsmen or acquaintances.

transporting goods for traders. Symbolically he has once more become a 'slave' of the Muslim Fulani traders. During this period David has also withdrawn from the activities of the Pere Cultural Association (MOLIM) and the Pere community in Ngaoundéré town. David's initial ambition to get a job as a state functionary had ended with him being a 'débrouillard', dependent on a day-to-day income, with no predictable future.

Commando: *'Rester comme ca, ce n'est pas bon'*[17]

In the Muslim quarter where Baba Hayatou lives, there is a milieu of 'runaway kids' from the Central African Republic (CAR) who have taken up the jobs manned by former household slaves in the neighbourhood.

Commando got his nickname due to his interest in war films. When he was nine to ten years old, he ran away from his parents to Ngaoundéré where he settled on the outskirts of town with some Gbaya *'frères'*. He cultivated and hunted as they did back home, while looking for something better or more 'modern' to do in town. After a while he met up with other 'runaway kids' who came from his region in the CAR. These worked as 'boys' in neighbourhood households or at the public water-tap where they transported water. In the neighbourhood, there are always some possibilities to earn a little money. Access to these opportunities depends on relations. Trust is a prerequisite for acquaintances to allow one to render them services such as ironing clothes, selling groundnuts, and chopping wood. Such trust is most often achieved through the recommendation of a third party that has relations to one who can offer a job. These relations are then developed through personal initiative. Commando was recommended by one *'frère'* to a truck owner who took workers with him once a week outside town to fill his truck with firewood. This solved Commando's problem as it gave him access to other work-relations.

Commando began to come to the neighbourhood regularly. People asked him for a helping hand in making bricks, digging toilets, washing and ironing clothes. After a while, he moved to town and obtained a job as a night watchman in addition to the day-to-day jobs he did in the neighbourhood. He was able to save earnings from his job as a night watchman job and to buy a handcart. With the handcart he started a new life, going into the bush every morning to fetch firewood that he sold in town in the afternoon. He gave up his other jobs, rented a small house and started to

---

17. French: To just hang around is not good.

pay the bride price for a girl he wanted to marry. The girl moved in with him.

After some months Commando's handcart was stolen, and he could not afford to run the house. The girl moved out and he had to start struggling all over again. He was back in the neighbourhood, hanging around, looking for work to do. His '*frères*' helped him by letting him have their handcarts when they were tired late in the day or when they were occupied elsewhere. Those who live as porters hardly get enough for a living, their stand-ins experience a hard time. His '*frères*' let him sleep on the floor in a room several of them rented. Times were difficult for Commando and there were days when he did not earn a single franc.

Commando was offered a position after some time as a night watchman. He went and saw the patron but turned down the job. He had learned from other watchmen working for the same patron that he did not pay their wages regularly, and sometimes he did not even pay at all.[18]

His brothers were however shocked. The fact that Commando refused to take a job, even though he knew it would not pay in financial terms, was close to a scandal in their milieu. They could not understand how he could say 'no' to an opening. Having a job meant establishing a relationship with someone better placed in society, thus a strategic and useful relationship. What his social milieu found surprising was that Commando had no other employment then. All he did they said was to sit, chat, hang around the neighbourhood. In Ngaoundéré, when foreigners (runaway children/refugees and others) spend their days hanging around, they are seen as deriving income from invisible work, in other words they are seen as potential or actual criminals. Such considerations posed a threat to one's respectability and one's own life. In the case of any misdemeanours in the neighbourhood, such a person is liable to suspicion. Commando had little option other than to leave. He went fishing in a lake with a friend for the rainy season. The following dry season, when it became possible to earn money in water-transport, he came back to Ngaoundéré, ready to start afresh.

Hamadou's respectful but unclear position

Hamadou is a native Kanouri, one of the ethnic groups that have been assimilated by the dominant Fulani (Waage 2002). He presents himself as a student, but mostly he spends his days in the neighbourhood, near the mosque or sitting in his house, reading. Hamadou does not do much other

---

18. This is a well-known phenomenon among night watchmen in Ngaoundéré.

than look around, discuss with his peer mates, correct kids during play, say the five prayers a day and eat his regular meals. He is his father's oldest son. There were not many cattle left for him when his father died. Furthermore, the father's heritage was divided among his four wives. Hamadou for his part received his father's house and the responsibility for his two unmarried sisters.

For the third year, Hamadou is trying to finalise his first year studies in economics at the university. The very first year, his professor was fired just before the exam because it was discovered that his PhD diploma was a fake. Consequently there was no exam that year. The second year, he had to go to Nigeria to do business during the exam period. Now he studies by making photocopies of notes other students took from lectures given. He does not have the money to go to the campus every day or to buy food there. He has to provide money for his aunt and food for his two sisters.

Hamadou spends most of his days 'hanging around' the neighbourhood. His way of hanging around differs considerably from what Commando and the other 'runaway kids' are doing. Hamadou is not working, not smoking, not shouting nor eating publicly. He follows the local Muslim behaviour, claiming respectability and dignity (Ver Eecke 1989). In contrast to Commando's way of "loitering" this adds to Hamadou's respectability. He and his age mates follow in the elders' footsteps. They spend their time between prayer and discussion. The elderly men sit together at specific places at the entrance to the neighbourhood. They are cattle owners and businessmen who have hired other young people (often from their families) to take care of their businesses. These elders are people with economic power. By imitating their way of life, listening to them, having them as Koran teachers, and praying regularly, Hamadou establishes relations with them, which he hopes will give him access to a similar business to theirs in one way or the other.

So far this engagement has not yielded any fruit except for an offer to be the 'accounts secretary' for a businessman in the nearby market. For a while, Hamadou spent his days from early morning to sunset in the small clothes' shop, noting everything the businessman sold. He soon gave up, since the work could be done every day after the shop was closed, besides which the monthly salary was as little as that of a night watchman. Hamadou says he sat in the shop so the old businessman could pretend that he could afford a secretary, and this, in open neglect of the relevance of his knowledge. Hamadou states he would not work for a 'slave's salary'.

He prefers staying at home with his age mates, discussing further business possibilities.

He complains that the elders ignore the relevance of modern knowledge, a situation that frustrates his personal attempts as setting up a business. When I ask him why he did not follow in his father footsteps as a businessman selling items for weddings, he responds: "I was in school when I had the possibility to learn my father's work. When he died, I had no knowledge of the art of selling and the relations he bought the goods from."

Hamdou is disappointed with his schooling. According to him education has only opened his eyes for possibilities that remain dreams at best (see also Mbere 1985). He explains his difficulty in obtaining gainful employment by the fact that potential patrons do not value his knowledge. The relevant identity trait in Hamadou's case is one of (Muslim and Fulani) respectability, which he hopes will give access to relations with elders that have an economic position to employ him.

Motorcycle taxi-drivers: Respectable criminals?

Motorcycle taxi-drivers are a common sight in Ngaoundéré as they cycle around and ferry passengers to various destinations. The bad roads and poorly organized taxi system make taxiing by cycle faster, cheaper and more affordable to the poorer masses. The success of most young men derives from offering this cheaper transport service, which is not so demanding in terms of investment and state taxes.

The business began in 1989 after the motorcycle manufacturer 'Honda' launched a model made on license in China. These cycles were sold at very cheap prices in Nigeria. The price for gasoline in Cameroon had also dropped due to the smuggling of cheap gasoline from Nigeria (Roitman 2005).

Baba Uba, a Hausa, was among the first who introduced the motorcycle as a method of public transportation in Ngaoundéré. Baba Uba was the president of the association of Ngaoundéré motorcycle taxi-drivers when a Cameroonian colleague and I began to study the group in 1996.[19]

Because Baba Uba did not want to go to school, his mother lent him money to buy a motorcycle. The first years saw him as one of a handful of motorcycle taxi-drivers whose services were limited to ferrying commuters from the big market in town to the suburbs just outside town. These were

19. Dr Mahmoudou Djingui.

very difficult years since people were not yet used to the service. Moreover the police were ceaselessly going after them checking their driving licenses, insurance and customs duty papers. As a result of these official hurdles, motorcycle taxi- drivers developed survival strategies – they started each ride by having the passenger reveal his identity. That way the driver and the passenger could present themselves as friends if they were stopped by police officers. The younger motorcycle taxi-men tell many stories of how police officers confiscated their cycles. At this point Baba Uba laid the foundation for his appointment by his colleagues as the president of the motorcycle taxi-men since he was unafraid of engaging in dialogue with the police. The other young men told me how one night Baba Uba took with him 20 motorcycle taxi-men to a small police station to confront the police who had seized four motorcycles claiming that their owners lacked customs and insurance papers. Baba Uba was able to negotiate with the police. The four cycles were returned.

He was the president of the motorcycle taxi-men in Ngaoundéré at the beginning of the 1990s, at the time when the democratisation process started up in Cameroon, and was invited to collaborate with the (then) illegal opposition party. During this period before democratic elections were established in Cameroon, the opposition party arranged many general strikes ('*villes mortes*'). In Ngaoundéré, motorcycle taxi-men driving through the town in groups announced the nation-wide strikes. They drove with their cycle lights during daytime. Baba Uba became engaged in this activity in solidarity with the people in the 'opposition' who faced daunting problems with the police,[20] just as the taxi-men did. Looking back, the motorcycle taxi-men saw that their engagement on the side of the opposition was good for business, because it made them popular in town. It was during this period that the young men were given the name '*moto-clando*' (clandestine taxi-men) or '*les attaquants*'.[21]

Many young men came to Ngaoundéré to work as '*moto-clando*' in the following years. Some of the traders around the crossroads where Baba Uba worked commented that many drivers drifted around, not even following the praying hours. This was one of the reasons for creating a new mosque

---

20. The police were associated with the Government which had mostly Christian members from South Cameroon, the opposition party UNDP, was a party with its source in Muslim milieus in the North.

21. This slang concept refers to the French word for attack. They are attacking people who signal that they want a lift, and they are thereby attacking money.

on the pavement nearby. The drivers collected money for prayer rugs and chose an Imam (a Muslim cleric) to lead the prayers.

The rapid growth of the number of new drivers has led to considerable increase in traffic accidents involving motorcycles. In addition, motorcycle taxi-drivers have become associated with much of the violent crime in town. These developments have changed the reputation of the *'moto-clando'*. They used to be called 'riders of metal horses' a reference to a proud Fulani past, when the Fulani conquered Northern Cameroon on horseback.[22] Today the *'moto-clando'* are occasionally referred to as *'vojo'*, meaning criminals in Fulani.

Baba Uba taught himself to be an excellent technician. He was known among the other drivers as someone who could repair their bikes when these broke down and he could also inform people on reasonable prices for particular bikes.

His knowledge about bikes was necessary for him when he started buying and selling motorcycles. Initially, he did not have enough money to go to Nigeria to buy a motorcycle. But since he was perceived as a good Muslim, was married, had a reputation as a good negotiator (for example with the police and the customs officials), had knowledge and respect as a person of moral repute, he was able to establish relations with rich Muslim traders in town, who invested in his business. In this way he was able to travel to Nigeria to buy motorcycles. Little by little he saved enough to import the cycles using his own money. Thus over the years, Baba Uba became an important role model for other *'moto-clandos'*.

The paradox for Baba Uba was that the *'moto-clando'* business was associated with crime in the public sphere, though to be successful within this specific field of activity, he had to be perceived as a respectable Muslim. This new economic adaptation entails new role-repertoires for young men, at the same time as it allows them to preserve traditional Muslim identity. Baba Uba's capacity to combine new technical knowledge with traditional Muslim respectability brought him success in the field of public transportation in Ngaoundéré.

Maimouna: New ways to traditional roles

Maimouna is a Muslim Hausa. She was born outside of marriage and grew up with her grandmother in Ngaoundéré.

---

22. Fulani: *putjo njamdi*. I am grateful to the late Professor Mohamadou Eldridge for this comment.

While selling doughnuts in town for her grandmother, she met the man who later became her husband. At the age of fourteen she married Baba Uba. She was happy, because her grandmother's husband had already agreed with a friend that she should marry him. Similar to Zeinabou, my first example, Maimouna wanted to marry for love rather than according to her father's (or grandfather's) wish. Luckily, Baba Uba had the money to provide for the bride price.

At the age of 18, after giving birth to two children, life became difficult. She felt that her husband treated her unfairly by not giving her sufficient money to cope with day-to-day expenses and to manage the household. Her mother-in-law constantly complained about deficiencies in the food she prepared and the manner in which she looked after her children. Maimouna was certain that her husband was saving money to marry a second wife.[23] She heard a lot of gossip about him taking out girls to restaurants and beer parlours. Her response was to refuse to have sex with him, which again made him angry. He began to stay away from home for days.

In her situation, Maimouna planned to acquire sufficient money to take care of her own needs, and to save enough to be able to leave her husband when he married a second wife. She woke up every morning at 3 o'clock to prepare local doughnuts and tea, with her baby on her back, until sunrise.

Since her grandmother had passed away, and she had no other family in town except her baby-daughters, she had to find someone outside the family to sell the food items for her. She did not want to use someone her husband knew for that would give him the possibility of knowing how much she earned. She found a Malian boy to sell for her. The boy was in Ngaoundéré in order to work and save enough money to travel to Equatorial Guinea, a rich oil-state just south of Cameroon. Before the boy left Ngaoundéré, he introduced Maimouna to another Malian. In 8 months, she had 17 different boys hawking for her. Some of them did not come back in the afternoon, though they would set out in the morning, disappearing with the money, the kettle and the plates. Others simply did not show up in the morning. In both cases she had to go out of the household to search for them. These instances made her husband and mother-in-law furious. Her husband was very strict with her when it came to her appearance in

---

23. She was right, her husband was often talking about getting money to have a second wife. He was asked by his family to take another wife. In discussions with me he would use a common friend of ours who had just married a second wife as an example of the importance of having two wives. Our friend was a successful Koran teacher and cattle-trader, a highly respected person in the local Muslim field.

the public space. He maintained Muslim rules about respectability that supported his public position. This gave him a positive reputation among the Muslim elite, and as we have seen access to relations that helped him into motorcycle trading.

One day Baba Uba died suddenly in a motorcycle accident. It happened just after it became known that he had made another woman pregnant. Maimouna was grief-stricken for a long time, a psychological situation that was worsened by her economic plight. She lived with her daughter in her husband's house for two years, before being obliged to leave. She left without being permitted to take her children with her and without any inheritance from her husband.[24] Since then, she has moved in with different family members, in different places in Cameroon. She also tried to live with girl friends in a similar situation to her though this was not without difficulties. Zainabou now lives with an uncle and is hoping to marry again.

Ambiguity in an unpredictable life situation

The recent socio-economic transformations in urban Cameroonian society have led to fundamental changes in the lives of young people in Ngaoundéré. The most obvious change in the surrounding society is the crises in the national economy and migration, which have generally weakened the family's position in marrying off their children, and transformed the significance of ethnicity in people's everyday lives.

These young people are excluded from many opportunities their parents had, but they also have a desire, and feel obliged, to carry on with life differently from their parents. Through a constant search for new knowledge and testing out new roles, they try out new possibilities and experiments to attain a more desirable future. In their endeavours they are sometimes successful but they also fail. Through improvisation, they constantly learn how to get by and to fend for themselves, with their personal savoir-faire and initiatives.

Bayart (et al. 1999) have written on flexibility and trickery as a cultural repertoire for social mobility, emphasizing these processes' contribution to the criminalization of the state in Africa. My point in this chapter, has been to show how creative their fending for themselves has to be for adaptation and survival in a harsh urban space. In these ongoing negotiation processes

---

24. Maimouna's mother-in-law had to pay back the bride price to the husband of the woman that was pregnant with Baba Uba's baby. That is an explanation of why Maimouna was not given any inheritance.

new social fields are established (Grønhaug 1978), like the field of motorcycle taxi-men, "boys" from RCA and Chad in a Muslim neighbourhood, female Muslim students at the university and urban ethnic organizations such as MOLNIM. Within these fields one finds very different potentials for succeeding in achieving the members' ideals of the "good life", due to their own very different proper dynamics. What I have discovered is how new knowledge and new roles must be combined with respectable identities, which are the opposite of criminality, if they want to get access to desirable social positions.

Family and kinship are relevant in understanding the changes experienced by young people. Baba Uba got started in life through a loan from his mother. Zeinabou secured economic help to study at the university. Hamadou is disappointed because his family was not able to provide for his economic needs, but provides for what he has as resources. Maimouna's situation is infected by the fact that she does not have her family in Ngaoundéré. As such she has to earn her own money. When her husband passed away, she was left with little. Daniel and Commando moved to Ngaoundéré and established 'families' or a network of '*frères*' as a supportive framework.

The founding of the university in Ngaoundéré has brought about a new field of formal knowledge in the vicinity. As shown above, the problem with this new kind of knowledge and the new roles it recruits, is that its social relevance is of unpredictable value for Christian and Muslim, female and male students. For Zeinabou and other Muslim girls, the possibility for study must be balanced with respectability. There is a limit to how long she can live as an unmarried woman without being able to provide for herself. For Zeinabou, just as for both Hamadou and David, formal education has been a disappointment because it has not given them access to the labour market. For David the consequences are dramatic. He has lost his respectability and has to start all over again.

Young people in Ngaoundéré, whatever background they come from, need useful relations. They require patrons to help them get started. To establish relations with a patron, two interlinked possibilities are open: the youths can either market their 'respectability' or their knowledge. Those without a patron, like David and Commando, are the very poor and vulnerable in this society. They have a difficult future in front of them since they have few roles and lack respectable identities that would afford them access to useful relations and new social positions. They are positioned outside social fields with proper dynamics with developmental potential.

They are now categorized as a *débrouillard* (in contrast to someone which is in the process of fending for himself (*se débrouiller*), in other words, as someone without useful relations that can be exploited. They are obliged to wait for something to happen.

Hamdou's case is similar. In spite of limited economic means and a narrow role repertoire, which does not open up for new opportunities, Hamadou is able to maintain his identity as a respected Muslim in the neighbourhood. For him access to future economic activities lies in his respectability, which is where he is positioned, a cultural repertoire where higher education is blocking more than opening up for access to new fields. Alternatively, it was Baba Uba's ability to acquire a respectable identity (which is defined within the local Muslim field dominated by the Hausa, the Kanouri and the Fulani) in combination with a very specific repertoire of new and relevant knowledge that led to his success.

The most important agents of change in relation to the established power structures in Ngaoundéré are those who acquire new formal knowledge and at the same time challenge the criteria for the definition of a respectable identity. Women with higher education occupy this critical position. Their future is unpredictable and it depends on the support of a patient father or a potential father-in-law. It appears difficult for women in this group to establish a viable relationship with a man that can lead to marriage. And outside the university arena their knowledge repertoire has little circulation potential.

Young people in Ngaoundéré are developing a new role inventory. They belong to a generation with a different sense of knowledge and different role repertoires than their parents. As we have seen, respectability is an important aspect of local identity management. Holtedahl and Mahmoudou (1997) have emphasized that influence in African contexts is dependent upon respectability. In this article I have presented constant negotiations concerning the relation between achieved roles and the management of a respectable identity. If there is no agreement between role repertoire and respectability, the young fail to find a predictable position. Young people often find themselves without roles that can be respected. Respectability is a condition for success, cultural continuity as well as providing a framework for the youth's own creativity.

Se débrouiller is a part of students', water carriers', motorcycle taxi-men's and other young people's cultural repertoire in making a life. It is a way of coping with challenges, which depend on role combinations and identity management that to a large extent is independent of ethnic and religious identities. They see 'fending for themselves' as using their relational knowledge to realize their dreams. The strategies they use differ, depending on gender and background. The major challenges they face are to balance new knowledge with respectability. In this struggle they employ their creativity and hopes for the future, but also their everyday suffering, frustrations and broken dreams.

For young people as different as Baba Uba, Hamadou, Maimouna, Commando, Zeinabou and David, life is challenging. They are all approaching adulthood. Baba Uba was seen as the most successful of them as he combined a new economic enterprise with traditional identities. Hamadou having approached "modern knowledge" at the university tends to experience a frustrated status quo. David is married, Maimouna was married, while Zeinabou had a fiancé. Commando for his part moved in with a girl. For all of them and for different reasons, things did not go as planned. Maimouna, Commando and David had to start over again, establishing new strategic relations, which they could exploit to start saving money again for their various purposes. They are still young. They find themselves again within a liminal space. They have to continue their journey as *debrouillards*. The implication is that they continuously develop their creative skills when it comes to handling new knowledge and coping with existing rules for identity-management.

I agree with Rudie (1994) that through studying role-negotiation we can identify transformation of cultural and social agreements. As I have shown above, there are dramatic changes when it comes to the construction of a person's role and knowledge repertoires. More significantly, there is an underlying continuity when it comes to the relevance of established identities. These identities are steadfast and they tell us about processes of continuity when it comes to the distribution of wealth and power in Ngaoundéré. Role-negotiations tell us about willingness and the need for new orientations in life-careers. These negotiations challenge established identities and run counter to important transformational processes between generations in the case of Ngaoundéré.

The youth in Ngaoundéré do what they 'see' is possible. When they lose track of opportunities they once 'saw', they tend to initiate the search for new knowledge through new relations of patronage. It is here that we locate the specific meanings and implication of *'se débrouiller'*. 'Youth' in Ngaoundéré could therefore be seen not only as a stage that one moves through in a single direction from childhood to adulthood, but also as one into which one can move back again – from adulthood back into youth.

The demands of the urban life's economy force them to move forwards and backwards, with periodic reversals of fortune thrusting them from 'adulthood' back to 'youth' as they struggle to establish firm identities for themselves.

Are their situations typical of youth in urban Africa? Perhaps. Again it may just be typical for life in urban Africa, here seen through the experiences of some young people.

References

Abdullah and Bangura (eds), 1997, "Lumpen Youth Culture and Political Violence: The Sierra Leone Civil War", Special Issue of *African Development*, 23 (3–4).

Abu-Lughod, L., 1991, "Writing against Culture", in Richard G. Fox (ed.), *Recapturing Anthropology. Working in the present.* Santa Fe: School of American Research Press.

Baker, J., 1997, *Rural-Urban Dynamics in Francophone Africa.* Uppsala: The Nordic Africa Institute.

Barth, F., 1981, *Process and Form in Social Life. Selected Essays of Fredrik Barth.* London: Routledge & Kegan Paul.

Bauman, Z., 2001, "Identity in the Globalising World", *Social Anthropology*, 9, 2, 121–129.

Bayart, E. and B. Hibou, 1999, *The Criminalization of the State in Africa.* Oxford: James Currey.

Bourdieu, P., 1998, *Acts of resistance: Against the new myths of our time.* Cambridge: Polity Press.

Burnham, P., 1980, *Opportunity and Constraints in a Savannah Society. The Gbaya of Meiganga, Cameroon.* London: Academic Press.

—1996, *The Politcs of Cultural Difference in Northern Cameroon.* Edinburgh: Edinburgh University Press.

Cohen, A., 1969, *Custom and Politcs in Urban Africa. A Study of Hausa Migrants in Yourba Towns.* London: Routledge and Kegan Paul.

De Boeck, F. and A. Honwana (eds), 2005, *Makers and Breakers: Children and Youth in Postcolonial Africa.* Oxford: James Currey.

Devisch, R., 1995, "Frenzy, Violence and Ethical Renewal in Kinshasa", *Public Culture*, 7(3):593–629.

Djedda, H., 1998, "Diko Yébe : Libératrice de peuple! Père de l'Adamaoua", in T. Bah (ed.), *Acteurs de l'histoire au Nord Cameroun. XIXé et XXé siècles.* Ngaoundéré : Ngaoundéré-Anthropos.

Eldrigde, M., 1981, "L'implantation des Peul dans l'Adamaoua: Approche Chronologique", in C. Tardits (ed.), *Contribution de la Recherche Ethnologique à la Histoire des Civilisations de Cameroun.* Paris: Centre National de la Recherche Scientifique.

Frølich, J.-C., 1954, *Le commandement et l'organisation sociale chez les Foulbé de l'Adamoua (Cameroun),* Études Camerounaises, No 45–46. Paris: Institut Français d'Afrique Noire.

Gecshiere, P. and J. Gugler, 1998, "The urban-rural connection: Changing issues of belonging and identification", *Africa,* 68:309–315.

Grønhaug, R., 1978, "Scale as a Variable in Analysis: Fields in Social Organization in Herat, Northwest Afghanistan", in F. Barth (ed.), *Scale and Social Organization.* Oslo: Universitetsforlaget.

Gugler, J., 1996, *The Urban Transformation of the Developing World.* Oxford: Oxford University Press.

Gullestad, M., 1984, *Kitchen-Table Society.* Oslo: Universitetsforlaget.

Hall, S., 1996, "Introduction: Who Needs 'Identity'?", in S. Hall and P. du Gay (eds), *Question of Cultural Identity.* London: Sage Publications.

Holtedahl, L., 1993, "Education, economics and 'the good life': Women in Ngaoundéré, Northern Cameroon", in P. Geshire and P. Konings (eds), *Itinéraires d'accumulation au Cameroun.* Paris: Karthala.

—1997, "Magic and Love on the Road to Higher Education in Cameroon", in E. Rosanders (ed.), *Transforming Female Identities. Women's Organizational Forms in West Africa.* Uppsala: The Nordic Africa Institute.

Holtedahl, L. and D. Mahmoudou, 1997, "Power of Knowledge: The life of Alhaji Ibrahim Goni, traditional judge, in Ngaoundéré, Northern Cameroon", in E. Rosanders and D. Westerlund (eds), *African Islam and Islam in Africa. Encounters between Sufis and Islamist.* London: Hurst & Company.

Kaplan, R., "The coming of Anarchy", *The Atlantic Monthly,* Washington.

Lee, N., 2001, *Childhood and society: Growing up in an age of uncertainty.* Buckingham: Open University Press.

Lode, K., 1990, *Appelés à la liberté : Histoire de l'Eglise Evangélique Luthérienne du Cameroun.* Amstelveen: IMPROCEP éditions.

MacGaffey, J. and R. Bazenguissa-Ganga, 2000, *CONGO-PARIS. Transnational Traders in the Margins of the Law, The International African Institute.* Oxford: James Currey.

Mahmoudou, D., 2000, *Le pouvoir, le savoir et la richesse. Les Fulbe du Ngaoundéré face au processus de modernisation, Tombe I and II, Thèse du Doctor Rerur Politicarum.* Faculté du Sciences Sociales, Université de Tromsø, Norvège.

Mbere, J.A., 1985, "Les jeunes et l'ordre politique en Afrique Noire", *Logiques Sociales,* Paris: L'Harmattan.

Mead, G.H, 1934, *Mind, Self and Society.* Chicago: University of Chicago Press.

Mitchell, C., 1956, *Kaela Dance. Aspects of Social Relationships among Urban Africans in Northern Rhodesia.* Manchester: Manchester University Press.

Munkejord, M.C., 2002, *Tout ce que je veux, c'est m'asseoir quelque part. Une étude anthropologique des discours et pratiques du Champ universitaire au Nord-Cameroun,* Master thesis in social anthropology, University of Tromsø, Norway.

Riesman, P., 1981, *Freedom in Fulani Social Life. An Introspective Ethnography.* Chicago and London: University of Chicago Press.

Richards, P., 1996, *Fighting for the Rain Forest. War, Youth and Resources in Sierra Leone,* Oxford and Portsmouth: Currey and Heinemann.

Roitman, J., 2005, *Fiscal Disobedience. An Anthropology of Economic Regulation in Central Africa.* Princeton: Princeton University Press.

Rudie, I., 1994, "Making sense of new experience", in K. Hastrup and P. Hervik (eds), *Social Experience and Anthropological Knowledge.* London: Routledge.

Shultz, E., 1984, "From Pagan to Pullo: Ethnic Identity Change in Northern Cameroon", *Africa,* 54(1):46–54.

Songo, N., 1993, "Le 'Labi', Rite d'initiation des Gbaya. Meiganga", in J. Boutrais (ed.), *Peuples et Cultures de l'Adamaoua* (CAMEROUN). Paris: ORSTOM/Ngaoundéré-Anthropos.

Stenning, P., 1962, "Houshold Viability among the Pastoral Fulan", in J. Goody (ed.), *The Devleopmental Cycle of Domestic Groups.* Cambridge: Cambridge University Press.

Turner, V., 1964, "Betwixt and between: The limial period in rites de passage", *The Proceedings of the American Ethnological Society.*

Ver Eecke, C., 1988, *Pulaaku: Adamawa Fulbe Identity and its Transformations,* Ph.D thesis. Pennsylvania: University of Pennsylvania.

—, 1989, "From Pasture to Purdah. The Transformation of Women's Roles and Identity among the Adamawa Fulbe", *Ethnology,* 18(1):53–73.

Waage, T., 2002a, *"Chez Nous On Se Débrouille." Om å håndtere uforutsigbarhet. Fortellinger fra syv ungdomsmiljøer i den polyetniske byen Ngaoundéré i Nord Kamerun,* PhD dissertation, *Visual Anthropology,* University of Tromsø, Norway.

—2002b, The Master Said That…, DVD/VHS, 49 minutes, *Visual Anthropology.* University of Tromsø, Norway.

—2003, Struggle for a living, DVD/VHS, 27 minutes, *Visual Anthropology.* University of Tromsø, Norway.

CHAPTER 3

Child Migrants in Transit
Strategies to Assert New Identities in Rural Burkina Faso

Dorte Thorsen

This chapter explores how adolescent children in rural
Burkina Faso use migration to renegotiate their social position. In contrast to the literature on children's work and
migration that focuses on fostering strategies or on children's
wish to migrate to escape poverty, this chapter seeks to enrich
our understanding of youngsters' migration from remote
rural areas to nearby rural towns and the capital by exploring the less visible elements of children's negotiations with
their parents and other seniors. The chapter thus focuses on
understanding children and adolescents' migration beyond
the usual economic rationale and on demonstrating the many
indirect ways in which youngsters may exercise agency despite the fact that they as a social category hold little social
and economic power. Detailed accounts by adolescent child
migrants from the Bisa region and their parents reveal that
although migration denotes the adventure of leaving home
for children and the opportunity to increase their income
compared to what they can earn by farming and trade in
the village, it is also a demonstration of a certain level of
independence. In addition to material benefits, migration
is perceived by young and old alike as a way for youngsters
to increase their social status and mature sufficiently to
take on adult responsibilities within the household. Consequently, to assert identities as successful migrants and mature
persons, adolescent child migrants are obliged to take on
adult roles and show responsibility towards their family.

Introduction

This chapter argues that children's migration is not solely an outcome of poverty; that is, of poor parents sending away their children to reduce consumption within the household or to receive much-needed cash from their children's labour, or of children being forced to migrate to meet their own needs because their parents are unable to do so. While much of the work underlying advocacy and international programmes seeking to eliminate child labour tends to see children as passive objects in their parents' coping strategies or as victims of poverty (UNICEF 1999, 2002, 2005), this study demonstrates that adolescent children make decisions about migrating not only for economic reasons but also to have more autonomy and to acquire new skills. Based on ethnographic material about independent child migrants from the Bisa region in south-eastern Burkina Faso who travel to rural towns in the region and to the capital, the chapter explores how adolescent children use migration to renegotiate their social position and accelerate the transition from childhood to adulthood.[1] I use the notion 'adolescent children' to denote that while young migrants are often perceived as children and treated accordingly, they are not small children; most of the youngsters in this study were in the age group 14–19 years.

The view on child migrants as docile victims of their parents' poverty is embedded in a primarily western notion of childhood which constructs all children as dependent, non-working children who go to school and play the rest of the day. In addition to treating children as if there was no difference between a child aged 7, 12 or 17, this construction sets up children's economic activities as an anomaly in contradiction to their parents' fundamental duties to provide for and support their children's development (Ennew 2003; Hashim 2005; Nieuwenhuys 1996). Finally, the failure to see children as proactive decision-makers, who pursue interests that may, or may not, coincide with those of their seniors, also ignores the formative aspects for the children of leaving home, working and earning an income (Myers 1999).

---

1. The research was funded and carried out under the auspices of the Development Research Centre on Migration, Globalisation & Poverty at the University of Sussex in the period October 2004–September 2005. The material was produced in interviews with 70 child migrants (under 18 years of age at the outset when they first left home) and 45 parents, as well as in casual conversations and repeated visits with a smaller number of them during four months in early 2005. Additionally, some of the material originates from field research funded by the Danish Research Agency that I carried out in one village in 2001–2002.

Although more nuanced views on childhoods have emerged within anthropology since the 1990s, the focus in the African context has mostly been on children's and youth's positions in societies experiencing rapid change, either due to armed conflict, HIV/AIDS or swift economic changes (De Boeck and Honwana 2005; Utas 2005). As a contrast, this chapter focuses on adolescent children's labour migration from quiet, remote rural areas where migration has long been an important source of livelihood and it explores the less visible elements of children's negotiations with their parents and other adults. The chapter thus aims at understanding children's migration beyond the usual economic rationale that explains children's mobility in terms of economic need. A second aim is to unpack the many indirect ways in which adolescent children may exercise agency, despite the fact that as a social category they hold little social and material power.

Negotiating identities, meanings and preferences

Recent theoretical insights into notions of childhood and the adjacent social categories of 'adolescence', 'youth' and 'adulthood' have moved away from the idea of universal, chronological life stages towards much more fluid definitions that foreground the historically and culturally constructed qualities of such categories (Bucholtz 2002; De Boeck and Honwana 2005; Durham 2000; Ennew 2003). Although a certain level of universality is accorded to the categories of childhood and adolescence as opposites of adulthood, the meaning of these categories varies from one social setting to the other and even from one person to another. While childhood generally is understood as a phase characterised by dependence, marginal social positions and asexual identity, and adolescence is perceived as a phase of increasing independence, gradual learning of adult social positions and developing sexual identities, the interpretations of these characteristics differ (Durham 2000:115–16). The degree of dependence, for example, does not simply decline as a child grows up and becomes able to provide for him or herself, it may shift back and forth depending on the economic, symbolic and ritual situations in which children and their parents or guardians find themselves at different times.

The shifting nature of dependency and its implications for children's social positions as children, adolescents or adults is the focus of Nyambedha and Aagaard-Hansen's (2003) study of orphans' spatial and social mobility in Western Kenya. They found children adapted to being orphaned by taking on adult roles and inventing new strategies for survival, such as taking up paid work in the community, migrating to work for fishermen at Lake Victoria or in the mines, or moving to urban areas where they often worked for better-off kin. Moving and earning money meant for the orphans a shift over to adulthood. But, argued the authors, if these children were given the opportunity, for example if an older relative took responsibility for them, they returned to their social position of being children. While Nyambedha and Aagaard-Hansen make an important point about the different paces at which children grow up within the same setting, their study also raises the significant questions of whether it is possible to jump between social categories at will, and how such positioning may be shaped by previous experiences.

Here it is useful to look at Durham's critical discussion of 'youth' as a social category. Earlier attempts to define youth refer to a period of early adulthood where individuals embrace many characteristics of adults but are still not accorded all the rights and responsibilities. This definition is problematic, argues Durham, because inclusion has depended on three slightly different demarcations. Accordingly, youth are:

> (1) those (either by their own claims, or by the impositions of others) who straddle kin-based, domestic space and wider public spheres; (2) those who have gained some level of recognized autonomy and take up public roles, but are still also dependants and not able to command the labour of others as superiors; (3) those who can be expected to act upon their social world and not just be the recipients of action (Durham 2000:116).

At the core of these demarcations is an evaluation and negotiation of *who* is included in the category and what it means to be youth, especially in relation to being adult. At the level of individuals, the evaluation often concerns the ability to take up particular social positions and with them bundles of responsibilities and rights within the family or in the immediate community, while at the general level, the evaluation aims at characterising youth as a social category in order to delineate who fits in and who does not. That is to say, in a given setting, evaluations at the individual level by youth and adults alike lean on the general views of what it means to be youth, views that in turn are shaped by the common practices at that particular time. A key point here is that such evaluations are not necessarily identical because they are made by several persons whose interpretations of the qualities ascribed to particular social categories and of the ability of the person in question to satisfy these qualities may differ. Evaluations are therefore part and parcel of negotiations over meaning, practices and individual strategies.

From this perspective, jumping between social categories at will – be they childhood, adolescence, youth or adulthood – requires a conscious casting by the individual as someone who, in his or her imagination, belongs to the desired social group. Whether the orphans in Nyambedha and Aagaard-Hansen's (2003) study slipped back into being children simply because they no longer needed to fend for themselves is uncertain. Rather, I suggest, they *chose* to position themselves as children in part because it was an implicit precondition for being supported by seniors in the extended family, and in part because fending for themselves had been difficult and lifting some responsibilities off their shoulders would ease their everyday lives. Along the same line, I argue, the choice for an orphan of returning to childhood may only last as long as he/she feels better off materially, socially or emotionally than during the period of taking on adult social responsibilities. In other words, the experience of managing on their own enters the children's repertoire and shapes how they subsequently respond to opportunities and difficulties, as well as to positioning themselves in other social categories.

The children in this chapter had migrated on their own to find work. Some of them worked in small food places and shops, while others tried hard to eke out an income from itinerant work such as shoe-shining and petty-trade. Among this group of young migrants, some were orphans of one or both parents, but none of them had been abandoned by their extended families. Hence the decision to migrate for all these children was shaped by their relationship with their parents or guardians, and by their own and others' evaluation of what would be in their best interest. Here their perceptions of the intergenerational contract, that is, of what obligations they had to their seniors and vice versa, were important elements in the decision-making.

The intergenerational contract as an analytical concept is based on feminist critiques of economic models of intra-household bargaining that stress negotiations at the level of individuals. The critiques counter among others the methodological premises in the economic models of seeing negotiation as a two-person game. Instead they stress that negotiation is bound up with the bundles of privileges and responsibilities of different household members in regard to one another, and that individuals take into account both immediate and future concerns, as well as past experiences when they make decisions (Whitehead 1984, 1991, 1998). While in most approaches the agency exercised by children, adolescents and youth is conceptualised at the macro-level with the effect that the way young individuals negotiate their everyday lives remains opaque, the intergenerational contract approach is valuable for understanding better the considerations that shape the interests of both children and their seniors and therefore their negotiations at the micro-level.[2] In farming households and poorer urban households in the West African savannah, the intergenerational contract links labour needs, separate economic spheres, and long term concerns about social security.

> Children have to ensure, on the one hand, that they fulfil their obligations to parents and seniors, while, on the other hand, they wish to carve out the space to pursue their own personal endeavours, which is both in their material interest, and also an aspect of [constructing] their identity and others' perceptions of them as *"a good child"*. For their part, seniors need children's labour to secure subsistence, while at the same time ensuring they provide children with the time and means for pursuing their own endeavours (Hashim 2004; cf. Whitehead et al. 2005:16).

The sometimes, but not always, overlapping interests of different generations allow some space for acting out choices that are not immediately palatable for the other party. In a study of children's migration in Karnataka, India, Iversen (2002; cf. Whitehead et al. 2005:4) argued that boys migrated without their parents' approval because they were dissatisfied with the way the intergenerational contract was functioning in their family, but neither the children nor their parents had an interest in terminating the contract. Firstly, the disregard of the parents' authority might be perceived as a minor offence, and secondly, for both children and parents it might be beneficial in the long term to maintain the contract. Although the parents did not agree to their children's migration initially, the children's proactive behaviour rarely had serious consequences for their relationships with their family. This raises the issue of how children negotiate with their parents to pursue their preferences, how their preferences are formed and to what extent children's interests are different from those of their parents.

While the notions of childhood, adolescence and youth are usually constructed as opposites of adulthood, they should not just be seen as liminal

---

2. Most definitions of agency focus on the ability and inclination to make choices and act upon them in the pursuit of one's interests and objectives, which may target one's own well-being as well as concerns related to others' well-being, social relationships, moral precepts for appropriate behaviour and the pursuit of particular values (Fabienne 2003:17; Kabeer 1999:438; Strathern 1996:28).

phases in the process of becoming adult. Each category "involves its own distinctive identities and practices, which are neither rehearsals for the adult 'real thing' nor even necessarily oriented to adults at all" (Bucholtz 2002:232). In other words, children and young people are not simply copy-cats. Being a child, adolescent or youth is, as the above discussion has implied, about creating, negotiating and renegotiating identities with adults in general, and with parents or guardians in particular, *as well as* with other children, adolescents and youth of a similar age and with those who are younger or older (Bucholtz 2002). So, even though the child migrants in part orientate their constructions of identities and decision-making to seniors, their peer-group is an equally important reference group in creating aspirations to specific lifestyles.

While at face value running away, as the boys in Iversen's (2002) study did, is the outcome of a conflictual relationship between generations, I argue that the reason for such behaviour is more complex. In social settings – such as the one I describe in Burkina Faso – overt expressions of feelings, preferences and decisions are restrained and often subdued by inequalities in power, hence children and other social categories holding little symbolic and material power cannot speak up against their seniors. Therefore, the exercise of agency happens mostly in indirect ways that can be difficult for an outsider to discern. This poses a methodological conundrum as to how we can discover and represent these not so visible forms of making choices and acting upon them. We must also not flatten out the differences in individuals' perceptions of their capability to act in certain moments, in their talents for strategising to meet their objectives, and in their courage to transgress boundaries or counter someone who is more powerful than they are. Abu-Lughod (1993:13), among others, argues that by stressing particularities and individual experiences, we may provide a window on social practice as well as on what different cultural habits and idiosyncrasies *mean* to the people who are living them.

Incitements to migrate in the making

Migration has long been a key source of livelihood for the rural population in Burkina Faso, which in 2002 comprised 83% of the entire population (UNDP 2004). Among other reasons, due to the prohibitive agro-climatic instability, people engage in a kaleidoscopic range of activities to meet their consumption and cash needs. Even before colonisation mobility was an important characteristic of the population in the West African savannah, but the heavy taxation and labour conscription, especially in the French colonies, gave rise to two types of migration: the expansion into unoccupied rural areas nearby and circular labour migration to the cocoa and coffee plantations in the forest zones in the Gold Coast (now Ghana) and Côte d'Ivoire (Breusers 1998; Cordell et al. 1996; Faure 1996). In the territory which today is Burkina Faso,[3] moves into areas not yet colonised or to the Gold Coast colonised by the British were popular strategies of resistance in the early 20th century. The proximity of the south-eastern region to the border made long-term resettlement in the Northern Territories of the Gold Coast easier, because people could still participate in all the important rituals and thereby maintain their network of kin through visiting.

After independence, circular migration from all over Burkina Faso continued, now mostly to Côte d'Ivoire, since the cocoa economy in the Gold Coast had stagnated in the late 1950s. Migration had become inscribed in rural livelihoods both as a source of income to subsidise the fluctuating farm production, and as part of young men's transition into adulthood (Breusers 1998:182-3). Today, a significant part of the population lives outside Burkina Faso permanently, or at least very long-term, and even though women migrate less than men do, there has been a general shift in the migration pattern since the 1960s. Not only has the proportion of female migrants risen because married women join their husbands instead of staying behind with his kin, many of them have become migrants in their own right to urban areas or to Côte d'Ivoire (Cordell et al. 1996:237). The implication of the civil war in Côte d'Ivoire, particularly since it escalated in 2002, varies greatly. Burkinabè migrants were forced to leave the country in large numbers, but many also remained, either because they were too poor to return or because they had invested all their savings in property or businesses with a view to remaining permanently.

The accounts given by people in the Bisa region in 2005 revealed that, throughout the crisis, both men and women continued to travel to and from Côte d'Ivoire because the wage levels and income from trade were still considerably higher than in Burkina Faso, in spite of the deteriorating employment opportunities. Of those migrants who had returned from Côte d'Ivoire, many tried to make a living in Ouagadougou or in the rural towns, while a few had taken up farming and trade in their village. Becoming farmers and villagers under their seniors' authority did not fit with

---

3. During the colonial era, this territory belonged to shifting colonies from Haute-Sénégal-Niger to Haute Volta (Upper Volta) to French Sudan, Côte d'Ivoire and Niger (Manning 1998).

the return migrants' aspirations for life, in part because the social status accorded to being a migrant was much higher than being a junior in the village. Tied to these aspects of identity and social position were material concerns of earning higher incomes in the urban areas than in the village. Furthermore, they would have more control over their time and income if they remained migrants within Burkina Faso than if they lived in the village, where they as juniors would be helping to grow crops on their seniors' farms every morning while only having the afternoon to work on their own farms.

When adolescent children migrate, they follow in the footsteps of their parents and often also their grandparents, and, as has been pointed out in other areas of repeated cycles of migration (e.g. Camacho 1999; Castle and Diarra 2003), they often join a network of relatives at the destination. This aspect of children's independent migration has received very partial and somewhat negative attention in the advocacy to reduce child migration and eliminate the worst forms of child labour. Firstly, parents' experiences of migration in the past, and the possibility of having spent the early years of childhood as a migrant or having lived with grandparents, uncles or aunts while the parents were away on migration, are rarely considered as an important influence on children's worldviews and on the aspirations they have in life. Secondly, the function of relatives at the destinations has been discredited in the national and international discourses on child trafficking, with the effect that relatives are now cautious about being publicly branded as intermediaries and/or guardians. And yet, the relatives operate within a cultural paradigm that defines their position as classificatory parents with the rights and responsibilities accorded to this position (for Mali: Castle and Diarra 2003; for Ghana: Hashim 2005; for Côte d'Ivoire: Jacquemin personal communication; for Burkina Faso: Terre des Hommes 2003). The first point especially is central to understanding the complexities of children's and adolescents' migration, while the presence of relatives at the destination may influence the likelihood of parents accepting their child's wish to migrate. It is important to stress that even though many of the young migrants in this chapter lived with kin, they were rarely part of fostering arrangements made between adults. They asserted their own social positions as juniors in their extended families by making claims on urban-based seniors to have a place to sleep for free.

Competing with children's desire to migrate to pursue the opportunities that many others had pursued before them – but in their own ways and often with the hope of doing better – are their obligations to and sentiments for their parents and seniors. Meanwhile their seniors must balance their needs for the children's labour and company with their obligations to the children and other family members, and with their own aspirations at that particular moment and in the future. These are of course linked with how rural childhoods and children's positions in the family are conceptualised in the West African savannah.

Fortes (1949) described in great detail how Tallensi children in northern Gold Coast were gradually incorporated in the social spheres of adults by steadily encouraging them to participate in farm and household chores, and in social and ritual events where families and the larger network of kin came together. Progressively, the encouragement of voluntary participation changed to expectations that the child would carry out tasks appropriate to age and physical ability. The fundamental principles in Tallensi childhoods as processes of learning the necessary skills to sustain a livelihood and of being drawn into the interdependencies between different members of the household and extended family are very similar to the prevailing notions of childhoods in south-eastern Burkina Faso today, despite the fact that new technologies and ideas have crept into the rural communities over the years.

From an adult perspective in these rural communities, having children is an important part of long-term happiness and security, since children are a means of gaining symbolic, material and ritual status within the community. The wish and need for children's commitment to their parents is reflected in the way they are socialised into becoming cultured and gendered persons just like in the past. One important change since Fortes' study of the Tallensi is the much higher frequency of long term migration that means families are spread out to several locations. But even absent children – young or adult – contribute to their parents' status if they have regular contact and the parents are able to demonstrate this contact to others by showing letters, photographs or gifts.

In south-eastern Burkina Faso today, children are still incorporated gradually in the farm and household chores but some of them also go to school if the father *or* the mother can afford to pay the school fees and related costs.[4] While tasks like looking after a younger sibling or herding goats and sheep may be asked of a child aged 8–10, heavier tasks are not forced

---

4. At the national level, the net enrolment rate in primary school was 35% in 2001/02 (UNDP 2004), and the remoteness of most village schools in the Bisa region both in terms of the distance to school for the children and of retaining school teachers implies that the regional enrolment rate was lower.

upon them though they are encouraged to participate in other activities if they show an interest. In those cases, tools like hoes and water containers are reduced in size to fit their physical strength. Even when they start being obliged to take part in agricultural work at the age of 12–13 years, children still gather fruit and leaves, they are asked to run errands with other children and they are given time to play. By expecting older children to participate in the farm work, they learn all the necessary skills by doing, but they are also important sources of labour for their parents both on the farm and in the house. To stimulate children from an early age to take up individual economic activities, they are given a small field of their own, or a hen, or are encouraged to sell the fruits they have gathered. Gradually as they grow up they are allowed more time to engage in their own activities, but are still required for household and farming tasks that normally are carried out by juniors. Adolescent children and youth are also given time to engage in various social activities. But while girls are often under adult surveillance, boys and young men have considerable freedom to explore the social and economic fields further afield. Parents rarely exert direct control on children's income but try to influence the way in which money is spent by encouraging certain purchases and expenditures while disapproving of others (Thorsen 2005).

Following the gradual learning of skills through the incorporation in dependencies, autonomies and interdependencies within the household and in the larger, extended network of kin, migration is just another step in the on-going acquisition of skills. What the child migrants learn by working and living in rural towns and urban centres, even when they work in low-paid and insecure jobs, increases their immediate and future opportunities for earning an income and for increasing their social relations and knowledge. In the remainder of this chapter, I follow closely the stories told by child migrants and their parents. The majority of these migrants were boys in their late teens who had left with or without their parents' knowledge. Although many of them spoke about their migration in material terms, it was clear from their ideas of how to spend their income and of what they gained by being away that they had left home for other reasons than destitution. They wanted to help their parents, not by meeting the basic consumption needs, but by constructing nice houses for them some day in the future; they wanted more freedom and they wanted adventure. Their migration was however not motivated solely by their individual aspirations to a better life but also encouraged by their parents, who hoped the children would support them later in life and perhaps also bring wealth to the family. These stories reveal much about how intergenerational negotiations take place and also how the migrant boys orientated their practices and identities to their peer-group as much as to their seniors.

Paths to new identities

The gradual integration into the adult social world, and thus into the interdependencies within extended households and kin groups, shapes children's and young people's perception of themselves, and consequently the way in which they seek to position themselves in relation to their family and friends. Here the process of positioning should be understood as individual projects of constructing particular identities rather than as transitions from incomplete to complete persons.

In rural communities in south-eastern Burkina Faso, with no electricity and a low level of literacy, the exposure to other people's actions and stories was still the main ingredient in children's imagination and identity-construction in 2005. Adult views on age-appropriate behaviour were important but by no means restricted to the ideas held by the children's parents. Others sources of inspiration were close kin, other villagers, schoolteachers, health workers, other non-local residents or visitors in the village, occasional visits to the nearby town, Tenkodogo, and the radio broadcasts that children and adults alike listened to whenever they had batteries for the radio. But perhaps most important for children and young people's decision-making were the ideas shared by friends of a similar age, as well as individual reflections, on the repertoire of social positions that were worthwhile to pursue.

The significance of migration as a source of livelihood meant the experience of urban lifestyles in Ouagadougou, Accra or Abidjan often figured in the tales told by young and old, irrespective of whether they had actually lived urban lives or worked in plantations in the forest zone. With few exceptions the current generation of fathers had been migrants to Ghana or Côte d'Ivoire, as had many mothers. Especially for boys, migration had almost become a rite of passage to adulthood. For this reason, decisions rarely concerned *whether* to migrate but *when* to go.

Deciding to leave home

In 2002, Yao, whose father had died two years previously, had itchy feet; at the age of sixteen he was stuck working on his mother's farm while his two older brothers had migrated and his younger brother was only 6 years old and too little to work. His oldest brother had been working on a plantation in Côte d'Ivoire for four or five years, while the other was at secondary school in Tenkodogo, some 20 km away. Yao was the only one left to help his mother farm, and since he had dropped out of school some years earlier because the teacher often beat him, his mother expected him to work with her on the household farm all the time. Once the harvest finished, he mostly hung out with one or two friends, catching bush rats which they roasted on a small fire while chatting in the shade of a tree. It was nice not having to slave away in the fields every day or invent ways to escape the work, but having nothing to do, no ways of earning a little money, was actually boring. A few weeks later he was gone.

Although his mother presumed he had gone to a cousin in Tenkodogo, she worried that he had gone further away. She now regretted having pestered him with angry questions ever since he sold the entire rice and bean harvest – the most valuable crops that *she* had counted on selling later in the year. Yao had disastrously reduced her key savings and hence the family's security for the coming year, but she was actually more concerned that the money could pay for his transport for quite a distance – at least to Ouagadougou. At sixteen, she felt, Yao was too young to migrate to distant destinations where he might suffer or get in the company of bad persons. Although she also needed his labour in the coming farming season and it was not sure that he would return if he had gone to Ouagadougou, she mostly worried about his well-being. After all, she could easily manage to grow enough food for herself and the little one.

Yao[5], on the other hand, may have felt entitled to a share of the harvest because not only had he worked hard on his mother's fields, other boys of his age had their own rice fields and sometimes also millet fields which they cultivated in the afternoons. His mother had not yet allocated him land so he could earn money for his own clothes, and the previous year she had spent everything on the construction of their new compound when his older brother returned briefly from Côte d'Ivoire for their father's funeral. Yao may have been torn between being like his friends who bought jeans or smart t-shirts with footballers' names and numbers printed on them and wanting to be praised like his brother had been when he returned from Côte d'Ivoire. Sometimes he felt that his mother treated him as a little boy, even though he had already shown that he was growing up when he had

---

5. As Yao had left, I was never able to discuss this episode with him, so I only know his mother's version of the story.

migrated to Tenkodogo in search of work during the previous dry season, where he had been unlucky with his employers and had not received a single wage.

The conflict between Yao and his mother underscores that children and parents may interpret the bundles of rights and privileges in the intergenerational contract differently, and that their expectations and strategies do not always concur. This does not only relate to resources like land, labour and crops, albeit they are important, the way one father spoke about his son in Côte d'Ivoire gave an indication that parents are very concerned about their children's welfare and ability to cope with the conditions at the migration destination. Although Hamadou was already 21 years old, his father described how somebody in the village had arranged to *steal* his son because a relative of theirs wanted a child to work on a plantation. As the conversation went on, he revealed that his son had actually talked about migrating but, in the end, had left secretly because he had felt the boy was too young to leave home. It is difficult to know whether the father recollected ancient practices of slave-raiding where children were stolen and sold as slaves by kin and by traders, the slavery-like conditions of both forced and voluntary labour during colonialism, or echoed recent campaigns to combat child trafficking funded by international organisations, government agencies and NGOs across West Africa. But his story brought into play the fine line between coerced and voluntary migration.

In the past, observed Dougnon (2002), migrants who voluntarily walked to the Gold Coast to look for work were frequently picked up en route by recruiters in trucks or by established migrants of their ethnic origin who gave them shelter on the way to the gold mines and cocoa plantations. Both recruiters and established migrants served as intermediaries between newly arrived migrants and employers but while some helped the new arrivals, others creamed off payments and literally left the migrants in slavery. Just like migrants who had been forcibly recruited by colonial administrators and fled the placement they did not necessarily return home immediately but found paid work. Although Hamadou's father knew that his son wanted to migrate and therefore could have been looking to others for information, placement and money for the transportation, he might have evoked malevolent practices and victimisation of migrants to evade the fact that the boy had chosen to leave in spite of his reservations. Moreover, he was genuinely worried that the boy would suffer because he was not skilled in growing cocoa and might not have the required physical strength, and ultimately he might not retain his job or get enough to eat because he could not keep up with the work.

Several boys described themselves how they had run off to Ouagadougou because they were convinced their parents would not permit them to go. Usually they sent a message with someone going back to the village to let their parents know where they were, or – as Hamadou did on arrival in Côte d'Ivoire – phoned an older brother who in turn acted as an intermediary in ironing out difficulties in the relationship with their father.

From the children's and parents' stories, it is clear that intergenerational relationships are arenas in which both children and adults exercise agency. On the one hand, parents evaluate their children's maturity on a yardstick combining the responsibilities they feel their children are able to take on, their wish to shield the children from hardship, and their desire to have the children around. On the other hand, adolescent children try to assert their identities as young adults by emphasising the characteristics they feel are central to being a grown up and which they think will convince their parents. Underlying the sometimes contradictory judgements made by parents and children regarding their maturity, are negotiations of the children's identities embedded in local ideas of age-appropriate behaviour, rights and duties. Yao and the other boys who had run away did not feel as immature as their parents judged them to be, and they wanted to prove themselves. Whether the decision about their migration was negotiated overtly or not, the parents had the upper hand because they were able to repeatedly remove it from issues that could be discussed. In these situations, some children would remain at home for another year or two, others might have tried to ask permission in different ways or asked other kin to mediate the negotiation with the father or mother. Yao, Hamadou and the other boys who left secretly may have tried these strategies too but, failing to get their parents' sanction, they defied their authority and ran away as a last option, knowing well that it was unlikely to backfire.

However, parents' and children's assessments of whether it is appropriate for a child to migrate do not necessarily conflict. At the age of sixteen, after a cousin had visited from Ouagadougou, Xavier decided he wanted to try his luck. He told his father that he too wanted to earn money to buy nice clothes and his father granted him permission to go. His mother even brewed beer to give him money for the transport, though his father did not know about this gift because, as his mother explained, if her husband knew and Xavier remained in the capital for a long time, he might accuse her of having sent his son away. The three boys, David, Pierre and Pascal, had also asked permission before going to Ouagadougou in search of work. Wishing them success, their fathers gave them the address of David's father's brother, money for the transport and advised them to take the time to find proper jobs instead of being satisfied with low-paid piece-work. They also told their sons to be polite, honest and well-behaved as they, the fathers, would not necessarily hear if their sons were in trouble. Finally, they stressed the importance of savings, however small they were.

Here the parents estimated that their sons were sufficiently mature to concretely test out their imaginings about being migrants. Having been migrants themselves, they knew what their sons were in for. The assistance with money, as well as the guidance on how to navigate in the urban setting, was in one sense an indication of the parents' support for their children's aspirations of getting new insights and adopting new social positions through which they would continue to construct their identities. On the other hand, the parents shifted negotiations from the decision of *when* to migrate to the implications for their children *of being* migrants. For the children, this shift amplified the future decisions to be made about maintaining family ties and meeting the expectations their parents had of them, while at the same time pursuing their own aspirations for the future. It opened an avenue for including new elements in their social positioning but also for more binding obligations.

Renegotiating social positions – asserting identities

When child migrants return home, they are usually obliged to strategise regarding how they straddle potential social positions and towards whom they aim their meagre resources that may increase their value in the eyes of others. The expectations of remittances are many but their means are limited, since in 2005 most child migrants earned 3–7,000 Fcfa per month (approximately £ 3–7).

Returning to the story of Yao gives us an idea of how children seek to renegotiate their social position in the family through migrating. Yao came back home after only one month. He told his mother that he had sold iced water[6] for his cousin, but when he was falsely accused of stealing from an

---

6. All over Burkina, it is very common to sell small plastic bags with cold drinking water, and sweetened drinks of roselle, tamarind and ginger for 10, 25 and 50 Fcfa. These drinks are either sold directly from the fridge in small shops along the road, from 'igloo' ice boxes tied on the back of a bicycle or to a little cart wheeled around town or from trays carried around within the market place or the neighbourhood.

elderly woman in the compound, he had decided to return home. As his cousin believed in his honesty, she had given him 7,000 Fcfa (approximately £ 7). He spent half the money on clothes and shoes for himself and gave the other half to his mother as a gift. Yao was imitating the practices of older return migrants. In a study of the Kasena in southern Burkina Faso, Hahn (2003) described how, in addition to presenting a lump sum to the household head on their return, the success and social position of young migrants was embodied in the clothing and gifts they brought home. The money Yao presented to his mother was, for him, a claim to his success as an adult son, as a migrant and as willing to contribute to the family's common well-being.

When Aïcha briefly visited her mother who had fallen ill, she also followed the practices of returning migrants and brought her mother a present of two metal serving-spoons, two plastic bowls and 350 Fcfa to buy clothes for her younger brother. Although the gift was small and her mother sold some rice to buy a nice set of clothes for the brother, she was very proud of her 17-year-old daughter, who sold iced water in a town some 40 km away. Aïcha's mother was also a widow but in a different situation than Yao's mother: she did not head the household, and as she worked on the household head's farm she received millet from him from time to time, though not enough to feed all her five children without the substantial contribution from her own farm. Despite the fact that Aïcha's labour was important for her, she had permitted her daughter to migrate in the dry season.

While Yao and Aïcha opted for similar strategies when they returned to the village, the outcome was different. Aïcha's mother was delighted by her daughter's demonstration of responsibility through visiting her sick mother, saving up money and contributing to her younger brother's upkeep. She actively supported her daughter's correct behaviour by financially backing her gift to her brother. In contrast Yao's mother dismissed his purchases as 'having spent money on nothing', either because she perceived him as only a messenger who should have brought the entire sum of money from his cousin to her, because she wished to punish him for selling the rice and beans, or because she would have preferred that he invested the money in a goat rather than spending it on clothes. Where she earlier was concerned about that Yao might suffer away from home, she was now worried that he was too selfish and would not learn to manage his money, save up and take on intergenerational responsibilities in the future. These examples illustrate how children's success in enacting particular social positions, for example as successful migrants, mature persons or young adults, is shaped by earlier choices and concrete acts.

Not all parents were as austere as Yao's mother in the judgement of their children's assertion of particular identities, even if the children had not listened to their advice. When David, Pierre and Pascal, whose fathers had urged them to find proper employment, returned to their village for a funeral after a less than a year in Ouagadougou, they were dressed up in new jeans and shirts, they had identical haircuts – the hippest ever – and flashy necklaces with a large scorpion as an appendage. They had spent almost all their money on clothing to look like smart urbanites. The fact that they had not found a job during their stay in the capital and therefore had worked as itinerant shoe-shiners was erased from their appearance. They radiated success like every other migrant returning to the village. But with no money left to give to their parents or to buy presents, their construction of a migrant identity did not impress their fathers, who once again sat down to invoke a different set of priorities and repeat the advantages of having a good job. In this case, the parents' evaluation of their migrant children's maturity was about their understanding of the principles in the intergenerational contract and thus of the bundles of responsibilities and privileges that were inscribed in being successful migrants back in the bosom of the family.

Presumably the boys were more successful in convincing their peer-group about their new identity, at least by prompting a measure of envy of their smart clothes. Another avenue for young return migrants to stress difference from their rural peers is to be extravagant. Paul did not bring back many gifts from Ouagadougou because the uncle he had worked for had bought him a pair of jeans and then given him a lump sum only on the day he departed. The uncle thought he would give some money to his father and then buy goats or sheep as savings, but Paul chose to keep most of the money and treat his friends to snacks and drinks in the market. He was thus able to be a big person, at least among his peers, and he had a great time socially until the money ran out. While seniors snigger at this squandering of money and explain it with the youngsters' immaturity, young returning migrants talk about how nice it is that their friends come along whenever they ask them. However, they also say that when the money runs out, some friendships cool off too.

The new skills they learn while away are valued by child migrants as much for what they symbolise as for their practicalities. When Aïcha described what she had learned in the three years she had stayed with a cousin in a rural town during the dry season, she represented the narratives of most girl migrants. She stressed her ability to cook urban meals – frying meat and using sauce ingredients such as oil, cabbage and Maggi cubes that were rarely used in the village – implicitly magnifying the social status she gained by having these qualities. The boys, like Salfo who worked as a kitchen hand in a small restaurant and Ibrahim who was an apprentice mechanic, dreamed about opening their own businesses one day using the practical and economic skills they had acquired from their patron. Additionally, both boys and girls pointed to all the things they had seen and experienced while away that their peers in the village could not even imagine. To their peers they recounted their experiences in vivid, story-telling traditions, describing how urban people behaved and, in whispering voices, how they misbehaved. They thus set themselves apart from their friends who had remained in the village by describing their impressions but they also reoccupied some common ground by offering their interpretations of spectacular events or odd attitudes and relating them to a mutual set of moral references.

Alisetta, who grew up in Côte d'Ivoire and only returned to the village with her mother at the age of 14, did not share any of the common reference points with the girls of her age. "The girls come around but they just sit without saying a word" she complained, "if only they would tell me about the things they know!" On the one hand, the other girls' stories would have helped her to clue in on how she in turn should tell her stories to position herself vis-à-vis her new peers. On the other hand, she did not give them much chance but left to work with a relative in a nearby town after less than a month in the village. Alisetta's story shows that the returning child migrants must refer to the local practices and moral order for their positioning to be effective, but as social mobility is a central element of migrating, their positioning may be oriented towards constructing identities that are distinctly different.

The high frequency of migration from rural communities means that the children's newly attained knowledge is not unique – in fact most of their seniors are former migrants, often to destinations further afield. Hence, the migration experience itself is only a valuable asset in social positioning vis-à-vis juniors and age mates. Convincing parents and other seniors that it ought to bring a higher and more mature status and another set of rights and more freedom requires returned child migrants to demonstrate that they have taken on board some of the adult views on the kind of behaviour befitting rural life and livelihoods, rather than colourful stories from the city.

Conclusion: Being in transit

For rural children in south-eastern Burkina Faso, migration represents an avenue to pursue their own desires of earning money, being independent and seeing some of the world, while at the same time fulfilling the expectations their seniors have of them materially and socially through promises of gifts and remittances that partially make up for their absence in the day-to-day work. Becoming migrants entails being in a state of transit at many different levels. Not only does the spatial move imply a physical transit from one place to another, it often sets in motion a trajectory of moves from rural towns to the capital, and later to neighbouring countries. This trajectory also involves moves from one employer to another. The adolescent child migrants frequently change job because they have troubles claiming their wages or feel the working conditions are too exploitative, but they also constantly look for work that is better paid and offers higher social status. These forms of transit reiterate the on-going transition from being small children with few obligations and limited say in decisions to being young adults with some responsibilities to their parents but also more opportunities to pursue their own interests. This chapter focused on the initial journeys and on the way in which adolescent child migrants use their newly acquired material status to renegotiate their identity back home vis-à-vis their parents and their peer-group. What I have described is therefore just the first step in a long process of being in transit.

In a social setting where juniors cannot voice their disagreements openly if they are to accord respect to their seniors, negotiation and decision-making unavoidably become less visible, because, in the end, decisions that counter the view of seniors are acted out rather than expressed in words. Keeping this in mind is central to getting a better understanding of how negotiations actually take place, and ultimately of how children's migration links in, or breaks, with the social and economic organisation of the family.

Looking at adolescent migrants' construction of identities through the lens of the intergenerational contract foregrounds that their decisions linked with the pursuit of particular identities and social positions are not simply individualist preferences of youth fleeing the rural areas, they are firmly tied into their relationships with their parents and seniors. The adolescent children's practices at the time of the first departure and when they returned home to visit, attend a funeral or to have a short break, demonstrated the kind of characteristics that *they* felt delineated the social categories to which they aspired. Their parents' mixed reactions, on the other hand, from entirely dismissing their attempts by either refusing them permission to migrate or thinking nothing of their efforts to claim success, to trying to adjust the youngsters' thinking and strategising, to encouraging them to continue along the path they had already chosen, reflected the constant evaluation and renegotiation of social positioning.

In the West African savannah, the relationships between successive generations are shaped by the complex organisation of large households containing many layers of sub-units.[7] The long-term security of the entire household is often the responsibility of the household head, while many of the immediate needs are met by wives and junior men. This is not to say that household heads are not concerned with everyday welfare, or that wives and junior men do not look ahead but that their decision-making is informed by the responsibilities associated with their social positions (Whitehead 1998:22–5). When adolescent children seek to assert their maturity, they do not aim at taking on substantial responsibilities but those linked with more immediate needs and with being young adults.

Although children and parents shared the general perceptions of which privileges and responsibilities were ascribed to being a child of a particular age, to being a young adult and to being a senior, their evaluation of what it took at a particular moment to be accorded the attributed privileges often differed. As Hashim (2004) has pointed out, such divergences are rooted in children's and parents' individual *and* relational interests in the intergenerational contract. While both juniors and seniors seek to reinforce their own positions and make claims on resources and privileges, they also acknowledge the need to give space to others' strategies. Along this line, children feel that it is important to fulfil their obligations to their seniors, though in practice they may only partially do so due to economic constraints. Likewise, parents and guardians balance their needs for their children's labour and presence with their ability to fulfil their obligations to the children and with the possibility of children absconding from home

---

7. In the Bisa region for example, many households comprise extended families of up to four generations and include both biological and classificatory siblings at all levels. Even when a household only consists of a monogamous couple and their children, it is typically linked with other households through kinship, marriage or other social ties (Thorsen 2005).

if they are not given sufficient space to pursue their own aspirations for the future. The way in which both adolescents and their parents spoke about migration demonstrated that these dimensions of the intergenerational contract produced ambiguous discourses and practices. Adolescent child migrants, for example, spoke about their obligations to their parents in terms of constructing new houses for them, but in practice they spent much of their money on satisfying their own desires for smart clothes, radios and bicycles or on buying treats for their peers while hanging on to the idea of helping their parents some time in the future. And parents like Yao's mother and Hamadou's father wove their preferences for having their children at home into worries about their children's well-being and, in the case of Hamadou's father, into narratives that refuted children's agency in the decision to leave. Those parents who were more willing, or able, to give space to their children stressed their own inability to meet the youngsters' needs but encouraged without exception *their* ideas of what obligations children had if they were to be seen as young adults.

While parents and seniors have an obvious – and with age increasingly visible – need for sustaining a relationship with the successive generations, the child migrants' interests are more ambiguous. In a study of street-working children and adolescents in Peru, Invernizzi (2003) pointed out that children's interests vis-à-vis their parents are relative to the protection they feel their parents offer, to the skills they gain by taking up independent economic activities and to the social recognition they earn. For the adolescent children in this chapter, the three concerns are linked with being in transit and with the dependencies, autonomies and interdependencies inherent in intergenerational relationships.

Firstly, in their search for more autonomy, the adolescent children do not always value the protection offered by their parents back in the village, at least not when they first leave. This may be the root of diverging evaluations by the children and their parents regarding their ability to endure possible hardships at the destination. Since adolescent children generally have little experience of migration, their stimulus is based on aspirations to future material and social wealth and on their perception of how migration enables them to fulfil these aspirations rather than on an assessment of the difficulties ahead. Consequently, they may overrate their own capacity to take up the responsibilities of young adults. In fact, several child migrants returned home if they could not find a job, were not paid, or experienced other difficulties such as falling ill or being accused of delinquency. One boy exclaimed on his return that Ouagadougou was not for children! The reintegration of the adolescent returning migrants in the household was similar to that of the orphans in Nyambedha and Aagaard-Hansen's (2003) study, but while they were slipping back into being juniors in their households, they continuously negotiated these positions. It was clear from Yao and his mother's conflict that she still saw him as a child, whereas he sought to assert himself as an almost adult son with the gift of money for his mother – and as a child, when he 'escaped' the farm work. The important point here is that social categories are fluid and both children and their parents may shift between seeing an adolescent as a child and as a young adult, depending on the situation. The transit from one social category to another is therefore neither a mono-directional process nor a wholesale shift. Another important point is the protection offered by the family when things do not work out and the children return home without a penny to their name. All the children I knew were welcomed back, often they were given more advice and sometimes some money for transport before leaving again. The family thus provides a space for concretely testing out the imagined benefits of being migrants without the detrimental costs. Such support demonstrates that children's migration is not necessarily an outcome of familial breakdown but can be a gradual incorporation into the repertoire of livelihoods practised by a large number of adults.

Secondly, the child migrants gained practical, social and economic skills which in turn boosted their social status and their ability to position themselves vis-à-vis both their family and their peer-group. The increased autonomy, especially if the child migrants were successful in acquiring material wealth, transformed their position when negotiating concrete matters as well as identities. While the way they invested their money was key to convincing others about particular identities, the ability to fend for themselves and endure the hardships experienced as young rural migrants in the urban areas changed their position in negotiations. Even if the seniors did not always approve of the adolescent migrants' social navigation as 'skills', they recognised the need to give their children some room for manoeuvre to test their ingenious pursuit of individual interests. Children as well as the antecedent generations were acutely aware of the options for leaving (again) on migration and for going to distant destinations, a knowledge that crept into negotiations as an asset for the adolescent children in strengthening their position. While difficulties experienced as new migrants put off some adolescents, most reflected on how they could be more successful in the future and solicited the advice of others. The taste of an increased social status, at least vis-à-vis the peer-group, as well as having located avenues to obtain practical and economic skills that might be useful in the future entered the adolescent migrants' and return migrants' evaluation of what it meant to be a young migrant.

Finally, the child migrants' interests were relative to the social recognition they gained through the demonstration of success by giving gifts, investing in resources for the future, showing off fancy clothes or items like bicycles and radios. While the desire to take responsibility for their own upkeep was a valid argument to obtain parents' and seniors' permission to leave on migration, buying clothes was also a means to construct success as a migrant. However, their limited material resources underlined the difficult challenge for young people of orientating their construction of identities towards both their seniors and their peer-group. For most of the children it was almost impossible to straddle their seniors' ideas of what it meant to be a successful, young adult, i.e. bringing small gifts for the many family members and binding the money in animals, with their own ideas of the need to impress their peers in order to be seen as worldly, experienced, and adult. If the clothing was too conspicuous, the older generation felt the children were too short-sighted and wasted resources that could have been put to a better use. Here they were not making claims on their children's means for their own use but sought to inculcate in their children the advantage of savings, but once the children were away from the village, it was difficult for parents to influence their children's spending.

In line with Iversen's (2002) study of migrant children in southern India, the patient guidance by parents in tying their sons and daughters into the interdependencies of successive generations makes obvious the resilience and elasticity in intergenerational relationships which means children can act out their choices, despite the fact that they cannot counter their seniors openly, for example by leaving secretly or by not following the advice they have been given. Furthermore, the elasticity in intergenerational relationships shows that the delineation of social categories at the general level is very broad. Although seniors may seek to impress on their children some of the issues that they identify as key in the intergenerational contract, the children's failure to meet particular expectations, or their different views on what the core issues are, does not necessarily imply that seniors judge them as immature or younger. They may also want to ensure that the children continue down the right path.

Acknowledgements

I would like to express my gratitude to all the child migrants and their parents who engaged in conversations about the migrants' aspirations and experiences despite the fact that they did not know me well. I also thank Kéré Zambende, Welgo Abdoulaye and Dindané Moumini in Zéké for facilitating contact with parents in neighbouring villages, and Daboné Dasmane, Welgo Zaccaria and Bebané Harouna in Ouagadougou for facilitating contact with adolescent migrants. Finally, I would like to thank Iman Hashim, Ann Whitehead, the editors and the anonymous reviewer for inspiring comments on the paper.

References

Abu-Lughod, L., 1993, *Writing women's worlds. Bedouin stories*. Berkeley, CA: University of California Press.

Breusers, M., 1998, *On the move: Mobility, land use and livelihood practices on the Central Plateau in Burkina Faso,* PhD thesis, Wageningen Agricultural University.

Bucholtz, M., 2002, Youth and cultural practice. *Annual Review of Anthropology,* 31:525–52.

Camacho, A.Z.V., 1999, "Family, child labour and migration. Child domestic workers in Metro Manila", *Childhood,* 6(1):57–73.

Castle, Sa. and A. Diarra, 2003, *The international migration of young Malians: Tradition, necessity or rite of passage*. Research report, London School of Hygiene and Tropical Medicine.

Cordell, D.D., J.W. Gregory and V. Piché, 1996, *Hoe and wage. A social history of a circular migration system in West Africa*. Boulder, CO: Westview.

De Boeck, F. and A. Honwana, 2005, "Children and Youth in Africa: Agency, Identity and Place", in F. De Boeck and A. Honwana (eds), *Makers and Breakers. Children and Youth in Postcolonial Africa*. London: James Currey.

Dougnon, I., 2002, Migration de travail ou "trafic d'enfant"? Mise en perspective historique: le cas du Pays Dogon. Paper presented at the 10th CODESRIA General Assembly, 8–12 December 2002, Kampala.

Durham, D., 2000, "Youth and the Social Imagination in Africa: Introduction to Parts 1 and 2", *Anthropological Quarterly,* 73(3):113–20.

Ennew, J., 2003, "Different circumstances: Some reflections on 'street children' in Africa", *Children, Youth and Environment,* 13. Retrieved 13.06.2005 from http://cye.colorado.edu.

Fabienne, P., 2003, "Gender and the foundations of social choice: The role of situated agency", *Feminist Economics,* 9(2–3):13–32.

Faure, A., 1996, *Le pays Bissa avant le barrage de Bagré.* Paris-Ouagadougou: Sépia-ADDB.

Fortes, M., 1949, *The web of kinship among the Tallensi.* London: Oxford University Press.

Hahn, H.P., 2003, "Return migration and consumption in the West African savannah", Paper presented to the African Studies Association 46th Annual Meeting "Youthful Africa in the 21st Century", Boston, 2003.

Hashim, I.M., 2004, *Working with working children: Child labour and the barriers to education in rural northeastern Ghana,* DPhil thesis, University of Sussex, Brighton.

—, 2005, *Independent child migration in Ghana: A research report,* Development Research Centre on Migration, Globalisation & Poverty, University of Sussex, Brighton.

Invernizzi, A., 2003, "Street-working children and adolescents in Lima. Work as an agent of socialization", *Childhood,* 10(3):319–41.

Iversen, V., 2002, "Autonomy in child labour migrants", *World Development,* 30(5):817–34.

Kabeer, N., 1999, "Resources, agency, achievements: Reflections on the measurement of women's empowerment", *Development and Change,* vol. 30:435-64.

Manning, P., 1998, *Francophone sub-Saharan Africa 1880–1995.* Cambridge: Cambridge University Press.

Myers, W.E., 1999, "Considering child labour. Changing terms, issues and actors at the international level", *Childhood,* 6(1):13–26.

Nieuwenhuys, O., 1996, "The paradox of child labor and anthropology", *Annual Review of Anthropology,* 25:237–51.

Nyambedha, E.O. and J. Aagaard-Hansen, 2003, "Changing place, changing position. Orphans' movements in a community with high HIV/AIDS prevalence in Western Kenya", in K.F. Olwig and E. Gulløv (eds), *Children's places: Cross-cultural perspectives.* New York, NY: Routledge.

Strathern, A.J., 1996, *Body thoughts.* Ann Arbor: The University of Michigan Press.

Terre des Hommes, 2003, "Les filles domestiques au Burkina Faso: traite ou migration?". Rapport de recherche, Ouagadougou, Terre des Hommes.

Thorsen, D., 2005, *Sons, husbands, mothers and brothers. Finding room for manoeuvre in rural Burkina Faso,* DPhil thesis, University of Sussex, Brighton.

UNDP, 2004, *Human development report 2004. Cultural liberty in today's diverse world.* United Nations Development Programme (UNDP), New York.

UNICEF, 1999, "Les enfants domestiques", *Innocenti Digest,* no. 5, International Child Development Centre, United Nation's Children's Fund (UNICEF), Florence.

UNICEF, 2002, "La traite d'enfants en Afrique de l'ouest – réponses politiques", *Innocenti Insight,* no. 7, Innocenti Research Centre, United Nation's Children's Fund (UNICEF), Florence.

UNICEF, 2005, *The State of the World's Children 2005.* United Nation's Children's Fund (UNICEF), New York.

Utas, M., 2005, "Victimcy, Girlfriending, Soldiering: Tactic Agency in a Young Woman's Social Navigation of the Liberian War Zone", *Anthropological Quarterly,* 78(2):403–430.

Whitehead, A., 1984, "'I'm hungry, mum': The politics of domestic budgeting", in K. Young, C. Wolkowitz and R. McCullagh (eds), *Of marriage and the market.* 2nd edition: 93–116, London: Routledge.

—, 1991, "Food production and the food crisis in Africa", in Tina Wallace and Candida March (eds), *Changing perceptions. Writings on gender and development,* pp. 68–78. Oxford: Oxfam.

—, 1998, "Gender, poverty and intra-household relations in sub-Saharan African small holder households: Some lessons from two case examples", World Bank Background Paper prepared for the 1998 SPA report on poverty and gender in sub-Saharan Africa.

Whitehead, A., I.M. Hashim and V. Iversen, 2005 (draft), "Child migration, child agency and intergenerational relations in Africa and South Asia", Paper presented at the conference "Childhoods 2005", 29 June–3 July 2005, Oslo.

GEN(D)ERATING ADULTHOOD

CHAPTER 4

Popular Music and Luo Youth in Western Kenya
Ambiguities of modernity,
morality and gender relations in the era of AIDS

Ruth Prince

Introduction

This chapter is based on ethnographic fieldwork during the period 2000-2002 around a Luo-speaking village I call Uhero in Nyanza Province, western Kenya, which is currently experiencing a serious AIDS epidemic. AIDS is seen by many as but one expression of a more fundamental loss of connection and moral direction, and of a profound doubt about social relations and historical continuity in Luo society. This is summed up in the expression, common among both old and young, "the land is dying" (*piny tho*) – *piny* meaning 'people' and 'community' as well as the land itself. This chapter examines contemporary Luo popular music as a social commentary on these changes – upon morality and gender relations, memory and continuity, 'tradition' and 'modernity', love and loss – issues that have long been a subject of debate among Luo people, but that have become particularly salient in the era of AIDS. It considers in particular how these songs speak to the experiences of youth in western Kenya. This is a generation born during the 1970s and thereafter, which has grown up and come of age in a country suffering economic decline and unemployment, and which has been heavily affected by the AIDS epidemic. Whilst Luo songs throughout the 20th century were concerned with issues of social change, many of the popular songs produced in the 1990s deal with the particular experience of decline and loss that characterises the present-day, and in particular the lives and trajectories of young people.[1]

---

1. I use the term 'youth' rather loosely, as a strict categorisation makes no sense. The *Dholuo* word is *jomatindo* ('small people'), which does not delineate a strict category but is rather relational, as it is often used in contrast to *jomadongo* ('old people' or 'big people') and it makes no distinction between children, youths and young

This chapter first situates the concerns that the songs express in the contemporary landscape of western Kenya and the lives of young people there. It then introduces Luo popular music, before going on to provide a textual analysis of songs that were particularly popular amongst the village youth. It considers the insights the songs give into the experiences, positions and pathways of Luo youth in present-day Kenya. In doing so, the chapter contributes to a growing literature on African youth that listens to their voices and seeks to understand youth not only as victims or perpetrators of societal breakdown or rapid modernization but as 'makers' (De Boeck and Honwana 2005) of socio-cultural realities, as active participants in societal transformation, and 'major players' in the delineation of alternative forms of modernity. In considering popular music not only as an expression of experience, but also constitutive of it (see Askew 2002) – a site where youth in particular are playing with different identities that draw upon global cultural forms while being distinctively local – the chapter contributes to an anthropology of youth (Bucholtz 2002) that explores how identities are being negotiated and produced in new cultural formations.

Piny tho: "The land is dying"

Laments that "the land is dying" or "the world is turned upside down" are a common feature of recent Africanist ethnography, conducted in societies emerging from war and famine (e.g. Gable 1995:243; Hutchinson 1996:40; De Boeck 1998), suffering economic decline and the effects of structural adjustment policies (Ferguson 1999; Sanders 2001) and experiencing the epidemic of AIDS (Bawa Yamba 1997; Dilger 2003). In an article on post-Mobutu Congo, De Boeck writes of a "deeply felt sense of personal and communal crisis which pervaded all levels of society" and of "the growing sense of loss of a viable basis of social relations" (1998:25; see also Devisch 1995). He traces this to a "crisis of postcolonial memory", as the rupture with social and symbolic systems and ways of life of the past that accompanied colonialism has not been filled by the promises of independence and development. Similarly, Ferguson describes a "crisis of meaning" among

---

married people. While in the past, youth appears to have been a life-stage clearly distinguished from adulthood, today pathways to adulthood are unclear and must be negotiated through a variety of trajectories, which may or may not include marriage, having children, having a job and economic security and building a rural house and a home. In this sense, Durham's conception of the category of youth as a 'social shifter', that is relational and indexical, rather than absolute, seems apt (2000:116).

miners in the Zambian Copperbelt, as unemployment drove city-dwellers back to the land and to a way of life they thought they had left behind in the heyday of Zambia's modernisation (1999). Rupture and fragmentation have been described as characterising the post-colonial condition in Africa (Mamdani 1996; Werbner 1998): a rupture not only from the past, which has been the experience of many African societies through the 20th century, but also from the future; an experience of dislocation and marginalisation in the present world economy, a loss of faith in modernisation and development and a breakdown of what Ferguson describes as the "teleological narratives of modernity" (1999:14). This has produced a sense of loss, in which nostalgia for a rural past underlies longing for an elusive modernity, causing, Mudimbe suggests, the context of daily life for many people to be situated within what he refers to as a space of marginality (1988).

A return to 'tradition'

Literature on Luo people suggests that nostalgia for the past and longing for cultural unity and a return to custom was a feature of Luo life during the 20th century, long before the era of AIDS. Already in the 1930s a mission-educated Luo, Paul Mboya, wrote a book called *Luo culture and custom*, expressing a fear that traditional cultural ways of life were being lost and forgotten, as people embraced Christianity and became labour migrants and city dwellers (Mboya 1983 (1938)). To judge by the amount of this kind of 'traditionalist' literature available in Kenya today (for example, Ocholla-Ayayo 1976; Ogutu 1995; Raringo 2001), this form of nostalgia has waxed and waned. However, it has clearly become prominent in recent years: since the 1990s there has been a proliferation of traditionalist publications, radio programmes and an internet site (www.jaluo.com) all concerned with how to follow Luo culture and traditions in the contemporary world and in response to particular situations brought about by AIDS, migration, Christianity and urban life. Young and old, women as well as men are avid listeners to these radio programmes and avid debaters in daily life about the merits of a 'return' to tradition.

A lost modernity

Alongside this resurgence of interest in 'tradition', many people in Uhero share a nostalgia for the heyday of modernisation in Kenya, the 1950s through to the 1970s, which is remembered as an era of new aspirations and opportunities (Hay 2000); a time of "dancing the rumba" as older Luo

– who spent much of their lives living and working across East Africa – recall. Formal education then led to secure employment, and geographical as well as social upward mobility. Black-and-white photographs on the walls of houses in Uhero, which show men in suits and women in 1960s and '70s mini-skirts; white weddings, Kenya Railways football club teams and family portraits in photo-studios in Mombasa and Nairobi, testify to the hopes and expectations of these times, in which the economy was buoyant, the government offered free education and stable employment, and mobility and connections with the emerging nations of East Africa expanded. From the perspective of the present, then, the future in those days appeared graspable. Such memories colour perceptions of the present as a period of decline and loss, and of the future as uncertain.

Nyanza Province was designated a 'labour reserve' by the colonial government in the 1920s, and already by the 1930s almost all men living there had entered the labour market at some point in the their lives (Stichter 1982:46). By the 1960s, the dominant pattern was for workers to spend the whole of their working lives in urban employment, returning to the rural home only for holidays and retirement (whilst their wives often moved between staying with the husband in town and taking care of the rural home) (Hay 1976, 1992; Parkin 1978; Stichter 1982). The dominant movement away from the 'reserve', and the location of economic opportunities elsewhere, together with the marginalisation of Luo in postcolonial politics, has meant that the area has continued to be underdeveloped (Haugerud 1993). However, although labour migration drained the 'reserve' of young men, during the heyday of independence and economic development, wages from labour migration also sustained rural life, and movements between town and village played a large part in transforming rural ways of life (Fearn 1961; Cohen and Odhiambo 1989; Hay 1994). Moreover, the movement to work in town expressed a faith in progress and development. As the economy expanded from the 1950s to the 1970s, people moved to towns and embraced urban life. Luo communities sprang up in the towns of Kenya and East Africa – as John Lonsdale wrote: "Nairobi, Dar-es-Salaam and Kampala were outposts of *Piny Luo*" (cited in Cohen and Odhiambo 1992:109; see also Parkin 1978).

Since the 1980s, however, falling real wages and growing urban unemployment have put a strain on the remittances that sustained rural households, and have led to a degree of reverse migration by men who have lost their jobs or have given up trying to find work in the urban labour market (Francis 1995). In this situation of decline, economic and gender roles are in flux. Gender roles established during the heyday of labour migration – of male breadwinner and dependent wife – are being challenged. At the same time, the 'reserve' remains just that, a place of poverty, malnutrition and struggle (see Cohen and Odhiambo 1989). The space of modernity, of progress and development is elsewhere, outside Nyanza, outside of Kenya and indeed Africa. Many of the Luo elite have studied in Europe and America and send their children to schools and universities there. However, most of those living in Uhero know about such places only through radio news, pop songs, second-hand clothes and what they see of urban and elite lifestyles. Europe and America promise a future that cannot be found in Uhero and that remains inaccessible – and the growing availability of images of this other world in advertisements, print, on Hollywood videos played in market centres, only exacerbates this experience of disconnection, of being left at the margin whilst the modern world moves on.

The road to modernity, on which the older generation have journeyed, is thus unavailable to the village youth – who instead now spend their time "tarmaccing", as they call it, a phrase that captures the endless movement back and forth along the pot-holed tarmac roads, between home and town, searching for work (see also Francis 1995). Even those with secondary-school certificates have few prospects of finding jobs in town, and fishing, once a relatively lucrative activity, is in decline. Many of the young people thus feel both disconnected from the optimism of the past and dispossessed of any future, and they express this as being stuck and directionless in the present: "we're just sitting" (*wabetabeta*), they say, or "we're just wandering around" (*wabayabaya*). This sense of immobility is spatial as well as temporal, and is captured in the colonial term for the rural area, 'reserve', which continues to be used in everyday conversations.

AIDS

This sense of being stuck is embodied and exacerbated by AIDS, which has hit Uhero hard. Our census data from November 2000 to December 2002 indicate that during this period there were 67 deaths in this village of approximately 1000 people, of which 30 were adults between 15–45 years of age.[2] UNAIDS statistics on HIV/AIDS in Kenya suggest that by the end of 2001, fifteen percent of the adult population (aged 15–49 years) were HIV

---

2. Thirty-six of those who died were female, while 31 were male. The actual number of deaths among *JoUhero* was probably higher, as we only registered people who had been resident in Uhero for more than six months prior to the census (six months

positive, and that at least 1.5 million people had died of AIDS (UNAIDS 2000, 2003). Western Kenya has been particularly hard hit by the AIDS epidemic and Nyanza Province has the highest prevalence in the country; in 2000, this was approximately 22 per cent among the adult population (UNAIDS 2000).[3]

In the village of Uhero, the effects of AIDS show in fresh graves and deserted houses, in homes inhabited only by the old and very young, by grandmothers and grandchildren (see Nyambedha et al. 2003), and in the weekly funerals that JoUhero attend. Many homes are struggling to look after sick sons and daughters who have returned from the town and hospital to seek care from their mothers. While people associate this sickness and death with AIDS, for many the death has another meaning; it is not understood as exclusively about AIDS. Some argue that it is form of *chira* – sickness arising from 'confusion' (*nyuandruok*) in social relations – as people either deliberately leave or forget to follow the relational acts or 'Luo rules' (*chike Luo*, often translated as 'Luo traditions' or 'Luo ways') that structure kinship and social life. But, whereas in the past there was medicine for *chira*, and meaningful and effective ritual means of addressing these ruptures in social relations, "these days", people say, "for this sickness, our medicine does not work". The fact that biomedicine also offers no cure for AIDS suggests the impotency of modernity itself; and the knowledge that even if treatment became available, few could afford it, presents an apt parable of the position of JoUhero in the world as, some put it, "us poor Africans". Thus, whether it is considered as AIDS or as *chira*, what is referred to as "this illness of ours" (*tuoni marwa*) or "the death of today" (*tho mar tinende*) is for many an expression of the lack of direction and the moral confusion of modern times, and it embodies the situation of JoUhero in the modern world: "it is our illness", they say, "not yours".[4]

---

being the time between two censuses), and thus missed those who returned from the city and died within half a year.

3. In 2001, the HIV prevalence rate among young people in Kenya aged 15–24 years was calculated as being between 12.5 per cent and 18.7 per cent for women, and between 4.8 per cent and 7.2 per cent for men (UNAIDS 2000, 2003). HIV prevalence among young people in western Kenya is much higher: 34 per cent among 19-year-old women in Kisumu compared to 9 per cent among 19-year-old men (see Appendix 3).

4. *Chira* is derived from the verb *chiyo*, 'to suck, or drain from', as it is a condition that drains life. It is similar to HIV/AIDS as the person gets thinner and weaker and finally dies.

When people in Uhero lament that the "land is dying" (*piny tho*), they thus refer to an accumulation of what they call "confusion" in social relations and in relations with place – *piny* meaning community and people, place as well as the land itself. That the land and the community, once the source of life-force, potency, generation, of fertility and well-being, is now said to be "drying up" or even to be "dead", refers not only to the literal loss of human life in recent decades, and the decline in the fertility of land, cattle herds and fishing stocks, which the area has experienced over the past century (Cohen and Odhiambo 1989), but also to the marginalisation and impotency of local forms of knowledge and power and the drying up of the roads to progress for many people in modern Kenya.

Youth and the crisis of social reproduction

Transformations in the colonial and postcolonial landscape – the development of labour migration, Christianity and education as pathways to modernisation, and the dissolving of these in the 1980s and 1990s in the context of economic decline and AIDS – have been closely bound up with profound changes in the younger generation's access to the means of social reproduction as well as with intense conflicts in gender relations. Today young men in particular face a double predicament. On the one hand they are unable to fulfil the role expectations of male breadwinner, established by their grandfathers and fathers through labour migration. On the other, their lack of access to cash means they face difficulties in finding bridewealth and keeping a wife, for who wants a husband without money? They thus remain socially immature; unable to gain access to pathways of what in Dholuo is called 'growth' (*dongruok*), a term that encompasses personal and family fertility as well as social reproduction in its broadest sense, and which is tied to the production of kinship and the socio-moral order. In the past, women were for the most part dependent upon husbands for access to land, and their children belonged to the husband's lineage – thus rural Luo women had limited opportunities for survival and for gaining social status outside of marriage (Parkin 1978; Pala 1980; Hay 1982). While this is still the case, due to the commodification and increasing scarcity of land, young men often find themselves either with a very small parcel of their father's land (too small to cultivate on), or with no land at all (Francis 1995).[5] In this context, young women prefer to become second or third

5. My survey of land transactions in the village where I did my doctoral fieldwork suggests that the crisis of unemployment and AIDS has placed additional pressure

wives of older men, who have land, or they are, like men, moving to towns to search for economic opportunities.[6] While the threat to the social order posed by women's economic independence and sexual mobility has long been a concern among Luo men (Parkin 1978; Francis 1995), the current situation, in which men are losing their foothold in both rural and urban economies, has intensified these anxieties.

Young lives in a fragmented landscape

Much of the literature on contemporary African youth documents their experiences of marginality, exclusion and frustration – where the trajectory of development and modernization has been disrupted by war, economic decline and AIDS (e.g. Richards 1995, 1996; O'Brien 1996; De Boeck 1999; De Boeck and Honwana 2005:11). This emphasis on marginality calls for a concomitant examination of agency: of youth as producers of new cultural and social forms in their exploration of new pathways and their creation of new social spaces (see e.g. De Boeck 1999). For instance, how do young people work upon experiences of loss and exclusion and how do they engage power and knowledge, memory and history, past and future under such conditions (see Durham 2000)? Young people do not only occupy a marginal space in-between, as Mudimbe (1988) suggests, but are actively negotiating and re-creating these spaces, producing new cultural and social forms, "searching for their own ways out of a life they feel to be without a future" (De Boeck and Honwana 2005: 8). In Uhero village and western Kenya more generally, there is no longer a clear road to development and what people call "growth", but young people are finding their own pathways through a revaluation of Luo tradition and culture, through different forms of Christianity, through various negotiations of gender relations, and through different patterns of migration and mobility. There is much debate among Luo people in everyday life about these transformations and contradictions, and Luo popular music is a major public forum where these issues are voiced.

---

on people to sell their land, as it is one of the few assets they have. While in the 1980s land sales were few and land was mainly sold for bridewealth, in the 1990s and in 2000 and 2001, land was sold in order to finance funeral expenses, medical treatment and school fees, and many more people were selling their land.

6. These patterns are shown in my census data of Uhero village and data on migration histories among youth in Uhero.

Luo popular music

At any time of day and night in the local marketplaces that punctuate the rural landscape, one can hear Luo pop music blasting out of minibus windows, from tailors' workshops, as well as from bars and, on weekend nights, the discos. This music is also played on the radio and at the many funerals in the village (during the all-night vigils before and after burial when the youth organise what they refer to as 'discos').[7] Audiocassettes pass between those people who own a cassette player and can afford batteries. People of all ages enjoy these songs: older people like the rumba or Lingala rhythms from the 1960s that recent bands have revived, whilst the youth prefer the influence of hip-hop and rap. People particularly enjoy listening to the lyrics, and many of the young people know the lyrics of popular hits by heart.

The music is played on western and Luo instruments and draws upon international musical styles, including Latin elements such as rumba, Zairian Lingala music and black American hip-hop and rap, alongside Luo elements.[8] It is performed by Luo musicians in urban and rural settings and is also recorded on audiocassettes in Kisumu and Nairobi (and, in a few cases, in the UK). Through the tapes, through radio and public transport and through itinerant DJs who arrange discos at the frequent funeral gatherings in village homesteads, the songs are distributed all over Luoland.

---

7. Disco music and all-night dancing are an accepted part of contemporary Luo funerals, which are always conducted in the rural home of the deceased. What people refer to as 'discos' are organised by youth who are relatives, friends or neighbours of the deceased. Not all funerals involve discos; this depends upon whether someone has access to a music system and a power generator. Although dancing appears at first sight to be rather inappropriate for a funeral, this may be a continuation of pre-Christian funeral practices. In the past, dancing and the staging of mock-fights by young warriors would accompany the burial of an elder (Mboya 1983). Many people told me that in the past funeral celebrations were most elaborate for elders and in their case, funerals formed an occasion to celebrate a long and fruitful life. During the 20th century, Luo funerals have moved to the centre of public life and have gone through a process of elaboration (see Cohen and Odhiambo 1992). Today, every family strives to conduct a large and impressive funeral, whatever the age of the deceased, and having loud music and dancing attracts more people (only babies and young children are buried with less ceremony, albeit with much grief).

8. Although I call them 'pop' groups to distinguish them from the more traditional, acoustic Luo musicians in the rural areas, the music of these bands is a fusion of traditional rhythms as well as Latin elements such as rumba (which have been transformed in West Africa and imported to Zaire/Congo and East Africa). It has been much influenced by Zairian/Congolese Lingala music, to a lesser extent by coastal Swahili Tarab, and more recently, by black American hip-hop and rap.

Songs are mostly in *Dholuo*, but are peppered with English and Kiswahili. The use of the mother tongue and the strong emphasis on Luo places and people in the lyrics means that the music is mainly for the Luo share of the national market, providing a shared cultural form for villagers, urbanites and cosmopolitans in the diaspora, and a forum to debate Luo concerns. Yet Luo musicians also sing in Kiswahili and in English; their songs are aired on the radio, and are popular among non-Luo Kenyans.

Most Luo pop bands started up in small rural market centres and retain rural and local roots (while the clubs in these rural markets are often named after famous tourist resorts or the venues of international stars in Nairobi). The songs make reference to familiar places in the rural landscape and are peppered with greetings to particular people from these places. At the same time they sing of mobility and migration and of urban life in Nairobi and Mombasa. The songs have roots in a pre-colonial and colonial Luo traditions of praise songs, composed to celebrate love for a girl or to sing one's own praises, as well as in social commentary (Cohen and Odhiambo 1989; Burton 2002). In East Africa, music has been an arena for public commentary on social issues and politics throughout colonial and post-colonial times (Mitchell 1956; Ranger 1975; Cohen and Odhiambo 1989; Odhiambo 2002; Gecau 1995; Askew 2002, 2003; Burton 2002; Nyairo and Ogunde 2003; Beez and Kolbusa 2003; for southern African, see Coplan 1994; Longwe and Clarke 1998). Today, Luo popular music provides a creative and multi-vocal commentary on Luo life and the transformations in the past decades and particularly during the past 15 or so years: on gender relations, morality, and the ambiguity of love and sexual relationships in the era of AIDS; money, politics, economic decline, migration and mobile lives; the relationship between town and village; the pathways of Christianity and the 'return' to 'Luo tradition'.

An exploration of Luo popular music does not only provide insights into the ambivalent and contradictory experiences of Luo people in contemporary Kenya; and into the debates about past, present and future that Luo are engaging in. Popular music, like other forms of popular culture, is not only expressive of sociocultural reality, but creative of it. It is a site where different imaginations are aired, new identities suggested, which may resonate with young audiences and listeners and be taken up and used to shape the sociocultural or political landscape (see e.g. Askew 2002, 2003; Ross and Rose 1994; Remes 1999; Nyairo and Ogunde 2003). There is no better example than the trajectory of the hit song 'Unbuogable' (a Luo-English hybrid meaning 'Unshockable'), a song of personal frustration and defiance created by two unemployed Luo musicians, which was aired on the radio and quickly taken up in the 2002 election campaign by the opposition coalition and used to express the defiance, strength and resolve of the political opposition and the anger of the electorate at corrupt government and the entrenched political class. This example shows that, once in the public domain, a song of personal experience may be interpreted and taken up in unexpected ways and used for political purposes; songs provoke debate; they enter political as well as personal relations. In this chapter however, I focus more on the textual analysis and interpretation of Luo popular songs. An exploration of their interactive, processual aspects and the ways in which songs themselves may shape social relations will be the focus of further fieldwork in this area.

Some themes of contemporary pop lyrics

The songs that I have chosen to focus on here were particularly popular with young people in Uhero; not only for their upbeat rhythms, but also for their lyrics – and many knew the lyrics by heart. The following analysis of the songs explores the issues they raise in relation to the lives and experiences of youth in Uhero. My analysis draws upon interviews and conversations with young people in Uhero, and with Luo and Kenyan colleagues and friends about the meanings and interpretation of the songs.[9] It places these interpretations in the context of broader histories, debates and tensions among Luo in Kenya concerning such issues as gender and generational relations, marriage, sexuality, youth, tradition, modernity and AIDS. The songs have been translated and shortened to bring out their main themes.[10] Thus I have taken out many of the salutations, greetings and praises, which are important aspects of their performance.[11] All of these songs were produced between the late 1990s and 2002.

9. In addition to the youth of Uhero, I am indebted to Emma Odundo, Philister Adhiambo, Collins Omondi, Reenish Achieng', Daniel Adipo and Eric Nyambedha for their interpretations of the songs and for their comments upon earlier drafts of this chapter.

10. I am indebted to Emma Odundo for her help with the transcriptions and translations of these recordings.

11. The agonistic and interactive aspects of these songs and their place in negotiations of social relations and subjectivities among youth will be the subject of another chapter.

The songs express different views and experiences, and contain much ambiguity and debate. Some songs sing directly of AIDS and promote safe sex; other songs celebrate lifestyles of bars and discos and lovers. Some bemoan the immorality of "these girls of today" and advocate a return to traditional gender roles; others celebrate the independent woman who earns money in town. Songs about love praise the innocence of the rural girls of the past or celebrate the excitement of urban life; others are stories of loss and death in the era of AIDS. Some songs explicitly link a return to what is conceived of as 'Luo Tradition' to the loss of hope in progress and modernity, to economic decline and to AIDS. In these different ways, contemporary pop songs capture the contradictions of modern life for people in Uhero.

1. *Return to the reserve: "Let's go back home"*

ASINO OSUNDWA BAND: "NYAR GEM"[12] ("DAUGHTER OF GEM")

(Male voice)

> Work is over, Daughter of Gem, let's go back home, so that we see how we can 'grow'.[13]
>
> The pleasure we have had is finished, and the money I was earning is running out.
>
> And you also know, Daughter of Gem from Oremo's place, that the house we had has fallen.
>
> People are laughing at us, Daughter of Gem, we are lost in town[14] and we don't even go home.
>
> It is now time to go back home so that we can make our home, as our people have done.

---

12. Married women, especially those who are young, are often called after the place they come from, that is, their father's homeland. Only later in life are they referred to as 'Mother of so-and-so'.

13. The Dholuo word is *dongre*, which literally means 'to grow' and is used to refer to a specifically Luo notion of 'growth' that implies well-being of family and social group, and cultural continuity, as well as modern notions of 'progress' and 'development'.

14. The term used for town here is *pango*, a Kiswahili word meaning 'work', which has been incorporated into Dholuo and come to stand metonymically for 'town' (*jopango* are labour migrants, literally: 'people of work') (Cohen and Odhiambo 1989).

Work is finished, Daughter of Gem, let us go back home!

When the money has run out, Daughter of Gem, let us go back home, so that we can make our home.

(*Female voice*)

We met in town so we should resolve our problems here,

I won't go back home, my children are going to die there.

I won't go back to Luo land, and I don't even know how to dig! Eh eh!

I won't go back home, my in-laws are going to laugh at me.

I won't go back home, my co-wives are going to despise me.

I won't go back home and I don't even know how to dig, mama! Eh eh!

We met in town, so we have to resolve our problems here.

A better solution, father of my children, (is to) give me money to trade.

Father of Sophie, you had better give me money to trade!

This song was very popular during the time of my fieldwork. When it was aired on the radio or on a cassette player, it would often provoke conversations and discussions among listeners and passers-by on the themes of gender conflict, urban-rural relations and the ephemeral nature of jobs and money. The argument between husband and wife that is played out in the song seemed to resonate with people's experiences and their observations of other people's experiences. The conflict between the husband's desire to return to the rural home (which, he argues, "will allow us to develop") and his wife's insistence on staying in town is linked to the morality of kinship and marriage and to concerns about belonging and continuity, Luo tradition and culture. In this morality of what are called 'Luo ways', the proper place for the Luo woman is in the rural home, dependent upon her husband for access to land (and, during the heyday of labour migration, for access to cash), and urban or economically independent women as a category are treated with suspicion. Yet in the song the wife argues that there is no future in the rural home, and that she would rather trade in town.

Several scholars have argued that the rural home became an object of cultural elaboration, nostalgia, memory, history, identity and belonging in response to the large waves of labour migration from the Luo homeland, during the 20th century (Parkin 1978; Cohen and Odhiambo 1989). They argue that the contemporary importance placed on giving birth and on being buried at home was part of an attempt to root identity and belonging in the Luo homeland. Based on his work among Luo migrants in Nairobi in the 1970s, Parkin argued that urban living led to reworking of Luo identity and ethnicity, with an emphasis on lineage ties in land and a valuation of the rural home as a place intimately tied to continuity, belonging, identity, kinship and marriage (1978). While in the 1970s and '80s, home was one theme of cultural elaboration alongside urban, cosmopolitan aspirations, in the 1990s, it seems to have become the overarching theme of Luo cultural production and debate, as expressed in the numerous printed pamphlets on the subject of tradition and the rural home (Ogutu 1995; Malo 1999; Raringo 2001), as well as in public debates on Luo radio programmes and even on an internet site (www.*jaluo*.com) as mentioned above. As there is today little hope for young people to leave the rural area and move out into the world, return to the rural home is the only pathway along which movement remains possible.

The reference to the house falling down needs some elaboration. Both linguistically and socially, the house stands for the creation and continuity of marriage and of children. A spouse is referred to as "the person of my house"; the house embodies the conjugal relationship and its fertility. Elaborate 'rules' (*chike*) surround the building of the house and of the home. Even if he resides in town, a man should build a house for his wife in his father's homestead, in order to lay the foundation for (lineage) continuity and fertility. After some years of family life in this house, he should move into his own homestead and build a new house for his wife. At each stage, the existence of a house is essential for the performance of ritual practices in the context of childbirth, death and funerals. Thus, not having a rural house threatens social death. In this sense the rural house and home contrasts with the temporary dwelling places of town. In the song, as well as in daily life, the term *pango* refers to town and has come to stand for the temporary nature of dwelling-places and the impermanence and fragility of marriage. *Jopango* (labour migrants) are laughed at as those who have no permanent home (Cohen and Odhiambo 1989). However, precisely because they are not 'real' houses and not identified with relations and tied to ritual rules, rented houses in town also offer a refuge for people who cannot or do not want to follow traditional rules, who wish to escape from the demands of rural kin, or for those who belong to no home, as is the case for some young JoUhero.[15]

The husband's plea "let's go back home", "our house has fallen down", "we are lost in town" thus captures a longing for a place of permanence, of belonging and of continuity between past and future. Yet the wife replies with fears of being laughed at, for her children's well-being in a rural setting, and with a practical problem: "I cannot even dig". Whilst the husband's plea to go home idealises kinship bonds, the amity of shared living on the land, the wife fears hunger and struggle for survival, the enmity of kinship, witchcraft and jealousy, and most probably her low status as a young wife in the home of her parents-in-law. "My children will die there" she says, contradicting her husband's belief that there "we can develop". The ambiguities of home captured by this song should perhaps also be placed in context of the 1990s AIDS epidemic and the reality of deserted homes and fresh graves that today mark a landscape of loss at the beginning of the century.

Finally, this song expresses historical changes as well as tensions in gender relations and marriage. The conventional picture of migrant men leaving their wives at home, and of men leading modern lives and women perpetuating tradition is turned around in the song: the husband is the one who longs for home, whilst the wife prefers to trade in town. This reflects contemporary gender stereotypes of townswomen who prefer urban promiscuity to a decent rural life (other songs are more explicitly nostalgic for a lost idealised rural past; they sing of the dangers of women's mobility, of girls who want only money, and the loss of the morality of the old days). At the same time the song reflects the fact that the 'traditionalisation' of Luo social life, in the sense of a growing codification (often in print) of customary rules rooted in the rural home, is driven by young men and returnees from town, who urge a 'return to tradition' onto their irresponsible fathers (see Gable 2000 for a similar situation in West Africa).

In summary, this song reflects an important trend in Luo life: the return to tradition, the importance of rural homes and houses for the continuity of marriage and kinship, as well as long-standing issues that have shaped 20th century Luo life: conflicts in gender relations, migration, and the relationship between rural and urban living. Thus this song seems to have struck a cord

---

15. For example, young women who have children but are not married (or refuse marriage), and young people born before their mother got married, who have no rights to land in their mother's husband's home.

with the young people living in Uhero, many of whom were constantly moving between places, searching for a living.

2. *Disillusionment with modernity and calls for a return to 'tradition': "The world is finished"*

The following two songs express the loss of faith in modernity, the sense of nostalgia and the movement towards what is now constituted as 'tradition'. *Piny Rumo* ("The world is finished / The world is ending") by Siyenga Dynamic Band captures the economic decline of the last two decades as well as the social tragedy of AIDS – experiences that people in Uhero are all too familiar with. *Kit Luo Machon* by the band of the late Luo 'superstar', Okach Biggy, argues for a return to the ways of the past; "the world of today is finished", he sings, expressing a sentiment shared by many. The world is finished; it is exhausted, dying or dead, and the past is the only source of consolation and (perhaps) of resurrection. Yet his idea of the morality of the past incorporates modern Christianity, as he ends his song with a call to 'follow Jesus'.

SIYENGA DYNAMIC BAND: "PINY RUMO" ("THE WORLD IS FINISHED")

Oya, why are we humans getting finished?
Ah, so AIDS is bad.

This world that you see is finished, this world that you love is finished,
I thought the world was good...
These human beings that I thought were good are the ones who are disappearing.
I thought our Kenya was bad, I have found our Kenya to be good.
These days it is diseases that have increased, and it is human beings that are vanishing...

Ah, friends all, you should be careful, AIDS is finishing us, yawa.
Kisumu, Siaya, Nairobi, we are all crying of AIDS. Kampala!

I saw an accident – and all these (accidents) are not discussed (in public).
Vehicles rolled over one another – and all this is not spoken about.
I thought aeroplanes were good – but now I hear that aeroplanes also burn.

I thought vehicles were good – but I have found that even vehicles
fail.

I thought trains were good – but I have discovered that they also de-
rail.

All these vehicles that you saw us buy – all those fall.

I heard that Scania was good – but I they also fall.

When we thought the Mercedes was good – they also fall.

I thought a motorbike would race – but all of them fall.

These bicycles that we think are good – I have found that all of them
fall.

The friends that I used to be with...

We used to roam with Omolo Ondigo – I heard that the son of Alego
is going (dying).

We used to drink with Omolo Simba – I heard Omolo is also going.

We used to roam with Fred Omolo, I understand all those people are
going...

ORCHESTRA SUPER HEKA HEKA: "KIT LUO MACHON"
("LUO CUSTOMS OF LONG AGO")

The Luo customs of long ago! The world is drunk!

Auja, the world is bad, there is nowadays only prayer and playing the
guitar.

Owiti son of Atek, I am playing music...I want to speak to the Luo
people.

(praise names and greetings)

Musician, son of Selina Atek, the boss is recalling our traditions and
wants to talk with Luo people, so that we help our Luo nation.

Those who want to 'develop', listen to these teachings: obstinacy is bad,
it is finishing the Luos

How were our grandfathers of long ago?

They were people who took care of the Luo community, they were people who got honorary positions.

They were people who respected their parents, they were people who respected God.

They were people who liked to drum, they were people who built a simba,[16]

they were people who paid bridewealth for their wives.

They were people who knew how to take care of homes, they were people who kept cattle,

they were people who drank curdled milk.

They were people who knew how to take care of many wives, they were people who built traditional huts, they were people who knew how to raise orphans.

They were people who followed the 'Luo ways', they were people who would return to funerals,

they were people who liked to educate their people.

They were people who liked the drinking straw, they were people who liked hunting.

They were people who had respect, they were people who liked wrestling,

they were people who didn't like mess...

Eh truly if the problems of today are compared with the ones of long ago, there are many differences.

Long ago, an old man had to build *abila,*[17] where he would educate children.

Long ago, women used to respect their husbands, but nowadays a woman will just oppose you in front of your age mates.

(Echo) There, there, there, there.

How do you see those issues, Owino prayer man?

(Echo) So difficult!

Owino son of Awasi, I see the world of today has come to an end.

Long ago young men used to help one another...

How do you see this world of ours, Daudi son of Adhila?

We don't agree with today's world.

Elders, mothers and girls, follow the 'Luo rules' of long ago.

Luos – you must know that we must follow our rules. Thank you!

---

16. *Simba* is a Kiswahili term that, incorporated into Dholuo, means the hut of a bachelor.

17. *Abila* is the 'traditional' round hut made of wattle-and-daub.

That is the son of Awasi. I believe that we have only Jesus now...
Songs like these are common, and they strike a cord not only with elderly
people. Many young people express a yearning for a past they have never
known. The time of the grandfathers, of the thriving village home, the
time of respect for people, of abundant herds of cattle, and strong, healthy
bodies – and underlying all this, the time when there was none of the
moral and social confusion that, for many Luo, marks the present day.
Such nostalgic songs are part of a broader cultural movement, briefly outlined above, which advocates a "return to tradition" and thus to a social,
moral and cultural order and which is spearheaded by youth. Through this
recourse to tradition, young people formulate an alternative utopia to that
of industrial, urban modernity, which many of their parents had striven for.
They mobilise the past in order to open up new forms of growth, continuity
and life.

3. *Defiance, and celebration of modern sexuality, mobility and
   the urban woman: "Adhiambo's buttocks"*

A song entitled "Adhiambo's buttocks", by Nyando Stars, was a 'hit' in
2001, its success spurred, perhaps, by its provocative title. Whilst many
Luo pop songs that we listened to and collected during our stay in western
Kenya sing of love and the excitement of travel, this song was particularly
controversial (according to local Anglicans, the Anglican Bishop suggested
banning it) and extremely popular (so popular, in fact, that a rival music
group came out with a similarly titled song, in which the singer accused
Nyando Stars of "stealing our song").[18] Many young people knew its lyrics
by heart. For some weeks, this song was played over and over again – on
matatus, blasting out of sound systems at local market centres or in people's homes, at local discos and at the all-night dances organised by young
people during funerals.

   Why did the song cause controversy and why did young people like it
so much? The title itself is provocative enough: the Dholuo word that the
singer uses for "buttocks", *sianda*, can also be used for the vagina; thus
indicating that the song is about sex. This kind of sexual talk and innuendo
is common practice among age-mates or between alternate generations

---

18. This song was the second explicit song after one by another singer called Okatch
    Biggy about a girl called "Helena the big eyed" ("*Helena Wang'e Dongo*") (an ex-
    pression for women who search for men). This song also referred to "*sianda*" (but-
    tocks") (Daniel Adipo, *personal communication*).

– those who are "free" with each other. However, its entry into the public sphere, where its potential listeners could include parents and children between whom there are taboos against speaking about sexual relations, was a risky move. As a Luo colleague explained to me:

> [E]ven on our vernacular radio stations the song was played carefully until the 10th line, then [it was] stopped since there were varied listeners. They would only have the whole of it late at night when it was presumed that the children slept. Luos are very sensitive about sex issues and it is almost a taboo to talk about sex. I don't know how the song managed to do this yet people still liked it. This song was always played in the bars. My opinion is that people like such dirty songs but get embarrassed when people they respect or who should respect them are also listening, like the children and the in-laws, who are respected. The first part is welcomed by the old; in fact the song starts in the conventional way – singing about a girl, praising her for being respectful and not like the modern girls "*nyiri ma kawuono*".[19]

The song begins in a conventional way, praising a girl called Adhiambo Rosy, the singer's lover: "there is no girl I can equate with her". Adhiambo appears as a good innocent rural girl who has "respect" for her parents. She has the qualities of the rural girls of the past, and the singer compares her to the "girls of today" who come and go.

NYANDO STARS: "ROSY (ADHIAMBO SIANDA)"
("ADHIAMBO'S BUTTOCKS")

> As I think of you, daughter of an old man, I see my tears streaming
>   down and I don't know why.
> Rosy sister of Amolo, hear my voice, hear the way I sing, I don't have hap-
>   piness in my heart.
> There is no girl that I can equate to you,
>   the girl has not been born yet.
> Akinyi's sister was far better than the girls of today
> who don't even smile when you talk to them.
> We get tired of girls of today (when they come to visit since they take
>   two weeks
>   and they just have to be sent away!)
> Rosy was respectful of her parents...

---

19. Daniel Adipo, *personal communication*.

Then the song becomes provocative and playful. "Adhiambo", the singer declares "is buttocks", but "I sing about her because of her deeds". The song moves on to describe drinking alcohol with Adhiambo, going to a bar, sleeping in a hotel – all of which Adhiambo pays for. Old people and the young girls, occupied in rural tasks (herding, fetching firewood, milling), wonder "why sing for this girl?". In the singer's celebration of this girl who pays, who takes him to Uganda, who drinks alcohol, goes to a bar and finally undresses him in a hotel, he seems to be contrasting her life with the rural life, and to be asking: Which is best? Who has the money? Who is paying? In the line "Such are the times that I have to sing for (i.e. praise) Adhiambo", he seems to be saying: "In these times of ours, this is what life is about? Adhiambo is a girl of these times, so let's celebrate her."

> This is my time that I should sing about a girl.
> (Adhiambo is buttocks.)
> No, such are the times that it forces me to sing for Adhiambo.
>
> Young girls fetch firewood as they ask,
>   (Adhiambo)
>   Why I am singing about the girl.
> Old women mill as they ask,
>   (Buttocks.)
>   Why am I singing about Adhiambo?
>   (Adhiambo is buttocks.)
> Old men herd as they ask,
>   The reason why I am singing about buttocks.
>
> I don't sing about Adhiambo because of buttocks,
>   (Adhiambo is buttocks).
>   I sing about the beauty of her deeds.
> I don't sing about Adhiambo because of buttocks,
>   I sing about the beauty for her respect.
>
> I took half a litre of Guinness,
>   Adhiambo paid for me.
> I took half a litre of Coke,
>   Adhiambo paid for me.
> When I reached Kisumu with Adhiambo,
> and when I took tea with Adhiambo,

when I took alcohol with Adhiambo,
when I slept in the hotel with Adhiambo,
And when the bill came,
Adhiambo paid for me.
When the bill was brought to me,
Beauty could pay for me.
    (Adhiambo could pay.)

Young girls turn around, asking
    why I am singing about a girl.

Her panties make me so happy
    (small and clean).
Her panties make me so happy.
    Your Intercooler kills me.[20]
    Your Intercooler makes me happy.

When I got to Ugunja[21] with Adhiambo,
 Boda Boda[22] could carry me happily.
Beauty paid for me.
When we got to Busia[23] with Adhiambo,
    I ate tilapia,
    bananas were prepared for me,
    groundnuts were fried for me.
When I stepped into Uganda with Adhiambo,
     The police arrested me with Adhiambo,
     And when this child looked at me,
     Adhiambo wept painfully.
     When the girl looked at me,

---

20. Intercooler refers to a prestigious off-road vehicle, which is usually driven by the Kenyan elite and expatriate workers. The reference to the Intercooler at this point in the song suggests that it is being likened to the vagina. Through this reference to the epitome of modernity in Africa – the car – sexual pleasure is linked to money, mobility and modernity (see Masquelier 2002).

21. A roadside town in Nyanza Province.

22. A bicycle taxi. This method of transport has been used for many years in Uganda and especially on the Ugandan-Kenyan border crossing (hence the name), but was only recently adopted in Kisumu and other parts of western Kenya.

23. The Kenyan-Ugandan border town, a lively place full of bars and hotels, black-market traders, lorry-drivers and prostitutes.

Adhiambo wept humbly,
(Adhiambo is buttocks)
and the handcuffs left my hands.

When we got to Malaba with Adhiambo,
    and when cassava was dug for me,
    Adhiambo could carry for me.
When we got to Butere[24] with Adhiambo
    sugarcane was cut for me.

Young girls run as they ask,
    why I am singing about a girl.

When I got to Komala with Adhiambo,
    pineapples were cut for me,
    potatoes were dug for me.
    Beauty carried them for me.
When we got to Bungoma with Adhiambo,
    young girls ran asking,
    why am I singing buttocks?

When we got to a club with Adhiambo,
    and when I took alcohol with Adhiambo,
    and when I was getting drunk,
    Adhiambo could lead me happily.
And when we entered the room with Adhiambo,
    Adhiambo could undress me by herself.
    And she throws the trousers away,
    She throws the coat away,
    (Isn't it?)
    She throws the underwear away.

And when Adhiambo could look at me,
    This child could kiss me with happiness.
    When the girl was looking at me,
    This child could pinch me with happiness.
    (Adhiambo is usually clean)

24. Butere and Malaba are towns along the railroad from Nairobi to Kampala.

> She takes white panties.
> She takes a white petticoat.
> She takes a white bra.
>
> God, I am now asking you
> To take care of Adhiambo.
> God I am asking you to help buttocks.
> Rosy, I am now leaving you like that, good-bye, good bye daughter of
> Urimba, we will meet...

Through his playful description of Adhiambo's "white panties", his reference to sexual satisfaction, his emphasis that it is she who pays and she who leads him, giving him alcohol, leading him to a room and undressing him – the singer subverts stereotypes of gender relations and celebrates the girl who leads. This celebration of urban life, mobility and money is underlined in the list of the places through which Adhiambo takes him, from Kenya into Uganda, and in which she buys him things. At the same time, he seems to say: Adhiambo Rosy, a girl of today, can love and respect and care. Moreover she knows how to behave like a proper woman and with respect, carrying food for him on her head. By praising a girl with money who pays for a hotel room, who is at the same time a girl who "respects her parents" and carries bananas on her head like the rural girls, and in the playful teasing of the listener "I am not praising her buttocks, I'm praising her character", the song plays with stereotypes of the 'traditional' and the 'urban' girl. He seems to suggest the rural/traditional and the urban/modern do not necessarily clash in values and that urban life and urban women can be respectful. The encounter seems to be brief: "I am leaving you like that", and the singer concludes by asking God to take care of her, adding cheekily "God I ask you to help buttocks". Here is another thrust at established morality. According to my Luo colleague, "[S]ex and Christianity in our culture do not so much go together, [so] when sex is mentioned so explicitly next to a reference to God, it sounds like mockery".[25]

In modern Kenya, sexuality has become the focus of different moral discourses and is as a result characterised by much ambiguity and uncertainty (Geissler and Prince, *forthcoming*; for elsewhere in Africa see Taylor 1990; Ahlberg 1994; Klepp et al. 1995; Setel 1996; Lebashira and Kaaya 1997; Leclerc-Madlala 1997; Nnko and Pool 1997; Rwebangira and Liljeström

---

25. Daniel Adipo, *personal communication.*

1998; Obrist van Euewijk and Mlangwa 1997; Dilger 2003). AIDS education promotes safe sex, the use of condoms and sticking to one partner, but is framed in terms of an ascetic public health discourse that emphasises disease prevention and ignores pleasure (for Uganda, see Gysels et al. 2004). Some of the Christian churches support this discourse on safe sex; others preach abstinence from sexual activity outside of marriage. At the same time, according to older cultural values, sexual intercourse in its 'proper' place, that is within marriage and kinship relations, is at the heart of social order, as well as fertility and growth (Ominde 1952; Ocholla-Ayayo 1976). In its tale of sexual desire, of bars, beer and money, of hotel rooms and in its explicit detailing of the undressing of each other's bodies as well as its provocative title, the song challenges, in a playful way, these different moralities. And while notions of respect within gender relations inhibit young people's ability to articulate and address these contradictions and dilemmas, the song insists on talking about sex and celebrating it. In doing so it poses a defiant attitude to love, sexuality and mobility in the era of AIDS – a stance that, given the song's popularity, seems to speak to the experience of young people.

4. *Anxieties about social reproduction: "Women who throw children away"*

Whilst *Adhiambo Sianda* playfully subverts gender stereotypes and celebrates love, sexuality and mobility, other songs convey an anxiety about the consequences of this pursuit of pleasure. In *From Man to Man* by Juma Toto, the singer complains about "women who throw children away, women who go to the disco". His lyrics convey a picture of social and moral confusion; here, the pursuit of pleasure is shown to be fruitless, a directionless wandering which overturns the social order. Women "give birth like animals" and thus upset the fundamental order upon which kinship and society are built. *Adhiambo NyaGot* likewise complains that "women are nowadays just roaming...bridewealth has ended...they just want people with money", and sets up an implicit contrast with an innocent past where girls had respect for their kin and stayed with their husbands. In this song, mobility and the pursuit of money are linked to the current illness and death ("the people with money have all died"), and the song ends with the ambiguous question in this time of AIDS: "Where are you people of

Nairobi, Mombasa and Kampala?". The third song, *Alecia Saloon* (a reference to the beauty saloons[26] where women go to lighten their skin and straighten their hair) by Osito Kale, a master of the nostalgic sound that makes middle aged men dream of their youth and evokes for young people tales of social and geographical mobility, sexual freedom and pleasure, ends with some advice for "your wives": "Even if you are looking for love, come back to the place where you will be buried...". In the fourth song, the singer Princess Jully, a rare female voice among Luo stars, counteracts this discourse on women with her complaints about the movements and unreliability of men.

JUMA TOTO: "FROM MAN TO MAN"

> Eh women who give birth like animals, women who throw children away, women who fly like a hawk in the sky, women who like going to the disco at all times.
> Women who give birth like animals, women who run away from homes, women who drink a lot, women who are found in discos at any time.
> Women who give birth like animals, women who waste time, women who prostitute themselves in Nairobi town,[27] women who have defied Jesus Messiah.

> She gives birth in this place, she starts to give birth in another place, she goes to get married and then she comes back, eh-----------

SIYENDA DYNAMIC BAND: "ADHIAMBO NYAR GOT"
("ADHIAMBO, DAUGHTER OF THE HILL")

> Musicians are murmuring that diseases and famine increase in the world,
> But it is not only we humans who suffer from the diseases.
> When I was still young (I am telling you my friend Omanyo son of Orido) it was easy to seduce girls. Nowadays they just want people with money (repeat).

---

26. A 'saloon' is a woman's hair and beauty parlour.

27. The Dholuo is: "*mon machodo kapango Nairobi*".

The people with money have all died. Elderly women are complaining that people don't pay bridewealth any longer. Women are nowadays just moving around[28] (repeat).

Where are you the people of Kisumu, all the people of Nairobi, Mombasa and Kampala?

OSITO KALE: "ALECIA SALOON"

Before I finish let me teach your wives for you:

You are wasting your time and you know the world is nowadays bad.

Even if you are looking (for love), try to come back to the place where you will be buried.

Get a place to stay before you spoil your life.

Understand what I am saying and don't forget my words,

It is the people who have sent me,

You know music is politics...

PRINCESS JULLY: "AGWENGE"

If men stop moving around the world would be a good place, (the world is bad),

What would be wrong if people just pray?

Agwenge a person from Rapogi do you know that I love you?

I gave you my love or you are cheating me (stay calm)...

....I gave you my love or were you punishing me?

These men of today have no truth.

When he is near you, he can cheat you: 'my beautiful girl you are the one I love!'.

When he finds another the next day, he loves that one too.

The following day he finds another and he loves her too.

The men of today have no truth.

The three male artists locate the source of what is often referred to as the "mess of today" (the stagnation of growth or social reproduction due, in large part, to AIDS) in the sexual mobility of women and their pursuit of money and pleasure. In this view, women pursue money and older, richer

---

28. To move around (*bayo*) has broad meanings, but in this context it refers to sexual mobility and thus promiscuity.

men in town, leaving young men without the means of marrying, gaining adult status and establishing a family. These anxieties about a loss of control over young women's bodies, mobility and even progeny were shared by many of the young men I knew in western Kenya, and similar concerns about social reproduction and the commodification of gender relations have been documented among male youth elsewhere in Africa (e.g. Cornwall 2002; Cole 2004; Masquelier 2005). Although such anxieties held by Luo men about Luo women predate the AIDS epidemic and the economic decline that has taken place since the 1980s (Parkin 1978), it may be that the current situation, where men are losing their foothold in the urban economy and returning to homesteads headed *de facto* by women, together with new concerns about sexuality, mobility and AIDS, has intensified conflicts between men and women. According to Francis (1995:212), the decline of real wages and urban employment, the return of migrant men, and the reduction in remittances to the rural households has meant that the onus of sustaining rural households is shifting onto women, whilst opposition among men to women's independent economic activities remains strong.

5. *Love and loss in the era of AIDS: "I am asking you the daughter of Seda… where did you get lost?"*

Many of the songs are situated between the defiance of "Adhiambo's buttocks" and the warnings about sexual promiscuity expressed in the songs above. These songs sing the praises of youth, lovers, particular friends and relations. They sing of the ambiguities of love and mobility (the excitement of travel with a lover through Nyanza, Kenya and East Africa) and of loss: travel turning to searching for a lost one. Nostalgia for the rural girls of the past is juxtaposed with nostalgia for the era of mobility and relative prosperity. They are love songs that sing of the threat of death embedded in sexual relations in the era of AIDS. Thus, Jaber Nyalego sings: "Oh Nora, come back now, this worry is making me sick. Where will I find you? Come back so we can see each other while I am still alive…". Another song praises a girl's beauty, promises to bring bridewealth and then warns the girl to: "accept to take care of our house, our children, AIDS is killing". This experience of love and loss is poignantly expressed in *Auma NyaSeda*.

OSITO KALE: "AUMA NYASEDA" ("AUMA, DAUGHTER OF SEDA")

Yes that is Auma, the daughter of Seda,
The black one with a soft body.
She insists that one kettle of water is enough for her bath.
She doesn't bother with those creams that women apply.
Yes the bow-legged one knows how to balance a water pot on her head,
Something that has defeated most of our girls,
And she balances it using a cloth...

I am asking you the daughter of Seda, the black one, where did you get lost?
Where are you?
And I'm telling you about her looks, she is a very beautiful girl.
I am telling you about her looks, she is a very humble girl.
I am asking you, the daughter of Seda, the black one, why don't you write to me?
(Echo: A letter!)
Or what has hurt Auma?
Or the man is more powerful than Auma?
Or is it love that has made my beautiful one get lost?
Or is it fun that has made Auma get lost?
(Echo: The way of fun!)
Or is it disease that has affected Auma; AIDS?
(Echo: Accident on the road!)
Or did an accident kill Auma? Or did Shaggy knock down the beautiful one?[29]
(Echo: There in Kericho!)[30]
Or did Shaggy kill Auma?
Or did the ferry capsize with Auma?

---

29. *Shaggy* is the name of a national bus company reputedly owned by ex-president Arap Moi's son, and feared for its reckless drivers who reputedly are above the law. In 2001, a Shaggy bus collided with another national bus and burst into flames, killing everyone on board.

30. Kericho is a town in Kenya in the highlands on the way from Kisumu to Nairobi. It is a hot spot for accidents, and it is where the fatal accident involving the *Shaggy* bus took place.

(Echo: Yes there in Likoni!)[31]
Or did the bomb kill Auma?[32]
(Echo: Bomb blast!)
Or did the bomb kill this beautiful one of mine?
Why didn't you bring me any word?
(Echo: Here in Nairobi!)
Or did diseases attack Auma?
(Echo: The world is bad!)
Or did diseases kill Auma?
Or did diseases kill this beautiful one of mine?
Or did AIDS kill Auma?
(Echo: AIDS that finishes!)
Or did AIDS kill this beautiful one of mine?
Or did AIDS kill this beautiful one of mine, and why didn't you send
     her back to me?
(Echo: Yes, I will bury her!)

This song begins as a praise song, in which the girl is praised not only for her beauty but also for her traditional skills: "She knows how to balance a water pot on her head, something that has defeated most of our girls." According to the singer, such skills are sadly lacking among contemporary girls, who are only interested in beauty creams. However, the song quickly turns into a search and ultimaly a lament for a love love, as the singer asks repeatedly: "Where are you Daughter of Seda?" By speculating about the cause of his love's absence, the singer weaves his fear and anxiety about his loved one into the dangers of life in modern Kenya. In this way he links her absence (and, as we learn in the last line, her death) to the deaths of others, whether through particular disasters such as the capsizing of a ferry in Momobasa in 1994 and the bomb blast in Nairobi in 1998, or through dangers and diseases that have almost become everyday events in contemporary Kenya, and which are bound up both with local politics and with the global economy, such as road accidents and AIDS. In this way the praise song weaves nostalgia for the innocence and purity of the girls of the past into a commentary on modern

---

31. Likoni is a settlement on the outskirts of Mombasa where many Luo migrants live and where the ferry linking Mombasa to the mainland departs from. In 1994, a ferry accident killed 200 of the 450 passengers.

32. The 1998 suicide bomb blast in Nairobi for which Al-Qaida was responsible, which killed more than 200 Kenyans.

womanhood and sexual mores, and he links the loss of his love to the condition of contemporary Kenya.

Conclusion

The chapter has explored the relationships between popular music and young people's lives in contemporary Kenya. It situates recent songs about love, death and gender relations, tradition and modernity in the uncertain context of postcolonial life and long-term economic decline. The selection of songs included here suggests the wide range of issues that are being debated among Luo people today, and the songs express the different, often contradictory, moralities and values that characterise life in modern Kenya – which include nostalgia for the supposedly morally coherent ways of the past and calls for a return to 'Luo tradition', longing for a return 'home', as well as a celebration of urban lifestyles, travel, sexual adventure, and mobility. Whilst Luo life in the 20th century has been characterised by major transformations in meanings and practices of social relations and moral values, AIDS – which poses a challenge to cultural and social continuity as well as to life itself – has rendered these issues particularly salient and hotly debated. Luo pop music is a vibrant arena of popular culture that provides a voice for these experiences as well as the desires of young Luo people.

Many of the songs produced in the 1990s are deeply shaped by the experience of AIDS. Many sing directly about the loss of loved ones, the death of friends and lovers. Others, such as "The world is finished", speak of a loss of faith in modernity and progress. Songs about love, pleasure and relationships are more ambiguous. A few songs (but significantly, those composed by women) take up public health messages about safe sex and the use of condoms (and in doing so, break through older Luo moralities in which sex is not a thing that can be discussed openly). Traditional taboos on discussing sex openly are also crossed in songs that celebrate sexual relationships, love and pleasure such as "Adhiambo's buttocks". There is also a streak of defiance in some of the songs towards the ascetic, medicalised discourse on sex promoted by public health campaigns and messages and church sermons, in which pleasure has no place, and only the negative aspects of sex (vulnerability to disease) are discussed (see Geissler and Prince *forthcoming*; Gysels et al. 2004). That Luo musicians are taking up these controversial issues and singing about them openly suggests that Luo pop songs represent a space where such issues can be expressed, thus opening them up to debate. As they are produced by Luo for Luo, and as they are accessible to and popular with young people, Luo pop songs represent an arena of popular culture that may have potential in the fight against AIDS.

Much has been written about the 'crisis' of youth in contemporary Africa (O'Brien 1996; Werbner and Ranger 1996; Durham 2000). This view is shared by many Luo themselves: in everyday conversations, young as well as old often talk about social change, the morality of the past and the 'mess' and 'confusion' caused by young people's behaviour. Yet young people are also actively trying to find ways of dealing with their situation. The range of issues that the songs take up gives us some insight into the moral dilemmas and societal transformations that young Luo people are currently facing in the era of AIDS; and into the particular challenges of postcolonial Kenyan and East African modernity. They also point to the multifaceted pathways young people are exploring – whether in relations between men and women, ideas about 'tradition' or in negotiations of kinship, place and belonging.

References

Ahlberg, B.M., 1994, "Is there a distinct African sexuality? A critical response to Caldwell", *Africa* 64:220–242.

Askew, K., 2002, *Performing the Nation: Swahili Music and Cultural Politics in Tanzania.* Chicago: University of Chicago Press.

Askew, K., 2003, "As Plato Duly Warned: Music, Politics and Social Change in Coastal East Africa", *Anthropology Quarterly* 76:609–638.

Bawa Yamba, C., 1997, "Cosmologies in Turmoil: Witch finding and AIDS in Chiawa, Zambia", *Africa* 67:299–223.

Beez, J. and S. Kolbusa, 2003, "Kibiriti Ngoma: Gender Relations in Swahili Cosmics and Taarab Music", *Stichproben: Wiener Zeitschrift für kritische Afrikastudien (Vienna Journal of African Studies)* 4:49–71.

Bucholtz, M., 2002, "Youth and Cultural Practice", *Annual Review of Anthropology*, 31:525–52.

Burton, A., 2002, *The Urban Experience in Eastern Africa*. Nairobi: British East Africa Institute.

Cohen, D.W. and E.S.A. Odhiambo, 1989, *Siaya. The Historical Anthropology of an African Landscape*. Nairobi: Heineman Kenya.

—, 1992, *Burying SM. The Politics of Knowledge and the Sociology of Power in Africa*. London: James Currey.

Cole, J., 2004, "Fresh Contact in Tamatave, Madagascar: Sex, Money and Intergenerational Transformation", *American Ethnologist,* 31(4):573–588.

Coplan, D.B., 1994, *In the Time of the Cannibals: The Word Music of South Africa's Basotho Migrants,* Chicago Series in Ethnomusicology. Chicago: Chicago University Press.

Cornwall, A., 2001, "Wayward Women and 'Useless' Men: Contest and Change in Gender Relations in Ado-Odo, S.W. Nigeria", in D. Hodgson and S. McCurdy (eds), *"Wicked" Women and the Reconfiguration of Gender in Africa,* pp. 67–84. Portsmouth, NJ: Heinemann and James Currey.

—, 2002, "Spending Power: Love, Money and the Reconfiguration of Gender Relations in Ado-Odo, Southwestern Nigeria", *American Ethnologist,* 29(4):963–980.

De Boeck, F., 1998, "Beyond the grave: History, Memory and Death in Postcolonial Congo/Zaïre", in R. Werbner (ed.), *Memory and the Postcolony. African Anthropology and the Critique of Power,* pp. 21–57. London: Zed Books.

—, 1999, "Domesticating Diamonds and Dollars: Identity, Expenditure and Sharing in Southwestern Zaire (1984–1997)", in B. Meyer and P. Geschiere (eds), *Globalisation and Identity. Dialectics of Flow and Closure,* pp. 177–209. Oxford: Blackwell.

De Boeck, F. and A. Honwana, 2005, "Children and Youth in Africa: Agency, Identity and Place", Introduction in F. De Boeck and A. Honwana (eds), *Makers and Breakers: Children and Youth as Emerging Categories in Postcolonial Africa.* London: James Currey.

Devisch, R., 1995, "Frenzy, Violence and Ethical Renewal in Kinshasa", *Public Culture,* 7(3):593–629.

Dilger, H., 2003, "Sexuality, AIDS, and the Lures of Modernity: Reflexivity and Morality among Young People in Rural Tanzania", *Medical Anthropology,* 22:23–52.

Durham, D., 2000, "Youth and the Social Imagination in Africa: Introduction to Parts 1 and 2", *Anthropology Quarterly* 2000, 73(3):113–20.

Fearn, H., 1961, *An African Economy: A Study of the Economic Development of Nyanza Province 1903–1953.* London: Oxford University Press.

Ferguson, J., 1999, *Expectations of Modernity: Myths and Meanings of Urban Life on the Zambian Copperbelt.* Berkeley: University of California Press.

Francis, E., 1995, "Migration and Changing Division of Labour: Gender Relations and Economic Change in Kogutu, Western Kenya", *Africa* 65:197–216.

Gable, E., 1995, "The Decolonisation of Consciousness: Local Sceptics and the 'Will to be Modern' in a West African Village", *American Ethnologist* 22:242–57.

—, 2000, "The Culture Development Club: Youth, Neo-Tradition and the Construction of Society in Guinea-Bissau, *Anthropology Quarterly* 73:195–203.

Gecau, K., 1995, "Popular Song and Social Change in Kenya", in *Media, Culture and Society* 17:557–75.

Geissler, P.W. and R.J. Prince, forthcoming, "Christianity, Tradition, AIDS and Pornography: Knowing Sex in Western Kenya", in R. Littlewood (ed.), *On*

Knowing and Not Knowing in Medical Anthropology. Festschrift for Murray Last. London: UCL Press.

Gysels, M., R. Pool and S. Nyanzi, 2004, "The Adventures of the Randy Professor and Angela the Sugar Mummy: Sex in Fictional Series in Ugandan Popular Magazines, Submitted to AIDS Care".

Haugerud, A., 1993, *The Culture of Politics in Modern Kenya.* African Studies Series 84. Cambridge: Cambridge University Press.

Hay, M.J., 1976, "Luo Women and Economic Change during the Colonial Period", in N.J.B. Hafkin and E.G. Bay (eds), *Women in Africa: Studies in Social and Economic Change*, pp. 87–109. Stanford University Press.

—, 1982, "Women as Owners, Occupants and Managers of Property in Colonial Western Kenya", in M.J. Hay and M. Wright (eds), *African Women and the Law: Historical Perspectives*, pp.110–123. Boston: African Studies Centre, Boston University.

—, 1992, *Who Wears the Pants? Christian Missions, Migrant Labour and Clothing in Colonial Western Kenya.* Discussion Papers in the African Humanities AH 23. Boston University, African Studies Center.

—, 1994, *Material Culture and the Shaping of Consumer Society in Colonial Western Kenya.* Working Papers in African Studies 179. Boston University, African Studies Centre.

—, 2000, "Historical context", in M.O. Macgoye, *Coming to Birth*, pp. 189–98. New York: Feminist Press.

Hutchinson, S., 1996, *Nuer Dilemmas. Coping with Money, War, and the State.* Berkeley, Los Angeles, London: University of California Press.

Klepp, K., P.M. Biswalo and A. Talle (eds), 1995, *Young People at Risk: Fighting AIDS in Northern Tanzania.* Oslo: Scandinavian University Press.

Lebashira, M.T. and S.F. Kaaya, 1997, "Bridging the Information Gap: Sexual Maturity and Reproductive Health Problems among Youth in Tanzania", *Health Transition Review* 7, (Suppl.3), pp. 29–44.

Leclerc-Madlala, S., 1997, "'Infect One, Infect All': Zulu Youth Response to the AIDS Epidemic in South Africa", *Medical Anthropology,* 17:363–380.

Longwe, S. and R. Clarke (eds), 1998, "*Women Know Your Place*". Lusaka: ZARD (Zambian Association for Research and Development).

Malo, S., 1999, *Jaluo* ('The Luo'). Nairobi: Joseph Otieno Malo.

Mamdani, M., 1996, *Citizen and Subject. Contemporary Africa and the Legacy of Late Colonialism.* Princeton NJ: Princeton University Press.

Masquelier, A., 2002, "Road Mythologies: Space, Mobility and the Historical Imagination in Postcolonial Niger", *American Ethnologist* 29(4):829–856.

—, 2005, "The Scorpion's Sting: Youth, Marriage and the Struggle for Social Maturity in Niger", *Journal of the Royal Anthropological Institute* 11(1):59–84.

Mboya, P., 1983 [1938], *Luo Kitgi gi Timbegi.* ("Luo Characters and Customs"). Kisumu: Anyange Press.

Mitchell, C., 1956, *The Kalela Dance: Aspects of Social Relationships among Urban Africans in Northern Rhodesia.* Manchester: Manchester University Press.

Mudimbe, V.Y, 1988, *The Invention of Africa: Gnosis, Power and the Order of Knowledge.* London: James Currey.

Nnko, S. and R. Pool, 1997, "Sexual Discourse in the Context of AIDS: Dominant Themes on Adolescent Sexuality among Primary School Pupils in Magu District, Tanzania", *Health Transition Review*, pp. 85–90.

Nyairo, J. and J. Ogunde, 2003, "Popular Music and the Negotiation of Contemporary Kenyan Identity: The Example of Nairobi City Ensemble", *Social Identities* 9:303–400.

Nyambedha, E.O., S. Wandibba and J. Aagaard-Hansen, 2003, "Changing Patterns of Orphan Care Due to the HIV Epidemic in Western Kenya", *Social Science and Medicine* 57:301–11.

O'Brien, C., 1996, "A Lost Generation? Youth Identity and State Decay in West Africa", in R. Werbner and T. Ranger (eds), *Postcolonial Identities in Africa.* London, New York: Zed Books.

Obrist van Eeuwijk, B. and S. Mlangwa, 1997, "Competing Ideologies: Adolescence, Knowledge and Silence in Dar-es-Salaam", in W. Harcourt (ed.), *Power, Reproduction and Gender: The Intergenerational Transfer of Knowledge,* pp. 35–57. London: Zed Books.

Ocholla-Ayayo, A.B.C., 1976, *Traditional Ideology and Ethics among the Southern Luo.* Uppsala: Scandinavian Institute of African Studies.

Odhiambo, E.S.A., 2002, "Gendered Discourses and the Countours of Leisure in Nairobi, 1946–63", in A. Burton (ed.), *The Urban Experience in East Africa.* Nairobi: British East Africa Institute.

—, 1992, "Kula Raha: Gendered Discourses and the Contours of Leisure in Nairobi, 1946-63", in A. Burton (ed.) *The Urban Experience in East Africa.* Nairobi: British East Africa Institute.

Ogutu, G.E.M., 1995, *Ker Ramogi Is Dead. Who Shall Lead My People? Reflections on Past, Present and Future Luo Thought and Practice.* Kisumu: Palwa Research Publications.

Ominde, S.H., 1952, *The Luo Girl from Infancy to Marriage.* Nairobi: East African Literature Bureau.

Pala, A.O., 1980. "Daughters of the Lakes and Rivers: Colonization and the Land Rights of Women", in M. Etienne and E. Leacock (eds), *Women and Colonization: Anthropological Perspectives,* pp. 186–213. New York: Praeger.

Parkin, D., 1978, *The Cultural Definition of Political Response. Lineal Destiny among the Luo.* London and New York: Academic Press.

Ranger, T.O., 1975. *Dance and Society in Eastern Africa, 1890–1970: The Beni Ngoma.* London: Heinemann.

Raringo. O., 2001, *Chike Jaduong e Dalane* ("The Rules of the Old Man in His Home"). Nairobi: Three Printers and Stationers.

Remes, W., 1999, "Global Popular Musics and Changing Awareness of Urban Tanzanian Youth", *Yearbook for Traditional Music,* 31:1–26.

Richards, P., 1995, "Rebellion in Liberia and Sierra Leone: A Crisis of Youth?" in O. Furley (ed.), *Conflict in Africa.* London: Taurus Academic Press.

—, 1996, *Fighting for the Rain Forest: War, Youth and Resources in Sierra Leone.* Oxford/ Portsmouth, NH: James Currey/Heinemann.

Ross, A. and T. Rose (eds), 1994, *Microphone Fields: Youth Music and Youth Culture.* New York and London: Routledge.

Rwebangira, M.K. and R. Liljeström, 1998, *Haraka, Haraka. Look Before You Leap. Youth at the Crossroads between Custom and Tradition.* Uppsala: The Nordic Africa Institute.

Sanders, T., 2001, "Save Our Skins. Structural Adjustment, Morality and the Occult in Tanzania", in H.L. Moore and T. Sanders (eds), *Magical Interpretations, Material Realities,* pp.160–183. London and New York: Routledge.

Setel, P.W., 1996, "AIDS as a Paradox of Manhood and Development in Kilimanjaro, Tanzania", *Social Science and Medicine,* 43:1169–1178.

Stichter, S., 1982, *Migrant labour in Kenya: Capitalism and African response, 1895– 1975.* Harlow: Longman.

Taylor, C.C., 1990, "Condoms and Cosmology: The 'Fractal' Person and Sexual Risk in Rwanda", *Social Science and Medicine,* 31:1023–1028.

UNAIDS, 2000, *Report on the Global HIV/AIDS Epidemic.* Geneva: UNAIDS.

—, 2003, *Report on the Global HIV/AIDS Epidemic.* Geneva: UNAIDS.

Werbner, R. (ed.), 1998, *Memory and the Postcolony. African Anthropology and the Critique of Power.* London, New York: Zed Books.

Werbner, R. and Ranger, T. (eds), 1998, *Postcolonial Identities in Africa.* London, New York: Zed Books.

CHAPTER 5

Industrial Labour, Marital Strategy and Changing Livelihood Trajectories among Young Women in Lesotho

Christian Boehm

Introduction

This chapter sets out to explore the changing pathways of young women and their implications for meanings of gender and 'youth' under current conditions of rapid change on the regional labour market in Lesotho, Southern Africa. Generally, and also amongst Basotho, youth and adolescence was long perceived as a 'transitional' phase, characterised by a certain degree of liminality (Bucholtz 2002; Gay 1980). In order to become a complete socially and morally accepted adult human being, marriage was, and still is, considered an essential precondition.

Yet Lesotho is currently experiencing what with some justification might be termed a crisis of marriage and dissociation between marriage and childbearing. Gender roles are changing and young people in Lesotho rarely engage in traditional marriages at present. Does this mean that the transitional phase of youth never ends for those Basotho who never marry? Not entirely! By drawing on case material from lowland Lesotho, I attempt to demonstrate how young women in this country are actively engaged in suggesting and negotiating new gender roles as well as cultural identities of adulthood under prevailing socio-economic conditions.[1]

In order to explore the implications of changing female life cycles (Lamphere 1974) for perceptions of youth and adulthood, I sketch out below some of the changes of labour migration patterns Lesotho has experienced in its recent past. I then discuss the cases of three young women in terms of

---

1. The data on which it is based emerged during eight months of anthropological fieldwork in a lowland village from September 2001 to May 2002. The fieldwork was supported by a grant from SLUSE, the Danish University Consortia on Sustainable Land Use.

the changing options and constraints they face today. A brief background of garment sector workers from Ha Sofonia is included. Subsequently, I explore some short- and long-term implications of the trend towards more female wage earners for intra-household relationships of gender, power and authority, as well as processes of household formation and marriage. Finally, I provide an interpretation of differences in male and female wage earning capacities in terms of the changing identities of youth and adulthood in Lesotho.

Mines and garments

During the past two decades, the small Southern African Kingdom of Lesotho has experienced some major changes in its regional labour market context. First, downscaling in the South African gold mines had meant that the number of Basotho men employed in the mining industry has been reduced from almost 130,000 during the 1970s and 80s to approximately 55,000 by 2002. Second, Lesotho has recently been caught up in processes of translocation of cheap labour within the global garment sector industry with the result that young women have entered the urban labour market on a large scale. As my main interest here is Lesotho's young women, I mainly focus on the latter aspect below.

The worldwide trend of Asian investors relocating the production of garments to cheap labour countries began to have an impact on Lesotho during the 1980s.[2] A number of conditions were important to Lesotho being relatively successful in attracting investors from the Far East, who control 90 per cent of the industry in Lesotho (Salm et al. 2002). First, Lesotho has preferential access to a number of important textile markets, most notably the United States (US). The signing of the Africa Growth and Opportunities Act (AGOA) has consolidated the US as the primary market for garments produced in Lesotho. This agreement is currently driving the growth of the industry. Second, corporate tax is very low and the Lesotho National Development Corporation (LNDC) does its utmost to please

---

2. In 1987, diplomatic ties between Lesotho and Taiwan were restored and the Lesotho National Development Corporation (LNDC) embarked on a strategy to attract investors in a manner very similar to the way the South African apartheid government sought investments for its economic decentralisation programme investments within the black 'Bantustan' areas (Baylies & Wright 1993). For a detailed analysis of Asian garment investments in apartheid South Africa under conditions of forced mass removals of rural populations into urban townships, see also Gillian Hart's book 'Disabling Globalisation', 2002, University of California Press.

investors in terms of capital investments, taxation, environmental legislation, service costs, etc. Third, labour is cheap and there is a large relatively well-educated labour force in Lesotho. Fourth, Lesotho can make use of a well-developed infrastructure in surrounding South Africa, an advantage, which makes Lesotho a preferred investment country in relation to other sub-Saharan African countries also included in the AGOA agreements.[3]

In 2003, it was estimated that more than 45,000 Basotho were employed in the garment industry and that there was potential for further expansion as a result of AGOA II, an extension of the existing trade agreement between the US and Lesotho.[4] 90 per cent of the employees in textile concerns are young women and wages are notoriously low at 27 US cents per hour (Salm et al. 2002).

The figure below consisely illustrates changes in the labour opportunities open to Basotho over the past three decades.

Figure 1: Lesotho Labour Market Developments

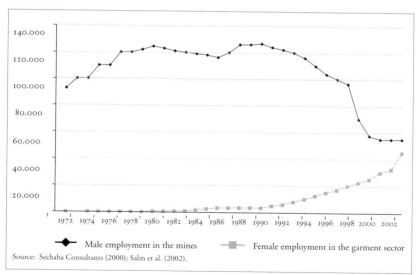

Source: Sechaba Consultants (2000); Salm et al. (2002).

3. For comparison, the value figures in mill. US$ for textile exports to the US in 2001 were 216.7 for Lesotho, 64.4 for Kenya, 178.2 for Madagascar, 238.3 for Mauritius and 173.3 for South Africa (Gibbon, P. unpublished manuscript: "Explaining responses to AGOA in the African clothing sector").

4. Mopheme, (daily newspaper in Lesotho), May 30, 2003.

As is apparent from the above graph, the emerging employment opportunities, which have come in the wake of the recent industrialisation of Lesotho, have come to a group, which is structurally different from that of men, the 'traditional' breadwinners and wage earners. Although far from all young women have been able or willing to take up wage labour in one of the Asian garment sector factories, the daily rush of tens of thousands of young women (and some men as well) to and from the industrial areas of Maseru, Maputsoe, Mafeteng and Mohale's Hoek has considerable implications for the social organisation among Basotho: young women's social position vis-à-vis men (their boyfriends, husbands, brothers, fathers or sons) and other women (girlfriends, mothers, sisters or daughters) is changing. Rising male unemployment combined with emerging female employment options has considerably changed young women's options in terms of their marital careers and affected processes of social reproduction and household formation.

Different interpretations and responses to young women's emerging options, especially the new employment opportunities, have led to an increased multiplicity of livelihood pathways among them. On the one hand, they try to integrate different cultural ideals and negotiate a possible life. On the other hand, they are also made up by the world they live in and through. The decisions they take throughout this process form both productive and reproductive activities, as well as cultural identities of youth and adulthood.

Changing female trajectories

Young women's lives take a different course nowadays compared to what was the case 20 years ago. An overriding theme in the literature on young women, a substantial part of which emerged during the 1970s, was the critical importance of marriage to them. In a situation where mainly men could gain access to cash through wage labour, marriage was the only means by which women could access it. Thus, marriage at an early age was the norm among young Basotho women. For Gay (1980), marriage was the single most important factor shaping a woman's life, mainly because marriage determines access to Lesotho's primary resource, men's remittances. The transition from a girl to an adult woman was perceived to be facilitated by three aspects: first, becoming a daughter-in-law; second, having the first child and becoming a mother; third, acquiring an independent homestead (Gay 1980). While the first aspect was linked to marriage with a man, the third aspect depended on marriage with a 'working man'. Unless the woman wanted to share her husband's remittances with her in-laws, moving to an independent homestead was essential to her. While it was possible to become a mother (*motsoetse*), it remained difficult for mother and child to thrive without remittances from a husband to cover essential items such as food, school fees and health care. Under conditions where both productive and reproductive activities were linked to, and determined by, access to cash resources from men's remittances, the need to gain some form of control over this source of cash became paramount. It was also important that marriage formed a way towards increased economic independence and 'freedom' from the natal home as a result of the husband's cash earnings and an independent household, perhaps a field, but also respect and the right to legitimate reproduction and formal protection by the husband and his kin.

The circumstances in which young women nowadays find themselves are in many aspects different from what their mothers (or even their elder sisters) experienced up to the onset of the labour market changes during the late 80s/early 90s. At present, the proportion of married women in Ha Sofonia within the age cohort 18–30 is as low as 22.5 per cent and corresponds well to that of the young men of the village. It is thus much lower than what was found by researchers such as Judy Gay (1980), who reported 80 per cent of all 21-year-old women to be married during the 70s or Robertson (1987), who gives marriage rates of 70–80 per cent for the female age cohort of 20–29 years. It would be misleading to assume, however, that marriage rates are declining only because young men cannot find wage employment, raise money for bride wealth and take on a role as breadwinner and provider, a status that is perceived to be a precondition for marriage among men. Cash remains the solution to (almost) all livelihood related problems in Lesotho but men are nowadays no longer the only means to access it.

While the majority of young men are unemployed at the moment, they witness how numerous young women have become 'new actors in the globalised economy', the new miners,[5] so to speak. In terms of accessing cash and creating an autonomous livelihood, for many young women, marriage is not a strict necessity any more. Long queues in front of the factory gates bear witness to that facts that, first, young Basotho women have enthusiastically taken on this new wage earning opportunity, second, that the need

---

5. The Asian factories are sometimes jokingly termed 'the new mines'.

for cash is urgent and that many families and individuals have no other choice than trying their luck at the factory gate and, third, that the number of job seekers far exceeds the number of job openings available.

The crowds at the factory gates might lead the observer to believe that the vast majority of young women want to work in the factory. Yet the perspective from Ha Sofonia is more diverse. Here, young women have reacted to the new labour market not in a uniform, but in a differentiated manner, depending on their particular individual and social situation as well as their personal and their surroundings' attitudes to gender roles and the sexual division of labour.

In order to explore this diversity and to show how young women in Lesotho make sense of the new employment options, I introduce below three young women and their families. The first woman is an active jobseeker and considers taking on factory work, the second woman rejects working in the factories while the third is currently employed in a textile factory.[6] With the help of these case studies, I want to show how and why young women may or may not strive to become 'new economic actors' as well as what their ideas and aspirations are concerning marriage and the often discussed 'feminisation of labour'.

Case 1: Litlokotsi Mofo

One of the families which are actively engaged in the new economic order is the one headed by 63-year-old Ntate Lekhlonoholo Mofo, who worked in the mines in Gauteng and Kimberley until 10 years ago when he stopped for health reasons. Their house was built in 1968, according to Me Mofo, 'at a time when we were all improving because our men worked in the mines'. The Mofo family manages financially by selling livestock and animal products, some occasional contributions from those children who are working as well as ploughing two of their four fields with the help of tractor owner Simon. Lekhlonoholo and Me Mamotebang have nine children, five daughters and four sons. All the daughters have left home, four for

---

6. Here, attention should be drawn to the methodological difficulties of interviewing young women working in the factories. As they leave early and return late, and because they are very busy and tired once they have returned home, access to them is limited. In the factories it is impossible to interview the workers because of strictly limited access. On Sundays, most of them are off work and chances are better. In general, young women were more difficult for me as a young man to interview because they were shyer and/or more protected by their parents. Female job seekers are easiest to interview on the spot within the industrial areas.

Maseru and one for Johannesburg. Two daughters work in the Asian factories. There are five grandchildren from three daughters left with the Mofos, because childcare is difficult for factory workers in Maseru. Me Mamotebang does not know their daughters' boyfriends and none of the girls are married. According to Me Mamotebang, the reason why they all stay in Maseru is that it is cheaper to rent a room at Ha Thetsane (80–120 Rand/month in 2002) than to pay transport costs for daily commuting. In addition and especially during the dark winter months, commuting is known to be dangerous.[7] Their firstborn son, the miner Motebang (born in 1965) has established his own household and family and is the only wage earner among four sons. Of the three remaining sons, the first is unemployed, the second chronically ill and the third still attending school. Besides the interviews conducted with both parents and Motebang's wife, Makhotso, I draw on conversations with 20-year-old Litlokotsi, the youngest daughter who has recently moved to Maseru in order to find a job. Below are some brief excerpts from an interview that dealt with the topics of female labour and marriage.[8]

> To be a real women, you should work on your own and not expect too much from your husband. I would like to work but I'd prefer office work rather than the factories. Now many women work and they work very hard because these Chinese harass and abuse our sisters. But we are strong because we can still do things under these hardships. ... I am really proud of being Mosotho. I don't want to lose my culture but that doesn't mean I have to put tradition into practice. We shouldn't be too much Basotho and we shouldn't act like Whites either. ... I want to get married, not with a miner but somebody who stays with me. If you are not married, you snatch away other women's husbands and I don't want to be like that. It is also good nowadays to be married because then you avoid this new disease. But as long as I am not married I have things under control. I hate these marriages where someone is called the 'head'. I don't want someone who is beating me. But once I am married I want the number of children I can afford to educate, perhaps two. Nowadays too many of our sisters fall pregnant very early.

---

7. The local daily newspaper '*Mopheme*' (in Lesotho), published an article on September 26, 2002, which describes the high frequency of mugging of female textile workers at month's end, especially around the banks and ATMs (Automatic Teller Machines), where most of the factory girls withdraw their salaries.

8. Most interviews were conducted with an assistant interpreting Sesotho and English.

The interview with Litlokotsi is a narrative characterised by the visions of a young woman, who has temporarily moved to town in order to escape her natal home and try her luck in town. Her chances to get the office work she dreams about are slim. Most likely and with the help of her sisters, she may only be able to get a factory job. Her ideas are of a fairly modernist nature, consisting of the desk job, two children, a faithful and kind husband who is willing to assist with domestic chores and the acquirement of the magic 'triple C' (cash, car and cellular phone). She thus belongs to a new generation of Basotho women for whom marriage is not a strict necessity to gain access to wages, but rather a possible and desirable option if a proper husband can be found. But it is difficult to imagine that any of the young men from Ha Sofonia would be able to fulfil her present ambitions concerning the financial capabilities of the ideal husband. Many of the young women of her generation, just like Litlokotsi's sisters, leave their chhildren behind in their own – or the father's – natal home[9] and strike out on their own to establish an urban livelihood based on factory wages, boyfriends, shebeening, etc. Hence, the Mofo family reflects the gender role implications of the new economic order and the changing employment situation well in that wage earners of the filial generation are to be found among both sons and daughters and that women have entered the previously male dominated urban industrial sphere. To call this family typical might be misleading though. Many other women and their families consciously oppose female wage labour in the garment sector factories, as the next case attempts to illustrate.

Case 2: Matseliso Khohloa

28-year-old Matseliso's household is formally headed by her uncle Daniel, who works on a farm in the Orange Free State in South Africa. She lives with two brothers, one working as watchman in Maseru while the other one is unemployed. The remaining household is made up of six children between 5 and 15 years of age. Two of the children are Matseliso's; the others are the offspring of one brother as well as relatives in the RSA. They make a living by financial contributions from Matseliso's brother combined with odd jobs, a bit of hawking and brewing as well as cultivating their large field. Matseliso has worked as a servant for one year but is in Ha Sofonia

---

9. By age 19, 52 per cent of all women in Lesotho are, or have been, pregnant (UN Integrated Regional Information Networks, June 16, 2003).

at the moment. On my enquiries concerning the factory job opportunities, she replied:

> Really, I suffer a lot. I am the de facto head here because my brothers are usually gone. People like me; we work for small money on the fields of the rich (Barui). Sometimes we can also wash their clothes. Or I can ask the other church members for help. With relatives it is difficult, they always want something in return, you see. They never just help. I really like it when women work for themselves but I cannot put up with the working conditions in the Chinese factories. There is so much hatred and jealousy there and the place is 'cold' and poisonous. You can hardly breathe there. If I go there, it won't take long and I am dead. We women are not meant to work that hard, we must do suitable work. It would be better if the men could do these jobs. ... I know some women who are fooling up and down in these factories. They should have improved by now but they are getting nowhere. They don't learn the lesson and their parents are drunkards. If I had a husband, he should be the one working while I keep the house. Even though I don't expect it to happen, I would like to marry. It wasn't my plan to have children early but now I have the two girls and no man would take that responsibility. ... But really, this thing you call marriage doesn't exist any longer. Last time we witnessed it was in our parents' generation. Today it is nothing but play. To be honest with you, people today don't last very long, either they run away or they die.

Like many others in Ha Sofonia, Matseliso rejects the idea of taking on factory work on the grounds that it is unhealthy, dangerous and does not conform to her ideals of gender roles. Childcare responsibilities might also be an important reason why she does not want to seek wage labour in the garment sector. Although she stresses the wish to work for herself, Matseliso's account is characterised by a much more conservative and traditionalist attitude to gender relationships and the sexual division of labour, in which women are said to belong to the rural and domestic sphere while men should go and earn wages. Yet at the same time, her household resembles a recent trend in Lesotho and beyond, namely the increasing occurrence of households where the centre of gravity rests on the sibling relationships. With the help of brothers and relatives, but also because Matseliso is a modest and hard-working individual, she manages to 'muddle through'. Her decision not to go to the factories is a conscious one and informed by the accounts of other 'factory girls', her own situation at present as well as the alternative livelihood options she has chosen to seize in Ha Sofonia.

Case 3: Aussi Skee

Aussi Skee is a member of the larger Skee family, consisting of three re-trenched brothers and their families. She stays with her parents, two broth-ers, one sister, her own child and a herdboy. Aussi has been married but is separated from her husband. Her eldest brother, a miner, is married and about to establish his own homestead within the site belonging to his fa-ther Ismael and his uncle Samuel. Below are a number excerpts from her account.

> I work at Stationeng, in a Chinese factory next to Lesotho Flour Mills. This is my first job and I have been there for three months now. My task is to do the quality check. We leave very early in the morning and return late. I am very happy for the job. But when I come home I am so tired I just sleep. My mother takes care of the housework and the children. Only on Sundays, like now, I work as well in order to help her. ... The money depends on the over-time we do. Normally it is around 500 Rand per month. Then I use 220 Rand for transport each month. It's a lot but I don't want to move to town. I have a home and here we can eat together. ... I have problems to solve now but in the future I want to put money in the bank account. I have a child and I am separated because my marriage didn't work. If there is some money remaining, it goes to the child. ... The money is very important. And I like it to have my own money. I'll work and do the housework when I come home. Some money also goes to the Funeral Association. Perhaps I'll have my own house one day. ... It doesn't really matter whether husband or wife is working, as long as there is one income in the house... For the future I don't know yet. I can lose the job any time.

With her new job, Aussi has taken on a position as a productive member in a fairly well-off and entrepreneurial family. Because of her work, she is an accepted and respected member. It is normally considered problematic to return to the natal home upon separation or divorce because the returnee may be perceived as an additional burden on a tight household budget. Yet Aussi's father assured me that this was not a problem in his house because of the contributions Aussi makes to the household economy. In that sense, the factory made it possible for Aussi to walk out of an unsatisfactory relation-ship and return to live in her natal home where she is a rather submissive and female role model despite her wage income. Thus, in her household, status and power come along with gender and age rather than wage earn-ing capacity. The wage has rather transformed her status from being a netdrainer of the household to a net-contributor.[10] Although she dreams about her own homestead, her chances to remarry are slim and she may remain a part of her paternal or fraternal household in the future where she can enjoy relative livelihood security as well as childcare assistance. The family nexus is her most important asset for security, which is one important reason why she has opted not to move to Maseru.

New options – new contraints

To further investigate the local dimension of the phenomenon of the 'feminisation of labour' in Lesotho and in order to move away from the individual cases, it might be worthwhile to explore briefly the social and economic background of the garment workers of Ha Sofonia. At the end of fieldwork in May 2002, there were around 26 women and one man[11] from Ha Sofonia working in the textile factories. Admittedly, these figures are subject to uncertainty and fluctuations because of the high staff turnover within the factory settings as well as variations in cash needs according to season.[12]

Yet it is evident that the number of textile workers exceeded the number of miners (22) in the community. Not surprisingly, given the fact that factories preferably hire young women, of 26 women working in the garment sector, 14 come from extended family-type households, where they normally constitute the middle generation, i.e. daughters to the head of the family and mothers to the small children. Concerning their economic background, only four can be said to come from households in a destitute condition. At the other end of the wealth spectrum, eight come from households, which

---

10. I am, of course, aware of the productive labour women put into their households. In a situation of acute lack of cash, however, it is higher valued than domestic labour.

11. This man got his job in a factory in Maputsoe with the help of his sister.

12. The period between January until mid-March used to be the financially most difficult time of the year because of Christmas, school fees, the recent investment in ploughing (usually between October and December) and depleted grain stocks as the coming harvest is approaching. Unemployment has meant that numerous households cannot afford to cultivate their fields any longer. Instead, they focus solely on odd job seeking as their prime livelihood strategy. In terms of the financial annual cycle, this has meant that the winter (May to September) with increased demands on fuel and clothing has for some become the most critical time of the year.

could be characterised as relatively 'well-off'.[13] This reflects, first, that only fairly resourceful women, in terms of transport investments, bribes, personal skills and education manage to get hold of factory jobs. Second, it also indicates that young women are not only *pushed* towards industrial labour due to economic hardships and the need for cash but also *pulled* towards the urban sector by factors such as economic independence, personal freedom and the adventure in town.[14] The fact that eight of the 19 households with access to factory income have another wage earner in the family illustrates that factory workers are concentrated in a few families and that factory work is conditioned by factors beyond pure economic need.

Gender, being female, is not only something they *are* but also something they *do*. Seeking factory work has become one way for young women in Lesotho to enact themselves and to realize the person they want to be. One characteristic, which most factory girls share, is that they are single mothers. But since most young women have children in Lesotho, the extent to which there is a correlation between motherhood and their occupation is hard to determine. While marriage is a point of withdrawal from the urban labour market in other developing countries where young women are employed in multinational industries on a large scale (Dyer 2001; Joekes 1985), this point is not valid for the case of Lesotho. First, many do not marry at all and, second, there are few working husbands available who could secure the young women's future livelihood upon marriage and an eventual withdrawal from the labour market. Dyer (2001) has argued that there are numerous single mothers in the factories of Lesotho, simply because there are no other livelihoods available to them. This is probably correct in many cases, but not in all. Matseliso is a good example of a single mother who refuses to take on factory work on practical as well as cultural grounds. Those single mothers in Ha Sofonia, who are really forced to go and seek factory work, are those who are positioned in a weak, unproductive and vulnerable social nexus, but who are able to solve their childcare problem at the same time.[15]

---

13. This categorisation is based on a number of wealth indicators from a census I conducted as well as my personal knowledge of these families.

14. Push-pull models of migration, as developed by Lee (1966) and elaborated by many others, are a cornerstone of the history of migration studies in social science.

15. One of my neighbours, 28-year-old Celina was such a case. Upon separation, she returned to Sofonia but found herself alone with two children, aged 8 and 11, in a poor house. She had found employment in a factory in 2001 and commutes daily. Her children are usually left alone in the village during the daytime.

Another interesting dimension concerning the background of factory girls is their unequal spatial distribution amongst the homesteads of the village. Most of them live in the village sections around *Moreneng*, the chiefly compound, while they are hardly found in the remaining village. In addition to that, the 27 workers come from only 19 households, meaning that 7 of the 19 households that have access to garment sector income have more than one and up to three daughters working in the garment sector factories. Assuming that there is a correlation between physical proximity and kinship ties in village neighbourhoods,[16] the physical concentration of factory workers in one part of the village as well as in a few families points towards highly differentiated and clustered access to the newly emerged wage labour opportunity in the form of kin and neighbourhood/friendship based job seeking networks.[17]

The empirical data concerning young women in Lesotho generally, and those working in the Asian factories specifically, presented so far points to a number of options and constraints critical to young women's lives today. First, marriage with an employed man is hardly an option for many of them. Rather, it has become more commonplace for young women either to never enter the state of marriage or to leave an unsatisfactory conjugal relationship with an unemployed husband who is unable to fulfil the obligations of the 'conjugal contract' (Whitehead 1981) or 'patriarchal bargain' (Sweetman 1995; Kabeer 1997)[18] and who is thus not in a position to claim her as a rightful conjugal partner. Competition for employed men is stiff and, as Litlokotsi explained, if you were lucky enough to have found an employed man, you would live in constant fear that he might be seduced by another women and snatched away.[19]

---

16. Although many of the families around Moreneng have different surnames (*fane*), many share their identification with a common ancestor. Over time, numerous lineages broke away, which has resulted in the variety of family names.

17. In practice, a job seeker can get help from a sister, cousin or friend in the following ways: first, once there are rumours of a job opening, the job seeker is told to queue up earlier than the others in order to be the first at the gate in the morning; second, the factory worker can manipulate the person responsible for hiring new staff by means of bribes in order to make them hire a specific person.

18. Roughly put, he offers access to wages, an independent homestead and formal protection, while he receives legitimate reproduction, access to her sexual services as well as childcare of his offspring.

19. This is said to be very common. Men, however, are not seriously blamed for this, because 'this is just how men are'. It is the very 'nature' of men, so to speak. Women, on the other hand can only be blamed to a certain extent because employed

Second, young women can nowadays go to the factory gates and attempt to find employment there. Those who persistently queue up for long periods (a costly affair in terms of transport) will often find some kind of employment, although it may only be for some months.[20] While some chose to stay at home (such as Aussi Skee), some move to Maseru, where they rent a 'flat' and, if lucky, may try to localise a more affluent man than the ones available in Ha Sofonia. But just like Matseliso, many women (and men) reject the disorder of men being unemployed and women working under poor conditions and for low wages. Those who reject factory work may 'muddle through' with a variety of other livelihood strategies, such as small-scale farming, gardening, brewing, hawking, odd jobs or receiving gifts from relatives. Basotho are experts in keeping going despite adverse circumstances, especially women who over generations have had to make ends meet with meagre and irregular remittances sent by their husbands in the mines.

Third, female rural-urban migration, often of a temporary nature, is an option closely related to the dimensions discussed above. Litlokotsi is a case in point here. Many young women, just like their male counterparts, move to town in order to try their luck. While most go to Maseru, a minority leaves for urban areas of South Africa, especially the townships in Gauteng and around Welkom, where many Basotho live. If job- and boyfriend-hunting does not prove successful and when the relatives where they reside during their urban adventure get tired of having an additional guest and extra burden staying with them, they often reappear in Ha Sofonia.

Fourth, few young women live in households of the nuclear 'compact type' (Robertson 1991) because only a small minority of young men can nowadays afford to finance household division together with a young bride. Instead, they either remain in their extended paternal households together with their children and one or both parents, or they maintain sibling households, often in cases where both parents have passed away. Strong sibling relationships are also a result of the migrant labour system, which left women with the entire domestic workload and children to look af-

---

men can be understood as a specific kind of common property, an item to be shared among Basotho sisters.

20. Staff turnover is high in general. In addition, Basotho girls are hired on a low apprenticeship wage, which after some months has to be raised according to Lesotho labour legislation. But instead of raising the wage upon completion of the 'apprenticeship', the Asian employers are accused of hiring new apprentices and dismissing the experienced ones.

ter for themselves and the others. As such, sibling co-operation builds on already existing social links. This trend indicates that the importance of husband–wife relationship decreases and is 'replaced' by the sibling relationship. Household fission in the manner it was observed and described during the 70s and 80s is often no longer possible because economic and childcare needs under changing labour market conditions demand new forms of co-operation. If more young people extend sibling co-operation well into adulthood and stay or move together, new patterns of household formation emerge. A trajectory different from the classical marital career has become common.

Fifth, it is important to consider the long-term consequences of young women's decisions. Due to the recent nature of the changed labour conditions, however, it might be early to determine these empirically. As former scholars of Lesotho have rightfully pointed out (Gay 1980; Murray 1981), marriage used to be a milestone in a woman's life. At present, this phase in her life has become a point of enhanced vulnerability (Peters 1983), where her marital options and ultimate decisions have far-reaching implications for herself and her offspring. Choosing an urban 'path' may have profound impacts on her entitlements and capabilities in terms of the necessary assets and social support networks of a later rural livelihood. It is important to remember that the notoriously low wages available to young women do not allow for any capital accumulation and that very little is remitted to the family or household. Remaining in the village without a reliable source of cash may leave her in destitution without any chance to accumulate wealth and security either. Because the decision-making process takes place in a state of knowledge and livelihood uncertainty (Mehta et al. 1999), most young women envision a life that keeps open as many options as possible and one that draws on both urban and rural spheres.

The feminisation of labour and changing gender roles

The picture presented thus far is one of social heterogeneity and differentiated interpretations as well as responses to the changing labour market conditions. Factory work is generally perceived as a low-grade job under humiliating conditions. Yet poverty in isolation cannot be seen as a satisfactory explanation to the recent participation of young women in the labour force of Lesotho. It might also be remembered that wage labour is not a 'cultural necessity' for women as it is for men. For many women, wage labour is one option among others, while unemployment is perceived to be predominantly a practical livelihood problem. Seen in men's, and also many women's eyes, being hired and earning a wage gives status primarily to men – and less so to women. At the same time, men 'cannot not work', so to speak. For them, wage labour is an absolute must and the lack of it can be a devastating condition undermining their male breadwinner identity.

For young women, factory work is also a means by which they strive for increased economic independence, social adulthood and personal freedom. Whether it also translates into changing gender relations and increased female independence is one of the key debates of the anthropological and especially feminist-inspired literature on the global feminisation of labour (e.g. Afshar 1985; Joekes 1985; Standing 1985; Humphrey 1985; Warren & Borque 1991; Baylies and Wright 1993; Goebel and Epprecht 1995; Kabeer 1997; Cairoli 1998; Dyer 2001; Dannecker 2002). In a nutshell, the discussion on whether the involvement of women from developing countries in the production lines of the translocated and multinational industries has 'empowered' women in societies which typically try to control their personal freedom, goes along two main strands. The protagonists argue that women have benefited as a result of their new employment options and that it is possible to maintain a constructive relationship with male-dominated family structures. The mere fact that any kind of wage represents some form of power in itself as soon as it enters social relations must create some additional personal freedom for these women, it is argued. This positive view is mainly found in studies on settings in the Far East, such as Hong Kong (Salaff 1981, cited in Warren and Borque 1991) or the Philippines (McKay 2003).

The proponents of the negative view argue that women are locked into new structures of inequality, that the double workload of factory and home further 'disempowers' women and destabilises families, and that the poor working conditions and discriminatory wage policies leave women disadvantaged and gender inequalities enhanced. Fernandez-Kelly (1983, cited in Warren and Borque 1991) with a case from Mexico and Joekes (1985) with a study from Morocco clearly support the negative view that the women in their cases have not benefited from an entry into the labour market. Amongst other reasons, they attribute this to increasing male-female tensions in a situation of, just as in Lesotho, massive unemployment among men. Joekes' study is particularly interesting here because, in her attempt to give an explanation of how such low wages can be maintained, she demonstrates that female workers in Morocco have similar family backgrounds to my cases from Lesotho. The female workers in Joekes' study are either single mothers who are extremely marginalized anyway and who cannot demand better wages, or daughters who are not considered as serious bread-winners and for whom nobody in this patriarchal society would ever expect a better salary. Wages, Joekes concludes, are thus always gender specific and never 'pure'. Another study from Morocco (Cairoli 1998) concludes that young women deliberately recast the patriarch power relations of their home within the factory space in order to create continuity between home and work, and to 'morocconize' their workplaces.[21]

Goebel & Epprecht (1995) look at the potential for transformation of gender roles among women employed in Lesotho's (fairly small) tapestry weaving sector and conclude that the exploitatively low wages actually pro-tect women from encountering a more violent and oppressive reaction from their husbands and fathers, and that female wage earning power does little to "mitigate the oppression and exploitation experienced by the majority of women in the region" (Goebel and Epprecht 1995:19).

Other authors such as Humphrey (1985), Standing (1985) or Kabeer (1997) are more ambivalent as to whether women really have benefited from becoming wage labourers. Kabeer (1997) offers a sophisticated analy-sis of the implications of female wage earning power on intra-household and gender relations. Drawing on economic notions of 'bargaining power' as well as Sen's model of 'co-operative conflict' (Sen 1990), she argues that Bangladeshi women do not challenge the patriarchal breadwinner model because of the general sense of insecurity and low status among women. Yet at the same time, she shows how the wage has significantly improved their bargaining position in the household and that it has opened other options in 'co-operation breakdown situations', where women, just as Aussi Skee in Case 3 above, can abandon an unsatisfactory relationship.

Dyer (2001) concludes that the situation in Lesotho is confusing be-cause "... the nature of the relationship between home and factory is cur-rently still in such a state of flux and contestation, that picking out overall trends from the idiosyncrasies of particular family and individual circum-stances is hazardous" (Dyer 2001:9).

As she correctly points out, it is also a question of to what extent the men at home co-operate and agree to live with the new employment situation or

---

21. It is worth noting here that the involvement of young women in the garment sec-tor occurs under different conditions than in Lesotho. The Moroccan situation is characterised by many smaller factories, which are owned by nationals. This has the implication that it is easier for workers to identify with the product. In addi-tion, employment periods are apparently much longer than in Lesotho.

if they perceive it as an attack on their male integrity.[22] It is obvious that the garment sector expansion has not solved the problem of male unemployment. By transforming women into an 'employable' category, while not providing employment opportunities for men, many of them feel threatened in their masculine integrity, which tells them that men are supposed to be hired while women belong to the domestic sphere. The emerging gender struggle has repercussions on the process of female 'empowerment'. As the studies discussed above demonstrate, equating female employment with either female empowerment or disempowerment is too simplistic to reflect the gender dynamics within households and conjugal relationships that emerge as a consequence of women taking up wage employment in the Chinese factories.

Perhaps, the modernist and 'empowered' attitude of Litlokotsi (Case 1) and the much more traditionalist and conservative role played by Aussi Skee (Case 3) point to the fact of residence as critical and make it necessary to differentiate between young women who set up their own independent household in town and those who remain part of the paternal or conjugal household in the village. For those women who commute on a daily basis, the factory practically functions as an extension of the household. Instead of going to the field to hoe, to the hillside to collect fuel or to the spring to draw water, they leave for the factory to earn wages. They cannot enjoy the 'freedom' of town, are left with the double workload of job and home and because their economic contribution to the household economy is very modest anyway, they do not challenge male authority within their homestead. These women appear to have penetrated the male sphere of cheap labour in the globalised capitalist production, but not the constructed male domain of culturally defined and ruled authority based on the accumulation as well as the diffusion of wealth by means of participation in both capitalist production and local economies.

Women who choose to leave home more or less permanently in order to work and live in town seem to be a different matter. Security reasons, commuting costs as well as the desire to leave an unsatisfactory social situation in the natal or conjugal home are often mentioned as reasons why girls move to a 'flat' close to the factory. A number of them were also able to leave an unsatisfactory relationship *because* of the factory income. While unequal gender relations still prevail within the Asian factory set-

---

22. Aussi Skee's family is a case in point here because the men in her homestead have taken a co-operative stance towards her wage labour efforts. This is certainly not the case everywhere.

tings (Warren and Borque 1991; Dyer 2001), freedom, empowerment and changing gender relations come through living in town, often with a new boyfriend and away from controlling and demanding household members and kinsfolk, who prevent them from becoming adults by treating them as minors. In the research site, 14 out of 26 young working women have set up a new 'home'[23] in town, left children with parents or siblings and pay irregular visits when they, according to their relatives back home, have little or nothing to contribute to the parental homestead.

Taking on factory work in Maseru may thus have different purposes. For many it is a livelihood strategy pursued due to economic needs and often put into practice when job-seeking efforts of their male household members have proved unsuccessful. Others look for personal freedom and/ or a boyfriend. Because factory work rarely takes on the form of a lasting career, we may view it in terms of a 'trajectory-loop' that is performed with the purpose of returning to a 'normal' female livelihood trajectory either with money or a man who has got some. For a few, factory work is a step towards a more lucrative, but also more dangerous, urban income generation strategy.[24]

Labour and social capital

The previous sections have presented ethnographic data concerning the changing position of young women and discussed some implications of their increasingly dominant role in the labour force for gender relationships in Lesotho. At this stage, a question that needs to be addressed is: What are the implications of increasing female wage earning capacity and decreasing male wage earning capacity in relation to livelihood strategies and age identities in a wider sense? Assisted by the notion of 'social capital', the next section attempts to suggest, perhaps not a comprehensive answer, but some main points of importance.

I suggest that social life in Basotho villages is considerably transformed as a result of the emergence of women as wage earners on a large scale. A society such as Lesotho, which – in theory and to a large extend also in

---

23. These 'homes' may only exist over a relatively limited time span and consist of one or more persons renting a 'flat' or staying with friends and relatives in town.

24. In 1999, I participated in a short study on prostitution as urban survival strategy and found that most 'upper-class' prostitutes working in the city centre of Maseru have a background as factory workers. See also: Sechaba Consultants, Maseru, *Poverty and Livelihoods in Lesotho*, 2000.

practice – is patriarchal, patrilinear and patri-virilocal, has to redefine its relationship between production on the one hand and social reproduction on the other in a situation where most men are unemployed and many women have become wage earners. Men's work determines a wide array of cultural themes and practices. Hence, the new economic order affects not only the livelihoods of particular households in Lesotho, but the cultural, social and economic order of society as a whole.[25]

Social capital, a contested key concept of social science in general, has found its way into livelihood thinking. Being so widely used (by e.g. Gilbert & Walker 2002; Scoones 1998 or Murray 2001), is has also been interpreted differently. One of the founders of the concept of social capital, Pierre Bourdieu (1986) defines the term as follows:

> Social capital is the aggregate of the actual or potential resources which are linked to possession of a durable network ... The volume of the social capital possessed by a given agent thus depends on the size of the network of connections he can effectively mobilize and on the volume of the capital ... possessed by a given agent, or even by the whole set of agents to whom he is connected (Bourdieu 1986:248–249, cited in Fine 2001).

Social capital as one of the non-economic capitals (social, symbolic and cultural) is thus about the extent of social connections or networks as well as group membership and how the above can be applied and put to work in particular practical circumstances. Social capital is what makes actors work together in order to pursue shared objectives and common goals.

Resources that are stored in human relationships have for some time also attracted the interest of development related research. Here, different forms of capital are seen to move within and between different spheres and circuits where they are evaluated by reference to local currencies and social values. These currencies establish the value of social capital and may render different benefits. The significance of a social relation is established, evaluated and maintained along the lines of social, symbolic and cultural codes, where gender, age, wealth and other parameters are important.

What is essential to my effort is that various kinds of social links, such as kinship, friendship, neighbourhood, patron – client relationships, etc.

---

25. The emerging perceived disorder of men in the village and women leaving for work, becomes even more obvious through a quick look at the Sesotho vernacular terms for man (=*monna*) and woman (=*mosali*). While the prefix '*mo*' stands for 'a person', the male '*nna*' means 'I', the female '*sali*' derives from '*sala*', meaning 'to stay behind / to remain' (Langston 1993).

can become mobilised and thus take on a form of capital to be applied in an action arena. Also critical is the moral dimension of social capital, meaning that social capital is frequently generated by some kind of reference to Sesotho custom and based on the lifestyle and social respect of the actors involved. Adulthood and gender roles are thus closely related to the potential of social capital.

An idea of social capital as something that can be 'stored' and used when necessary seems, however, to miss its dynamics. As it lies in the relationship between people it is rather a matter of a potentiality to be mobilised under certain conditions during the process of social management. This acknowledges that the parameters of social capital and the different forms of social currencies change alongside conditions of social life in general. In other words, as different social positions and trajectories are changing, so are different forms of capital as well as the nature of social relations including the rights and claims therein. The methodological challenge that remains is to define the 'social', i.e. the content of the relationship and/or network.

The concept of social capital might be usefully applied as an analytical tool to grasp what happens to both male and female wages once they are earned and enter a social life in household and community. Especially in a situation of rapid social change, investigating social capital can show existing disorder and anomy, or identify new emerging orders. Once wages are earned, they take on a particular social life, depending, amongst other dimensions, on the sex of the earner or nature and form of social capital at work within the networks of which the wage earner is an active member. Therefore, it is important to incorporate the structural position of men and women into an analysis of the impact of labour market changes and look at what happens to wages, once they are earned. Such an approach is informed by Appadurai's (1986) argument that the value of a commodity or of money itself is never just pure value, but value governed by a specific value regime. In other words: the movement of monetary wealth as, in principal, a free-floating commodity is restricted by gender specific (cultural) boundaries. Methodologically, this requires a strategy, which follows money, maps its trajectory in social life and uncovers the values attached to it.

At this stage, I do not want to completely abandon the concept of 'household income', and even less so the concept of household as such.[26]

---

26. There exists a significant bulk of literature that problematises the concept of 'household' from an anthropological perspective. To refer to it in detail here goes beyond the limits of this article. See for example: Guyer and Peters (1987); Moore

Yet to disentangle 'household income' in practice is very difficult. Rather than being the context for altruism and conjugal harmony, marriages and households in Lesotho and the wider Southern African region are widely known as sites of mistrust, fear, suspicion, competition or domestic violence. Frequently wives do not know how much their husbands earn. While it certainly is a normal practice that members of a given household put some of their earnings in a common pot and co-operate in order to cover expenses such as schooling or fertilizers, one has to be wary of treating the household as a homogeneous economic unit. There appear to be joint and individual spheres of consumption and responsibility in households, i.e. household members both 'pool' and 'hide' money simultaneously

Male income, on the one hand, is widely, and not only among men, associated with building the homestead, which includes agricultural investments as well as some form of livestock purchases. All of these activities are of a social and co-operative nature because no household controls all the means of agricultural production. Most of them need labour for activities such as ploughing, weeding, harvesting, herding livestock as well as cash and other inputs, which necessitate co-operation with other households. Once a man starts earning wages, the social claims that are laid on male income are numerous. These claims, which are partly constituted by culturally defined forms of relatedness, are frequently contested and resisted. Meeting and creating mutual obligations by means of dispersing wage income creates positions from where social capital can be mobilized. In that sense, miners' remittances and male income in general have strong connotations of 'common property' to the extent that many individuals can negotiate culturally defined access. This implies that it is inherently different from wages earned by women. As men's wages enter a social life in the community, they create mutual claims in their circulation. Their ratings according to the local social currency mobilise 'social capital', which becomes potentially accessible to the wage earner as well as individuals near to him. Men are frequently accused both in the literature on gender as well as amongst women in Ha Sofonia of spending money selfishly on items such as 'booze' and cigarettes. Yet at the same time, senior women are frequently the ones to benefit from male forms of consumption, whereby money is redistributed to women.

Female income, on the other hand, is locally, and by many men dismissively, considered as 'petty money'. While I listened to women complaining

---

(1988); Folbre (1994); Kabeer (1994); O'Laughlin (1995); Ferguson (1999); Mackintosh (2000); Ngwane (2003).

about their husbands ridiculing their meagre incomes with remarks such as, "keep your change" or "she's just helping out", I also heard women giving accounts of their fathers or husbands taking their money by force. Owing to an ideal of men's money being saved and stored in durable values, such as housing,[27] female earnings are earmarked and used for daily needs, such as food and fuel. Women have a different position (daughter, daughter-in-law, wife or mother) in household and community, which means that fewer people can legitimately claim women's earnings. In looking at the patterns of cash dispersal within the community, it is obvious that Sesotho custom prescribes that men assist a wider group of community members consisting of kin and neighbours, while women as outsiders[28] are supposed to primarily assist their own household, especially their children and in-laws. Their money does not enter the same avenues of diffusion as men's money. Hence, seen from a male perspective, female money is rated lower according to the local social currency. It generates fewer social claims and mutual obligations and is considered as private rather than common property. While local values prescribe that the 'good husband' helps his wider kin and neighbours as well as the poor in the community, the 'good wife or daughter' is supposed to primarily help her own household, especially her children, husband and in-laws.

To illustrate this point further, I sketch below Aussi Skee's (Case 3) social situation and show that her wage may legitimately only be claimed by her parents, her child and her father's brother's daughters.

1. After having stayed with a young man for a while, she returned with the child to her natal home. Her parents have accepted her back but have certain rights to her labour and other contributions.

2. Her child. Basotho women are supposed to be, and take pride in being, caring mothers.

3. Her father's brother's daughters, with whom she has an intimate relationship, were the ones helping her into the factory. Job-seeking networks are important in creating claims and obligations.

---

27. Practice was frequently very different. First, only very little money was remitted in many cases. Second, pressing financial needs at home did not permit for the saving of any money. Both factors led to frequent arguments within conjugal relationships.

28. Due to it being a patri-local society, many married women originate from other, sometimes fairly distant, regions.

Figure 2: Claims on Aussi Skee's Wage

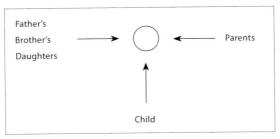

This is of course not meant as an underrating of the social significance of female income. In contrast to men's perceived 'selfish' consumption patterns, women are generally believed to act more 'altruistically' and in favour of their household and children's welfare (Whitehead and Kabeer 2001). Female support networks play a considerable role in the persistence, resilience and survival of a great number of households. Rather than male breadwinners doing it, they frequently cover the costs of caring and dying during the current AIDS epidemic. This is less due to the altruistic nature of women, but more due to the sexual division of labour, which gives Basotho women greater control over field and garden crops and how they are distributed within the domestic group. But the capacity of women to participate in female support networks of mutual obligation is often closely linked to their husband's wage earning ability, which is why the husband's lack of income can seriously affect his wife's social position and thus access to social capital. Wages earned by factory girls, most of whom are fairly young, rarely enter local networks of social cohesion, as do the wages earned by their fathers and brothers. Their contributions to the household economy may seem modestly, yet at certain times of the year, their earnings can make the difference between complete destitution and a minimum supply of daily needs.

However, the spheres of male and female money are not exclusive and female money can cross culturally defined boundaries, enter spheres of male money and mobilize social capital linked to male networks. Intrahousehold cooperation, as in the case of the Skee family, is one example of this. Home brewing and giving credit can be other examples where female money enters a wider social realm within the community. Yet in many households where a daughter works in the Chinese factories, this is rarely the case, as the modest earnings are used for urgent daily needs such as food from the shop.[29] This money is not brought into circulation in local circuits of social and cultural significance. It constitutes instead a kind of 'dead money'. Compared to the social life of men's wages, the larger part of female money is not invested in social networks, it does not create mutual obligations of reciprocity and it does not put existing social networks and values to work or maintain them.

The fact that some women are in a better position to transform their income into social capital than others, is intimately linked to their household and family position. Drawing on case material from the Tswana, Jean Comaroff (1985) argues that female production occurs in its own space and that female produce has to be ritually and politico-economically transformed in order to be incorporated. Yet here, men are by and large still the ones who control the means of transformation. A not dissimilar situation seems to prevail among the linguistically and culturally closely related Basotho. This may explain why many women are not interested in openly challenging male authority. Part of the explanation why women hold a weak 'bargaining position' (Sen 1990) despite their current access to wages is that they are still dependent on men and that they are the first ones to suffer when co-operation breaks down. Women cannot hold land, cattle or homesteads in their own right but only through a position as wife, mother, sister or daughter within a given household unit.[30] Even though the majority of women working in the Asian factories do not belong to the poorest economic strata, they still find themselves in a position where the bulk of their earnings is immediately consumed by pressing daily needs, such as food, transport and health expenses. Only where their earnings enter a productive nexus, can their income enter wider social networks of male connections.

---

29. The budget of one such household for a four month period looked approximately like this: income: 4 times 400 Rand plus small income from the sale of pumpkins and peaches. As the family could not afford to plough their field during the previous season, they were forced to purchase mealie meal for almost 700 Rand, oil, sugar and vegetables for 280 Rand, pay approximately 700 Rand for the minibus-taxi and use 195 Rand at the hospital in Maseru. Their diet was supplemented with vegetables from their garden. The informant claimed that the emerging deficit was an outstanding debt at a shop close to her workplace.

30. This is outlined in detail in the so-called 'Laws of Lerotholi'. All customary laws were written down in the 'Laws of Lerotholi' at the beginning of the 20th century. Today, many of these laws are contested as discriminatory.

Conclusion

The increasingly unequal access to social capital has resulted in accelerated processes of differentiation as compared to the situation during the 1970s, when most households had direct or indirect access to cash through men working in the South African mines. While the institutionalised diffusion of miners' remittances shaped a situation where men's income had a social nature and common property qualities, factory money earned by young women can only gain the same qualities when it enters joint expenditure pools and/or can become channelled into the means of transformation from 'private' to 'common'. The implications are the marginalisation of a certain category of households within Lesotho's rural economies, which means that the nature of differentiation moves towards a more linear nature. Poor households are thus poor not only because of their temporal position on a 'developmental' or life cycle, but increasingly also because of their spatial and structural position within the community.[31]

I have shown how uneven access to Lesotho's 'new mines' is distributed within the community. One result of some households being able to put their income into circulation within the local village economy and others not is the further 'clustering' of social capital, a process by which groups of households and families form and reinforce networks and social situations of mutual support in general or job-seeking and agricultural strategies in particular. In a situation of unemployment and general scarcity, the social embeddedness of Basotho's livelihood strategies has resulted in social capital becoming even more critical for survival. It is difficult to overemphasise the critical importance of potential allies in putting together and timing the various implements and activities necessary to Basotho's livelihood portfolio. 'Being near' to a person with material and/or social resources is key today. The differentiated success of job-seeking among young women is a case in point here.

Regarding gender roles, age-related identities and household formation processes it is worthwhile to recall Bourdieu, who has argued that marriage is not the obedience of a set of normative rules but rather the outcome of an array of distinct strategies (Bourdieu 1976). While marriage used to be an outcome of key livelihood strategies among Basotho women, marriage to unemployed husbands is apparently seen as 'useless'. The newly emerging livelihood options among young women in contemporary Lesotho result

---

31. I deliberately avoid the notion of 'class', because it cannot possibly capture the dynamics and uncertainty inherent in contemporary livelihood trajectories in Lesotho.

in new forms of female life courses, changing patterns of accumulation and investment as well as new forms of households and social reproduction in general. While marriage used to be a key indicator of the leap from adolescence to adulthood, the decreasing importance of it and the dissociation between marriage and childbearing means that young women, just like young men, are in search of alternative adulthoods without marriage. Whether they succeed or not depends on their ability to navigate the shifting cultural meanings of adulthood in contemporary Southern Africa.

References

Afshar, H., 1985, *Women, Work and Ideology in the Third World*. London: Tavistock.

Appadurai, A. (ed.), 1986, *The Social Life of Things: Commodities in Cultural Perspective*. Cambridge: Cambridge University Press.

Baylies, C. and C. Wright, 1993, "Female Labour in the Textile and Clothing Industry of Lesotho", *African Affairs*, 92:577–591.

Bourdieu, P., 1976, "Marriage Strategies as Strategies of Social Reproduction", in R. Forster and O. Ranum (eds), *Family and Society*. Baltimore: Johns Hopkins.

—, 1986, "The Forms of Capital", in J. Richardsen (ed.), *Handbook of Theory and Research for the Sociology of Education*. Westport: Greenwood Press.

Bucholtz, M., 2002, "Youth and Cultural Practice", *Annual Review of Anthropology*, 31:525–52.

Cairoli, M.L., 1998, "Factory as Home and Family: Female Workers in the Moroccan Garment Industry", *Human Organisation*, Vol. 57, No. 2.

Comaroff, J., 1985, *Body of Power – Spirit of Resistance: The Culture and History of a South African People*. Chicago: University of Chicago Press.

Dannecker, P., 2002, *Between Conformity and Resistance: Women Garment Workers in Bangladesh*. Dhaka, Bangladesh.

Dyer, K., 2001, *Gender Relations in the Home and the Workplace: A case study of the gender implications of Lesotho's current economic development strategy for the clothing industry*. The Institute of Southern African Studies, National University of Lesotho at Roma, Lesotho.

Ferguson, J., 1990, *The Anti-Politics Machine: Development, Depoliticization and Bureaucratic Power in Lesotho*. Minneapolis: University of Minnesota Press.

—, 1999, *Expectations of Modernity: Myths and meaning of urban life on the Zambian Copperbelt*. Berkeley: University of California Press.

Fernandez-Kelly, M.P., 1983, "Mexican Border Industrialisation, Female Labour Force Participation and Migration", in J. Nash and M.P. Fernandez-Kelly (eds), *Women, Men and the International Division of Labour*. Albany: State univ. of New York Press.

Fine, B., 2001, *Social Capital versus Social Theory*. London: Routledge.

Folbre, N,. 1994, *Who Pays for the Kids? Gender and the Structures of Constraint*. London, New York: Routledge.

Gay, J.S., 1980, *Basotho Women's Options: A study of marital careers in rural Lesotho*, PhD thesis, University of Cambridge.

Gibbon, P., Unpublished manuscript, "Explaining Responses to AGOA in the African Clothing Sector", Centre for Development Research, Copenhagen.

Gilbert, L. and L. Walker, 2002, "Treading the path of least resistance. HIV/AIDS and social inequalities – a South African case study", *Social Science and Medicine*, 54:1093–1110.

Goebel, A. and M. Epprecht, 1995, "Women and Employment in Sub-Saharan Africa: Testing the World Bank and WID Models with a Lesotho Case Study", *African Studies Review*, Vol. 38, No. 1, April 1995.

Guyer, J. and P. Peters, 1987, "Introduction", *Development and Change, Conceptualising the Household: Issues of Theory and Policy in Africa*, Vol. 18, No. 2.

Hart, G., 2002, *Disabling Globalisation*. Berkeley: University of California Press.

Humphrey, J., 1985, "Gender, Pay and Skill: Manual workers in Brazilian industry", in H. Afshar (ed.), *Women, Work and Ideology in the Third World*. London: Tavistock.

Joekes, S., 1985, "Working for Lipstick? Male and female labour in the clothing industry in Morocco", in H. Afshar (ed.), *Women, Work and Ideology in the Third World*. London: Tavistock.

Kabeer, N., 1994, *Reversed Realities: Gender Hierarchies in Development Thought*. London: Verso.

—, 1997, "Women, Wages and Intra-Household Power Relations in Urban Bangladesh", *Development and Change*, Vol. 28, No. 2.

Lamphere, L., 1974, "Strategies, Cooperation, and Conflict among Women in Domestic Groups", in M. Rosaldo and L. Lamphere (eds), *Women, Culture and Society*, Stanford: Stanford University Press.

Langston, A., 1993, "The Ties That Bind: Marriage and Dependency in Basotho Women's Lives", Unpublished BA dissertation, Harvard University, Cambridge, Massachusetts.

Lee, E.S., 1966, "A Theory of Migration", *Demography*, 3(1):47–57.

Mackintosh, M., 2000, "The Contingent Household: Gender Relations and the Economics of Unpaid Labour", in S. Himmelweit (ed.), *Inside the Household: From Labour to Care*. Basingstoke: Macmillan, New York: St Martin.

McKay, D., 2003, "Reading Remittance Landscapes: female migration and agricultural transition in the Philippines", in Proceedings of the International Conference 'Local Land Use Strategies in a Globalising World: Shaping Sustainable Social and Natural Environments', Copenhagen, Denmark.

Mehta, L., M. Leach, P. Newell, I. Scoones, K. Sivaramakrishnan and S.A. Way, 1999, *Exploring Understandings of Institutions and Uncertainty: New Directions in Natural Resource Management.* Discussion Paper 372, Institute of Development Studies, University of Sussex.

Moore, H., 1988, *Feminism and Anthropology*, Minneapolis: University of Minnesota Press.

Murray, C., 1981, *Families Divided: The Impact of Migrant Labour in Lesotho*, African Studies Series. Cambridge: Cambridge University Press.

—, 2001, "The use of livelihood frameworks to investigate poverty", Draft Paper, Manchester.

Ngwane, Z., 2003, "'Christmas Time' and the Struggles for the Household in the Countryside: Rethinking the Cultural Geography of Migrant Labour in South Africa", *Journal of Southern African Studies*, vol. 29, no. 3.

Obbo, C., 1980, *African Women: Their struggle for economic independence.* London: Zed Press.

O'Laughlin, B., 1995, "Myth of the African Family in the World of Development", in D.F. Bryceson (ed.), *Women Wielding the Hoe.* Oxford: Berg.

Peters, P., 1983, "Gender, Developmental Cycles and Historical Process: A Critique of Recent Research on Women in Botswana", *Journal of Southern African Studies*, vol. 10, no. 1.

Robertson, A.F., 1987, "Lesotho: Seahlolo and lihalefote", in A.F. Robertson, *The Dynamics of Productive Relationships: African share contracts in comparative perspective.* Cambridge: Cambridge University Press.

—, 1991, *Beyond the Family: The Social Organisation of Human Reproduction*, Cambridge: Polity.

Salaff, J., 1981, *Working Daughters of Hong Kong: Filial piety or power in the family?* New York: Cambridge University Press.

Salm, A., W. Grant, T. Green, J. Haycock and J. Raimondo, 2002, *Lesotho Garment Industry Subsector Study for the Government of Lesotho.* Maseru.

Scoones, I., 1998, *Sustainable Rural Livelihoods: A framework for analysis,* IDS Working Paper 72. Brighton: Institute of Development Studies.

Sechaba Consultants 2000, *Poverty and Livelihoods in Lesotho 1999: More than a mapping exercise,* Lesotho.

Sen, A.K., 1990, "Gender and Cooperative Conflicts", in I. Tinker (ed.), *Persistent Inequalities: Women and World Development.* New York: Oxford University Press.

Standing, H.,1985, "Resources, Wages and Power: The impact of women's employment on the urban Bengali household", in H. Afshar (ed.), *Women, Work and Ideology in the Third World.* London: Tavistock.

Sweetman, G., 1995, *The Miners Return: Changing gender relations in Lesotho's ex-migrants' families.* Norwich: University of East Anglia, GAID, 9.

United Nations Integrated Regional Information Networks, June 16, 2003.

Warren, K. and S. Borque, 1991, "Women, Technology, and International Development Ideologies: Analyzing Feminist Voices", in M. di Leonardo (ed.), *Gender at the Crossroads of Knowledge: Feminist Anthropology in the Post-Modern Era*. Berkeley: University of California Press.

Whitehead, A., 1981, "'I'm hungry mum': The Politics of Domestic Budgeting", in R. McCullagh, C. Wolkowitz and K. Young (eds), *Of Marriage and the Market*. London: Routledge & Paul Kegan.

Whitehead, A. and N. Kabeer, 2001, *Living with uncertainty: Gender, livelihoods and pro-poor growth in rural sub-Saharan Africa*, IDS Working Paper 134, Institute of Development Studies, Sussex.

CHAPTER 6

Relocation of Children
Fosterage and child death in Biombo, Guinea-Bissau

Jónína Einarsdóttir

The Convention on the Rights of the Child (CRC) states that each child has the right to life and to grow up with its parents. In this chapter I examine relocation of children from their parents in a rural village in Biombo region, Guinea-Bissau. Three different forms of displacement are identified. First, the child is relocated to others, most likely the maternal grandmother, who will foster the child. Second, a girl whose maternal family has suffered high child mortality is relocated to a religious specialist for ritual services in order to counteract child death. Third, child death is interpreted as relocation to the other world. Child death implies definitive disruptive family relations, despite death in itself being conceived of as a temporary displacement of a human soul from this world to the other world. Finally, I discuss the alleged ethnocentric spirit of the CRC and the sad fact that after its ratification the former decline in child deaths levelled out and even reversed in those parts of the world with the highest rates of child mortality.

Introduction

The Convention on the Rights of the Child (CRC), adopted by the General Assembly of the United Nations on November 20, 1989, confirms that "every child has the inherent right to life" (Article 6). Further, the Convention states that a child has the right to grow up with its parents unless separation of the child from his/her parents is deemed necessary for the best interests of the child by competent authorities (Articles 7 and 9).

Separation or relocation of children from their parents occurs for various reasons. Millions of children are affected by 'trafficking', a term which implies exploitation of a displaced individual (Boonpala and Kane, 2002: 4). Irrespective of whether or not the child itself or some family member is involved in the 'trafficking' the most common causes of these "demand-driven phenomena ... matched by an abundant supply of children, most from poor families" are likely to be hope for better life, improved access to education and shelter from or involvement in war (Boonpala & Kane, 2002:23). Adoption or fosterage is another form of relocation of a child from his or her parents, and as with trafficking most fostered or adopted children come from poor families.

Various forms of transferral of parental responsibilities and rights are practised world-wide.[1] Scholars concerned with the history of childhood in the Western world have at times treated fosterage as identical to infanticide (Badinter 1980; de Mause 1974; Shorter 1975; Stone 1977). The historical literature tends to see parent-child relations as having improved through time, and, accordingly, Shorter (1975:168) claims that "good mothering is an invention of modernization". Good mothering came to imply that the biological mother, who was both white and married, almost exclusively took care of her child during the so-called formative years (Glenn 1994). According to Solinger (1994), in the period 1945–1965, unwed, white mothers were assumed to lack the potential for good mothering and were urged to give up their children for adoption by white couples unable to conceive children. This was made possible by treating illegitimacy as a temporary and treatable mental disorder rather than a sign of inborn decadence as had been the custom earlier. On the other hand, the black unwed mothers were classified as "ex-Africans and ex-slaves, irresponsible and immoral, but baby-loving" (1994:298). Their culture was treated as inherited and unal-

---

1. See Goody (1977) for a cross-cultural perspective of adoption and fostering.

terable.[2] Further, blacks were assumed to be unwilling to adopt children, thus black mothers should take care of their own illegitimate offspring.

Fosterage is widely described in ethnographic and demographic studies from West Africa. The mutual economic and social advantages for all involved are stressed as well as maintenance of kinship relations and their role in sustaining high fertility among the poor (Bledsoe 1993; Bledsoe and Isiugo-Abanihe 1989; Goody 1984). Fosterage is reported to give poor children the opportunity for social and economic mobility often denied to those who come from rural areas (Eloundou-Enyegue and Stokes, 2002). At the same time, the harsh treatment of fostered children and their disadvantage in relation to the foster parents' own children is documented (Bledsoe 1995; Bledsoe et al. 1988; Castle 1995; Oni 1995). Yet, fosterage is not solely documented as motivated by economic concerns. Until recently the majority of Baatombu children in Northern Benin used to grow up with foster-parents due to the shame attributed to biological parenthood (Alber 2003). The foster practices imply that all parental duties and rights for children are transferred to foster-parents who are most likely the grandparents, in particular the grandmother, of the child. Fosterage among the Baatombu, primarily sending children from towns to live in the rural areas, is gradually declining with negative affects for the social situation of the older generation and changed intergenerational relations. Verhoef (2005) shows how children's residence in an urban community in north-western Cameroon is highly influenced by the relationships of adults and that there is a diversity of fostering arrangements.

In this chapter I will discuss the relocation of children from their mothers in a rural village in Biombo region in Guinea-Bissau. The ethnography presented is based on fieldwork conducted in the region during the period 1993–1998 (Einarsdóttir 2004:20–25).[3] Guinean Creole, which was the language used for communication during fieldwork, has its origin in the early contacts of the Portuguese and the West African inhabitants. Creole is widely spoken among the Papel population who are approximately three-quarters of Biombo's roughly 60,000 inhabitants. In fact, a minority of Papel do not speak their vernacular language. Child mortality is high in the region and about one third of all children born alive are likely to die before they reach the age of five years (Aaby et al. 1997).

---

2. See McDaniel and Morgan (1996) for similar racist arguments.

3. Fieldwork was made possible through the support of DanChurchAid (DCA), Copenhagen.

The Papel divide themselves into seven matrilineal lineages, thus children belong to the lineage of their mother. Residence is ideally patrilocal and polygamy is common. Most of the Papel who reside in Biombo practise religion according to what they call the "original law" or in Creole *lei di primudu*. They believe in reincarnation, which implies that human souls circulate through deaths and births between "this world" (*es mundu*) and "the other world" (*utru mundu*). The Creole word *mufunesa*, which literally means misfortune, is central. It carries with it a notion of a mishap or a tragedy that is caused by an intentional agent, either a human being, dead or alive, or a supernatural force. *Mufunesa* cannot be alleviated without an identification of the agent through divination and a ritual action has to be carried out to eliminate it. There are various types of religious specialists who specialize in such work. One type is called *balobeirus*, women and men, who are capable of communicating with the one and only God of the Papel through the mediation of an ancestral soul who resided in a kapok tree, a *baloba*. Each *baloba* belongs to the lineage of the ancestral soul that has settled in it, as does its respective *balobeiru* or "owner" (*donu*). Papel women are highly involved in religious life and their involvement, both as providers and users of ritual services, is centralised around questions related to fertility, children's wellbeing and their survival.

Fosterage

Mpona, who states she is 16 years old, lives in a rural village with about 700 inhabitants. Villagers make their living mainly from agriculture, fishing and migrant labour. Women also take part in commerce in the capital, Bissau. The school is situated in a nearby village five kilometres away and provides grades 1–4. Like most of the girls in the village, Mpona never attended school. Only three girls, aged 13–15 years old, attend school compared with thirty-nine boys or young men. Only one of the mothers in Mpona's village attended school before marriage. She is in-married and comes from the regional centre of Biombo.

Mpona has been married for four years back and she has two co-wives. She lives in what she refers to as "her husband's home". Her first co-wife has already left their shared husband. Mpona's husband, who is 33 years old, has attended school for four years and he has already inherited land, goods and compound from his mother's brother. He also inherited his senior wife, who is Mpona's second co-wife. Despite her young age, Mpona has in one way or another responsibility for five children. She takes care of her first co-wife's two children, four and seven years old, after their mother's departure. Mpona is also responsible for a seven-year-old boy who belongs to her husband's family. In addition, a five-year-old motherless child, a relative of Mpona's second co-wife, is also under her supervision. Mpona is herself already a mother of two. When I met her she was breastfeeding her second-born child, only a few weeks old. Mpona told me she had "given" her first-born child, a three year-old son, to her mother who had taken her grandson with her to the interior of the country.[4] She stressed that "they will not stay there forever". Mpona emphasised that "this is our custom." Her mother had the right to have one of her daughter's children and if she refused to give her mother a child something bad might happen.

In a survey I conducted in Mpona's village, I asked eighty-three mothers or caregivers of children younger than five years of age if they took care of all of their children. I also asked for the ages of children staying elsewhere, with whom they stayed and the reason for their not living with their own mothers. I found that about one third of the mothers who had at least one child younger than five years had one or more of her children staying with others. About three-fifths of these children stayed with their maternal grandmother, as did Mpona's first-born. Close relatives, mostly maternal or paternal aunts, took care of about one fifth of them, and another one fifth of the children stayed with their father and *madrassas*, that is their mother's co-wives. The children who were younger than five years usually stayed with their maternal grandmother or on rare occasions with a mother's co-wife, while all the children who stayed with aunts and other close relatives were nine years or older. The mothers I interviewed were more likely to have their own children staying with others than to take care of others' children.

Mothers most commonly gave two reasons for relocation of their children. First, in nearly half of the cases of fosterage mothers said they needed someone to feed and/or take care of the child. Second, for roughly two-fifths of children fostered mothers explained they had given a child to their own mother because it was the custom to do so. Maternal grandmothers claim they have the right to take one of their grandchildren, and should a woman refuse to give her own mother a child, something bad might happen to her family, for example death or illness, as a punishment for breaching a kinship obligation. Further, elderly women may also take care of grandchildren to help their daughters to terminate breastfeeding or be-

---

4. See Layne (1999) for reference to an adopted or fostered child as a 'gift'.

cause of their work or if the daughters find themselves in a difficult situation. The maternal grandmother may live in the same village as the mother or in a nearby village but sometimes they live far away. Children were said to weep for their mothers for the first few days away, thereafter they become accustomed to new people. Several times mothers told me that the grandmother and the child had become too fond of each other to take the child back later.

The third most common reason for children not living with their mothers is divorce. In such cases the child is most likely to stay with the father under the responsibility of the mother's co-wife. In fact, formally a husband who has paid the bride price has the right over all the children of his wife. Nonetheless, a mother is unwilling to leave her children with him if she is on bad terms with her co-wife. Most men are neither willing to have their children brought up with another man, nor are they willing to live with children their new wife had with a former husband. Therefore, a woman who moves to live with a new man will preferably not bring her children from a previous relationship to that man. She may leave the children with her own mother or somebody else, most likely an aunt (her own sister or a sister of her husband) or a paternal uncle of the children. No mother said she had given a child to one of her brothers, but at the same time he is likely to live in the same compound as her mother, the child's grandmother. A Papel man will preferably not foster his sister's son likely to become his heir.

In addition to the reasons for children staying away from their mothers mentioned above, i.e. mothers' need for help, the maternal grandmother's right to claim a child from her daughter and divorce, two mothers in the survey mentioned education as a rationale for fosterage. One other mother had given a child to a barren female relative.[5] A mother of many children is in particular expected to give her barren sister a child of her own.

Mothers expressed various feelings about giving their children to others. They said they would continue to keep contact with their child and the time perspective was most frequently seen as temporary or not defined. As did Mpona, they often stressed that the child would only stay away for a short period of time. Some mothers mumbled "there is nothing to do about

---

5. At times, fostering is an alternative for infertile women when they may have the right to claim a child from their kin (Bledsoe and Isiugo-Abanihe 1989; Goody 1982:44; Riesman 1992:96). Infertile Borana women (East Africa) or women whose children left home or have died can ask a relative for a child to secure their own subsistence and respect (Dahl 1990). It is difficult to reject such a request since people fear the evil eye of a woman without a child.

it," others argued that the arrangement would allow them to enter into a new relationship or start some income-generating activity, in other words, to "look for life" (*buska bida*) or "make a living" (*fasi bida*). Many claimed the child would be better off staying with others. Mothers were aware that fostered children might be treated badly and often obliged to work hard. Life is tough and mothers said the children would at least learn to work properly and be better prepared for real life than children brought up only by their own parents. Grandmothers are also considered to be bad educators, nonetheless, they are the caregivers most commonly resorted to and they are considered to be bad educators.

A grandmother's love for her grandchild is taken for granted and she is assumed to do her best to ritually protect her grandchild and to feed him or her the best she can. The problem is that she loves her grandchildren too much and spoils them, people agree. Mothers are at times concerned about other problems than those related to a proper upbringing of their children. Grandmothers are sometimes elderly, their health may be frail and they lack awareness of changed times, in particular as regards health care services. Sometimes they were said to be already "more in the other world." If the mothers live far away, for instance in the capital Bissau or another distant village, they are unable to intervene in the case of sudden illness of the child. This may leave the child in a precarious situation. The other women in the compound are not likely to take the child to the health centre or advise his/her grandmother to do so; that would make them responsible if the child dies. It is safer not to interfere in the affairs of other people, particularly when relations are constrained. Accusations of sorcery are common and nobody wants to become involved when death is a possible outcome.

If a misfortune (*mufunesa*) befalls their lineage mothers sometimes fear that it might cause their child's death when staying with maternal grandmothers. In such cases the *baloba*, a kapok tree where an ancestral soul has settled, might see the child and take it to punish some maternal lineage member for ritual failure. On the other hand, it may be safer for the child to stay with the maternal grandmother or elsewhere than close to a jealous co-wife, who might want to kill the child with sorcery. In extreme cases, with repeated deaths of children without the cause of death being found, a mother may decide to give her child to a person living far away from matrilineal hazards and envious co-wives. Such a person could even be someone belonging to another ethnic group.

The fosterage practices explained above are characterised by foster-parents' prior relations with the child's biological parents and an initial time-frame that is likely to be either short-term or uncertain. The child will keep contact with the biological parents during the fostering period if possible. Adoption, that is permanent legal transfer of parental rights and responsibilities from biological parents to adoptive parents, is rare. The only accounts of adoption I was informed of involve the Catholic mission in a nearby village. One such story was about a girl who was brought to the mission hospital for health care as she was suffering from a severe infection. The girl was presented as a fostered child. The nun who treated her gradually understood that the girl had been left to stay day and night under a kapok tree. In addition she was maltreated and obliged to work hard. In response, the nun decided to take action and give the girl to a Christian family for adoption. Despite the efforts of the girl's biological parents, they were not allowed to get her back or even to see their daughter. The girl in question was a so-called *katandeira*, a girl who had been "given" by her matrilineage to a religious specialist (*balobeiru*) to serve at ceremonies.

To give a girl for child survival

Celeste, who is in her forties, has given birth to six children and happens to be the mother in my survey that has most children staying with others. Three of her children, who are four, seven and nine years old, stay with their maternal grandmother and two stay with her co-wife and father. One child died at one year of age after a persistent period of diarrhoea three years ago. Celeste told me that since she was a *katandeira*: "It is difficult to combine child care with my duties." In particular this applied during the raining season, when some important ceremonies were to be performed. Celeste's mother had lost many children, which prompted senior members of her maternal lineage to make a visit a to powerful *baloba* belonging to another lineage and ask for help. They asked the ancestral spirit to ensure that their lineage's women would conceive many healthy children who all would survive. In turn, they promised to send a girl from their lineage to serve the *baloba*, that is, to become a *katandeira*.

A *katandeira* has a lifelong obligation to "fetch water" or *kata iagu* (hence the name *katandeira*) and cook rice to offer at the *baloba*. The religious specialist who collaborates with or "owns" the ancestral spirit residing in the *baloba* has the right to wed the girl or arrange her marriage. If a mother does not agree to send a daughter to serve a *baloba* that has fulfilled a request to prevent child death she risks losing still more children as a punishment for her refusal. Many women think it is a good thing for a girl to become a *katandeira*. It gives a respected social position and can be favourable in economic terms, in particular if they come from a poor family. They may have access to better food and sometimes they travel a lot. They also become respected as they perform important religious services, though that respect may be associated with fear. I was told about an elderly female *balobeiru* without children of her own who treated a young *katandeira* serving her *baloba* as if she was her own daughter. However, not all the girls are as lucky. Some *balobeirus* are men who are drunkards. They may marry all the *katandeiras* themselves while others give them to their sons or other men.

Mothers are said to be increasingly unwilling to give their daughters as *katandeiras*, I was told. Impors, who has lost all her children, explained her misfortune with the fact that she had refused to give a girl as a *katandeira*. Her children had died at different ages without signs of disease. In contrast, Zinha told me she had given her second-born daughter, who was the only surviving child after five births, as a *katandeira* to serve a *baloba* where her family had asked for help. Zinha's first-born had died after four days without a disease, the third child got convulsions three days after birth and died, the fourth died from measles at six years of age, and finally the fifth child died four days after birth without a sign of disease. After her second-born and only surviving child began to serve the *baloba* she gave birth to five more children who all survived and thus escaped relocation to the other world.

Child death

According to the Papel religion God decides who is to enter the other world. Those who die old, die when the time is ripe and God calls them. They are said to die from God's diseases and are welcome to settle in the other world. Those who die untimely deaths are not welcome because God has not asked them to come. They are victims of misfortune. Such is child death, which is never attributed to God's diseases. Mothers tend to explain the death of a child by sorcery or ritual failure. However, before death is a fact a warning is normally given through certain symptoms of disease that allow mothers and others to act. On the other hand, when older children die without symptoms of disease mothers attribute the cause of death to an extraordinarily serious ritual failure. Among other reasons, refusing to give a daughter as a *katandeira* classifies as such an oversight.

Child death is interpreted as a sign of *mufunesa* whose origin must be identified and acted upon to prevent additional deaths. The question is always: Why did that particular child die? "A child is born to live, not to die," mothers say. While a child's death is never a good death, the afterlife can, at best, be accepted through the knowledge that some family member will take care of the child in the world of the dead. Yet, a child who dies will only be allowed to stay there for a while before returning. There is however no agreement whether a dead child will be reborn in this world with the same mother, or even within the same lineage.

It is recognized that certain newborns will quickly return to the other world after birth, through their own desire, or because somebody in the other world has sent them over to bring things back from this world. Children who die during the first days of life without a disease are so-called "come and go" (*bim-i-bai*) infants. While infants in general are described as innocent, not yet capable of doing much harm, such infants are described as deceitful. Preventive action can be taken to stop these infants from continuing with such tricks. After death a suspected *bim-i-bai* infant can be buried naked, with the aim of not satisfying its intention to return with something valuable to the other world. Only elderly women are allowed to be present at such a funeral to prevent the child from entering the womb of some fertile woman. The body is sometimes even burnt to extinguish that child forever.[6] A mother may also mark the ear or cut a piece from the ear of her live newborn. The child is said to be more likely to stay with the mother rather than risk embarrassment for such an ugly ear when "returning back from where it came." A mother may also cut a sign into the ear of her dead infant in the hope of recognizing it when it comes back to this world. I have, however, never heard about the success of such an effort.

Humans weep for the dead in both this and the other world. "When somebody dies in this world we cry and those in the other world laugh. When a child is born in this world we laugh but those in the other world cry. Such is life," says Imburquenha, whose children have all been relocated to the other world. Mothers whose children die, and in particular those mothers, who have lost all their children, have an indisputable reason to grieve. A mother grieves because she has lost a child she loves. That love is based on affection related to knowing, becoming accustomed to, the child, but may also be based on a loss of something that never became. A mother may also be worried about not having children to take care of her in her old

---

6. See Allotey and Reidpath (2001), Argenti (2001), Gottlieb (1998, b2000, 2004), Gupta (2002) and Leis (1982) for similar descriptions.

age, in practical, economic and emotional terms. Furthermore, if the cause of a child's death is unknown the mother may be worried about her future births or the life of those other children she may have. The cause must be identified and acted upon so as not to risk their lives.

Preventive measures against grief are taken. For instance, when a mother loses her child, in particular when it is her first child, she is supposed to stay in her parental home for a couple of weeks "to forget her child" and "calm down." Indeed, it is recognized that the first child dies easily, which means that many mothers experience child loss at a young age. Isabel, barely twenty years old, is one of them. Her first-born daughter died at two years of age. The daughter was taken away from her through what Isabel refers to as a "satanic act." Her death was only one of many tragic events that had happened to the family. Therefore, Isabel, her younger co-wife and her husband all decided to escape their destiny within the Papel custom through conversion to Protestantism. Those who convert to a Protestant religion have to dissociate themselves quite extensively from their former religion. They are not supposed to participate in any kind of ceremony that does not belong to the Protestant religious practices, for instance funerals, and they are not allowed to drink alcohol. In return, they are told they are immune to sorcery and ritual punishments. According to Isabel, her husband, despite being Protestant, was still allowed to keep the wives he had when he converted, but he was not allowed to arrange for additional wives.

Isabel reacted to the loss of her daughter with religious conversion. Since the conversion, she has given birth to her second child, a son, and this time she has faith in the Protestant Spirit. Isabel hopes she will be allowed to keep her son with her in this world. Some other women, who after the death of their children considered conversion to Protestantism, told me they had decided to wait. They wanted first to give their mother a honourable burial and contribute to her entry to the other world.

Children's rights and survival

The CRC states that the child has the right to be taken care of by his/ her parents. In literature on fosterage in Western societies, lack of parental dedication and in particular maternal neglect is frequently highlighted.[7]

---

7. Both African American and Euro-American women alike, who in the 1990s fostered children in temporary need were continuously reminded of the view within their society of foster mothers as "non-mothers" and foster children as "failed" children (Wozniak 1999:92). Nonetheless, they described fostering as both a "gift"

In contrast, in Africa the economic and social benefits of fosterage for all involved are stressed (Bledsoe 1993; Bledsoe and Isiugo-Abanihe 1989; Goody 1984). The sustenance of intergenerational and kinship relations is highlighted, in line with studies from West Africa and beyond, where it is a frequent custom that grandparents raise their grandchildren, in particular the grandmothers (Alber 2004; Bledsoe and Isiugo-Abanihe 1989; Notermans 2004). As evidenced above Papel mothers emphasize the positive aspects of giving or lending a child for proper upbringing, better social and economic conditions for the child, as well as their own possibility to engage in work or enter a new relationship. The importance of kinship relations is evident. Research from Guinea-Bissau on children who had lost their mothers also demonstrates the importance of extended family relations for child care and children's well-being. Motherless children have been shown not to differ from other children as regards feeding, school enrolment, quality of housing, and possession of clothing (Masmas et al. 2004a). However, they experience more frequent movement between relatives than other children and tend to live in smaller families, often with a grandmother (Masmas et al. 2004b). On the other hand, motherless children under two years of age have an increased level of mortality due to premature weaning.

The custom to give a girl as a *katandeira* aims to counteract child death. Some Papel mothers in Biombo underline the positive aspects of following this custom, not only for the sake of the urgency of impeding the high child mortality but also for the benefit of the girl herself. At the same time they are highly aware of the possibility of abusive treatment of the girls. Thus, some mothers refuse to give their girls, despite the inherent risk of dire consequences. In Ghana, Benin and Togo there is a similar practice to give girls referred to as *trokosis* to serve religious shrines to counteract the sins of family members and thereby save the family from misfortune, diseases and repeated deaths. *Trokosi* means "wife of the gods" in the language of the Ewe, who reside in the Volta region of Ghana (Owusu-Ansah 2003). The children the priests beget with the girls become the property of the shrine and they are supposed to have particular power to compensate for human wrong-doings. In contrast to local opinions, children's rights advocates take this custom to be a form of ritual slavery and combat it (Hawksley 2001; Owusu-Ansah 2003; Rinaudo 2003).

---

and a "burden", and they emphasize having "experienced themselves as mothers in relation to their foster children and developed kinship bonds based on affective claims of belonging" (Wozniak 1999:89).

In similar fashion, in Senegal children's rights groups have become engaged in programmes targeting the *talibés*, young boys who spend hours each day begging for money and food while they live under the guidance of a religious specialist called a *marabout* to learn the Koran. Donna L. Perry (2004) contrasts the intentions of Wolof parents of *talibés* to give their son an opportunity to become "a virtuous adult able to withstand the difficult life that awaited him" with the discourses of abuse of the children's rights advocates. Perry highlights the difference in the presentation of culture given by groups that advocate indigenous rights and those engaged in women's and children's rights. According to the former, culture becomes "a marker of indigenous identity" and indigenous peoples "emblems of a pristine, ecologically sustainable lifeway". The latter group focuses on abuse, for instance trafficking of women and children, violence, circumcision, slavery, rape and prostitution, something that easily "develops into disdain for the cultures under scrutiny".[8]

The CRC has been criticized for ethnocentrism and warnings given that the public's attraction to scandals and exaggerations of abuse have drawn attention from political questions and the role of inequality and poverty in the adverse situations of many children (Ennew 2002; Scheper-Hughes and Sargent 1998; Stephens 1995). According to UNICEF, the decade for child survival in the 1980s was followed by the decade for children's rights (Bellamy 1996). In the wake of the adoption of CRC children's rights have been given increased attention and priority by international agencies and non-governmental organizations (Horton 2004). At the same time, reduction of child mortality has not been given the same consideration as compared to the 1980s. This shift in priority may have had a negative effect on child mortality rates. UNICEF confirms that reduction of child deaths has slowed down since 1990 with the highest child-mortality rates found in Africa (Bellamy 2004). Thus, the fourth Millennium Development Goal to reduce the under-five mortality rate by two-thirds by 2015 as compared with 1990 is unlikely to be met.

---

8. See Basu (2003) for discussion about the success of Western human rights groups in building up public opinion against violations of women in Islamic societies and sexual abuse.

Conclusion

In this chapter I have discussed relocation of children from their mothers in a rural village in Biombo region, Guinea-Bissau, and identified three different forms of displacement. First, the child is relocated to others, most likely the maternal grandmother, who will foster the child. Second, the child is relocated as a *katandeira* to improve the likelihood of child survival. According to local understanding, these forms of displacement aim to promote intergenerational relations and the maintenance of the matrilineage, as well as to enhance the child's well being and chances of survival. Both practices are opposed to the spirit of the CRC. The third form of displacement, which implies that children are relocated to the other world through death, is also against the intentions of the CRC. Although death in itself is conceived of as a temporary displacement of a human soul from this world to the other world it is the most definitive form of relocation of a child. Child death contributes to disruption of family relations, and for mothers it implies broken promises and the loss of a beloved child.

Ironically, after the adoption of the CRC the former sharp reduction in child deaths levelled off and even reversed in those countries of the world with the highest child mortality rates. The international aid agencies and non-governmental organizations are too often far too trendy, which is reflected in shifting priorities and ever-changing slogans (Einarsdóttir and Gunnlaugsson 2005). There is no doubt that the Convention diverted support from programmes aimed at child survival to programmes fighting for children's rights. I am not willing to trade children's rights for child survival or vice versa. However, I tend to agree with the pointed comment of a recent editorial in The Lancet that states "a preoccupation with rights ignores the fact that children will have no opportunity for development at all unless they survive. ... The most fundamental right of all is the right to survive" (Horton 2004:2072). Biombo's mothers seem to agree. They are tired of weeping for the death of their children who were denied the right to live.

References

Aaby, P., J. Gomes, L. Høj, and A. Sandström, 1997, "Estudo de Saúde de Mulheres em Idade Fertil e os Seus Filhos. Dados de 1990–1995." Bissau: UNICEF/ Projecto de Saúde de Bandim, Bissau.

Alber, E., 2003, "Denying biological parenthood: Fosterage in Northern Benin", *Ethnos*, 68(4):487–506.

—, 2004, "Grandparents as foster-parents: transformations in foster relations between grandparents and grandchildren in northern Benin", *Africa*, 74(1):28–46.

Allotey, P., and D. Reidpath, 2001, "Establishing the cause of childhood mortality in Ghana: the 'spirit child'", *Social Science and Medicine*, 52(7):1107–1112.

Argenti, N., 2001, "Kesum-body and the places of the gods: the politics of children's masking and the second-world realities in Oku (Cameroon)", *Journal of the Royal Anthropological Institute*, 7:67–94.

Badinter, E., 1980, *Mother Love: Myth and Reality*. New York: Macmillan.

Basu, A., 2003, "Globalizing local women's movements", in A. Mirsepassi, A. Basu and F. Weaver (eds), *Localizing Knowledge in a Globalizing World: Recasting the Area Studies Debate*, pp. 82–100. New York: Syracuse University Press.

Bellamy, C., 1996, *The State of the World's Children 1996*, pp. 43–73. Oxford: The United Nations Children's Fund/Oxford University Press.

—, 2004, *The State of the World's Children 2005, Childhood under threat*. The United Nations Children's Fund.

Bledsoe, C., 1993, "The politics of polygyny in Mende education and child fosterage transactions", in B.D. Miller (ed.), *Sex and Gender Hierarchies*, pp. 170–192. Cambridge: Cambridge University Press.

—, 1995, "Marginal members: children of previous unions in Mende households in Sierra Leone", in S. Greenhalgh (ed.), *Situating Fertility. Anthropology and Demographic Inquiry*, pp. 130–153. Cambridge: Cambridge University Press.

Bledsoe, C., D.C. Ewbank and U.C. Isiugo-Abanih, 1988, "The effect of child fostering on feeding practices and access to health services in rural Sierra Leone", *Social Science and Medicine*, 27(6):627–636.

Bledsoe, C. and U. Isiugo-Abanihe, 1989, "Strategies of child-fosterage in Sierra Leone", in R.J. Lesthaeghe (ed.), *Reproduction and Social Organization in sub-Saharan Africa*, pp. 442–474. Berkeley/Los Angeles: University of California Press.

Boonpala, P. and J. Kane, 2002, *Unbearable to the human heart. Child trafficking and action to eliminate it.* Geneva: International Labour Organization (ILO).

Castle, S., 1995, "Child fostering and children's nutritional outcomes in rural Mali: The role of female status in directing child transfers", *Social Science and Medicine*, 40:679–693.

Dahl, G., 1990, "Mats and milk pots: The domain of Borana Women", in A. Jacobson-Widding and W. van Beek (eds), *The Creative Communion. African Folk Models of Fertility and the Regeneration of Life*, pp. 129–136. Uppsala/ Stockholm: Uppsala University/Almqvist & Wiksell International.

de Mause, L. (ed.), 1974, "The evolution of childhood", in L. de Mause (ed.), *The History of Childhood*, pp. 1–73. New York: Harper Torchbooks.

Einarsdóttir, J., 2004, *Tired of Weeping. Mother Love, Child Death, and Poverty in Guinea-Bissau*. Madison, Wisconsin: University of Wisconsin Press.

Einarsdóttir, J. and G. Gunnlaugsson, 2005, "International aid, partnership, and child survival", *The Lancet*, 365(26):1135–1136.

Eloundou-Enyegue, P. and C.S. Stokes, 2002, "Will economic crisis in Africa weaken rural-urban ties? Insights from child fosterage trends in Cameroon", *Rural Sociology*, 67(2):278–299.

Ennew, J., 2002, "Future generations and global standards: children's rights at the start of the millennium", in J. MacClancy (ed.), *Exotic No More. Anthropology on the Front Lines,* pp. 338–58. Chicago: University of Chicago Press.

Glenn, E.N., 1994, "Social construction of mothering: a thematic overview", in E.N. Glenn, G. Chang and L.R. Forcey (eds), *Mothering. Ideology, Experience, and Agency*, pp. 1–29. New York/London: Routledge.

Goody, E., 1984, "Parental strategies: calculation or sentiment? Fostering practices among West Africans", in H. Medick and D.W. Sabean (eds), *Interest and Emotion. Essays on the Study of Family and Kinship*, pp. 266–278. Cambridge: Cambridge University Press.

Goody, E.N., 1982, *Parenthood and Social Reproduction: Fostering and Occupational Roles in West Africa*. Cambridge: Cambridge University Press.

Goody, J., 1977, *Production and Reproduction: A Comparative Study of the Domestic Domain*. Cambridge: Cambridge University Press.

Gottlieb, A., 1998, "Do infants have religion? The spiritual lives of Beng babies (Côte d'Ivoire)", *American Anthropologist,* 100(1):122–135.

—, 2000, "Luring your child into this life: a Beng path for infant care", in J.S. DeLoache and A. Gottlieb (eds), *A World of Babies. Imagined Childcare Guides for Seven Societies*, pp. 55–89. Cambridge: Cambridge University Press.

—, 2004, *The Afterlife Is Where We Come from: The Culture of Infancy in West Africa*. Chicago: University of Chicago Press.

Gupta, A., 2002, "Reliving childhood? The temporality of childhood and narratives of reincarnation", *Ethnos*, 67(1):33–57.

Hawksley, H., 2001, *Ghana's trapped slaves*, BBC.

Horton, R., 2004, "UNICEF leadership 2005–2015: a call for strategic change", *The Lancet,* 364(9451):2071–2074.

Layne, L. (ed.), 1999, *Transformative Motherhood: On Giving and Getting in a Consumer Culture*, p. 222. New York: New York University Press.

Leis, N.B., 1982, "The not-so-supernatural power of Ijaw children", in S. Ottenberg (ed.), *African Religious Groups and Beliefs. Papers in Honor of William R. Bascom*, pp. 151–69. Berkeley/Meerut, India: Folklore Institute/Archana Publications.

Masmas, T.N., H. Jensen, D. da Silva, L. Hoj, and A. Sandström, 2004a, "The social situation of motherless children in rural and urban areas of Guinea-Bissau", *Social Science & Medicine*, 59(6):1231.

Masmas, T.N., H. Jensen, D. da Silva, L. Hoj, A. Sandström and P. Aaby, 2004b, "Survival among motherless children in rural and urban areas in Guinea-Bissau", *Acta Paediatrica*, 93(1):99–105.

McDaniel, A. and S.P. Morgan, 1996, "Racial differences in mother-child co-residence in the past", *Journal of Marriage and Family*, 58(4):1011–1018.

Mirsepassi, A., A. Basu and F. Weaver, 2003, *Localizing Knowledge in a Globalizing World: Recasting the Area Studies Debate*. New York: Syracuse University Press.

Notermans, C., 2004, "Sharing home, food, and bed: Paths of grandmotherhood in East Cameroon", *Africa*, 74(1):6–27.

Oni, J.B., 1995, "Fostered children's perception of their health care and illness treatment in Ekiti Yoruba households, Nigeria", *Health Transition Review*, 5:21–34.

Owusu-Ansah, A., 2003, "Trokosi in Ghana: Cultural relativism or slavery?", *The African Symposium*. An On-line African Educational Research Journal 3(4): African Educational Research Network (AERN).

Perry, D.L., 2004, "Muslim child disciples, global civil society, and children's rights in Senegal: The discourses of strategic structuralism", *Anthropological Quarterly*, 77(1):47–86.

Riesman, P., 1992, *First Find Yourself a Good Mother*. New Brunswick: Rutgers University Press.

Rinaudo, B., 2003, "Trokosi Slavery: injustice in the name of religion", in T. Lyons (ed.), *The Twenty-Sixth Annual Conference of the African Studies Association of Australasia: Africa on a Global Stage: Politics, History, Economics and Culture*. Flinders University, Adelaide Australia: African Studies Association of Australasia and the Pacific.

Scheper-Hughes, N. and C. Sargent, 1998, "Introduction", in N. Scheper-Hughes and C. Sargent (eds), *Small Wars: The Cultural Politics of Childhood*, pp. 1–33. Berkeley and Los Angeles: University of California Press.

Shorter, E., 1975, *The Making of the Modern Family*. New York: Basic Books.

Solinger, R., 1994, "Race and 'value': black and white illegitimate babies, 1945–1965", in E.N. Glenn, G. Chang and L.R. Forcey (eds), *Mothering. Ideology, Experience, and Agency*, pp. 287–310. New York/London: Routledge.

Stephens, S., 1995, "Introduction. Children and the politics of culture in 'late capitalism'", in S. Stephens (ed.), *Children and the Politics of Culture*, pp. 3–48. Princeton: Princeton University Press.

Stone, L., 1977, *The Family, Sexuality and Marriage in England 1500–1800*. London: Weidenfeld & Nicolson.

Verhoef, H., 2005, "'A child has many mothers': Views of child fostering in northwestern Cameroon", *Childhood*, 12(3):369.

Wozniak, D.F., 1999, "Gifts and burdens. The social and familial context of foster mothering", in L. Layne (ed.), *Transformative Motherhood: On Giving and Getting in a Consumer Culture*, pp. 89–131. New York: New York University Press.

INCLUSION / EXCLUSION

CHAPTER 7

Meaningful Rebels?
Young adult perceptions on the Lord's Resistance Movement/Army in Uganda

Sverker Finnström

Low-intensity armed conflict has shaken northern Uganda since 1986. The Ugandan army is fighting the Lord's Resistance Movement/Army (LRM/A) rebels. Especially affected is Acholiland (Gulu, Kitgum and Pader districts). This chapter shows that rebels and non-combatant young adults alike experience a diffuse yet very real discontent and disenchantment because of increased marginalisation. Despite the internecine and counter-productive violence committed by the rebels, it is argued that there is nevertheless an increasing frustration among young adults over the fact that the political issues the rebels address are left without commentary in the public realm. Given its experience of being silenced, many young adults claimed, the LRM/A's effort to articulate politically viable statements made sense. Young people's stories, in public only too commonly sidestepped or reshaped, are comments on contemporary Ugandan society as such which place the rebel manifestos in relief. Their stories can deepen the understanding of contemporary African societies in emerging global realities.

Opening: Conflicting discourses

As it is now... the bush is almost better than home.
Otto, 28 years, unmarried,
representative to the National Youth Council,
Gulu town, February 2000

In this chapter, I delineate the image of the Ugandan rebel group known as the Lord's Resistance Movement/Army (LRM/A) as it is presented in what I will call, somewhat crudely perhaps, as I lack any better alternative, the official (or public) discourse. The LRM/A has been fighting Yoweri Museveni's no-party rule, the so-called Movement, ever since the latter captured state power in 1986, and Acholiland in northern Uganda has been the immediate war zone. I will soon proceed to introduce the official discourse. Towards the end of the chapter, I also delineate what the LRM/A rebels have written in their manifestos. Throughout, I investigate how these two different representations, which for heuristic reasons I will present as rather neat counter-discourses, relate to the opinions and experiences of young adult non-combatant informants.[1]

Material for the chapter was collected in Acholiland (Gulu, Kitgum and Pader districts), and more particularly Gulu town, where I conducted anthropological fieldwork for a total of one year, in three phases (1997–1998, 1999–2000, 2002). The principal method was participant observation, or better, participant *reflection* (Århem 1994:25; Finnström 2003:23–35). I spent a great deal of time with a limited number of young adults, and throughout the research I had continual conversations and meetings, rather than formal interviews, with them. This was supplemented with more formal conversations and interviews with other people as well, including young people. The chapter obviously reflects the situation during the years when the material was collected.

Knowing very well that job opportunities in contemporary Uganda are very few, and that education may not deliver anything concrete, young adults still regard education as important. It is not that these young people had unrealistic dreams for the future, or even, to draw a parallel with

---

1. This chapter is an abridged version of a text which previously appeared as chapter four in my PhD thesis in cultural anthropology (Finnström 2003). I thank Michael Whyte and the editors of this anthology, whose perceptive comments encouraged me to rework some of the arguments from my thesis. Most of all, however, I thank Jimmy Otim, my close Ugandan friend and partner in research, for all those long hours and endless conversations.

Sierra Leone, that there was a "poignantly impossible gulf between their dreams and their reality" (Jackson 2004:148, 176). Rather, for many young Africans, education rather than a military career represents the hope for a better future on the continent, and perhaps more importantly, for the African nations at large. The young Ugandans I encountered were frustrated, struggling hard, *but doing so with a critical and informed mind*, and like the great majority of young Africans, their choice is not to embrace armed struggle, but instead search for "societal hope, these social routes by which individuals can define a meaning for their lives" (Hage 2003:15, passim; see also Jackson 2005:xxiv).

In his description of today's global empire of disorder, Joxe (2002) notes that some people in Serbia supported (or still support) chauvinistic and violent militia groups – not because they liked what these groups do, but because they disliked even more what they experienced as an imperial, neo-liberal American world order imposed on theirs lives. "In sympathy," Joxe (2002:201) suggests, "there is *common suffering.*" In a similar way, but perhaps less straightforwardly, the LRM/A rebel manifestos made sense to many young Ugandan adults, as the manifestos locate the lived predicament in northern Uganda in relation to the wider, global political order.

To sum up the argument, I will highlight below efforts of young non-combatant people to find societal hope and make political sense out of what is going on in war-torn northern Uganda as they aspire to adulthood and citizenship. To pay attention to young people's efforts to enter into political space, Durham (2000:113) has argued, is to pay attention to the topology of the wider socio-political landscape. I will thus ask, as young adult Ugandans do in their lives, if the rebels' activities and claims can be regarded as meaningful, despite their violent tactics. The word meaningful, as I want to use it, simply indicates that a phenomenon is situational and can be made comprehensible and comparable with other phenomena and that people who live together articulate and mediate experiences and stories among themselves in a patterning and systematic manner.

To find common ground is a principal concern in cultural life everywhere in the world. And the voices of young adults, I suggest, can provide a widened understanding of *changing and evolving political motivations* that sustain war in northern Uganda. Young adults' stories are not only the expression of their effort to navigate youth and adulthood, to allude to the title of this anthology, nor are they only the expression of their "struggle to recognize themselves in relation to society" (Durham 2000:114). Their stories are also comments upon contemporary Ugandan society as such, and they place the rebel manifestos in relief. In other words, young people's stories express their engagement in "sustaining a sense of agency in the face of disempowering circumstances," but they also exemplify "a strategy for transforming private into public meanings" (Jackson 2002:14f., passim).

Young adults and the official discourse

In a new preface to his comparative account of nationalist violence in Australia and Sri Lanka, Kapferer (1998:xi) argues that written material and media accounts "are crucial adjuncts to anthropological work." More importantly, he continues, "the analysis of textual materials is the beginning and not the endpoint of anthropological investigation" and texts are therefore "to be related to their context and interpreted through the everyday worlds for which they may be relevant" (Kapferer 1998:xi). Following Kapferer, I suggest how the LRM/A manifestos are socially embedded documents, of relevance to young adults, more than they are diaspora fantasies, disconnected from Ugandan realities. I also argue that the war in northern Uganda exemplifies how forceful international policies such as economic liberalisation implemented in the 1990s have promoted the conditions of political violence in Uganda's marginalised regions and among its marginalised peoples, especially the young.

Before I proceed, let me explain what I mean by the official discourse. A number of influential stakeholders seem to have the upper hand in defining this discourse. Of these, I will provide examples from media, international human rights organisations, and the Ugandan government. In introducing the notion of an official discourse, I will refer to issues that these stakeholders disseminate, from the local level in northern Uganda to worldwide media networks, and which tend to completely overshadow other aspects of the social and political reality. The official discourse defines and structures the ways in which the world, or parts of it, is to be understood and talked about.

To illustrate the point: the LRM/A's mass abduction of minors into its fighting ranks is a dominant issue in the official discourse (see notably Amnesty International 1997; Human Rights Watch 1997), which has totally drowned out the rebels' efforts to launch their political agenda. For many years, the rebels' gross violence has "drawn much international sympathy for the government" (Mwenda and Tangri 2005:466), and the focus on the child abductees has even justified a non-negotiation stance by the Ugandan government (Dolan 2002). The crisis is held to be humanitarian rather than political.

There is an irreducible contradiction here which needs to be recognised. Over the years, the armed struggle of the LRM/A has taken on a most violent logic of its own which in many respects contradicts, sometimes even nullifies, the political aims that the LRM/A has claimed to be fighting for. Paradoxically, the violent practices conform to the official discourse, and sometimes I am left with the feeling that most rebels aim at nothing more than to sustain themselves, or to remove a government which they regard as corrupt, but really not to offer any alternative political representation. This development is similar to what has been reported from civil wars elsewhere on the African continent (see, for example, Jackson 2004; Nordstrom 1997; Vigh this volume).

But also, as Aretxaga notes for the conflict in Northern Ireland, for a state to recognise insurgents is to recognise a legitimate player in the arena of international politics. "The British refusal to characterize the conflict in Northern Ireland as a war, despite the continuous presence of an inordinate number of military troops, aims at erasing the IRA [the Irish Republican Army] as a political subject," Aretxaga (1997:85) writes. She concludes that the British government refused to acknowledge that the IRA had a political voice, thus excluding them "from the sphere of legitimate discourse" (Aretxaga 1997:172). In other words, I argue that despite the gross and counterproductive violence committed by the LRM/A rebels, there is nevertheless an increasing frustration among non-combatants, and especially among young adults, over the fact that the political issues the rebels have tried to address are left without commentary in the official discourse. Given its experience of being silenced, young adults claimed, the LRM/A's continuous struggle to articulate politically viable statements made sense. Durham again: "New forms of political participation and authority exclude and include youth in novel ways, and debates about those forms are debates about the nature of citizenship, responsibilities, and the moral, immoral, and amoral nature of social action" (2000:114). Indeed, for many young adults growing up in war-torn northern Uganda, the issue of citizenship is a most important issue, and, as Durham suggests, youth "are central to negotiating continuity and change in any context" (2000:114). But at the same time, for young adult Ugandans, war rather than citizenship has always been the main reference in life. In the words of an 18-year-old woman:

> Everyone … wants peace. Me, even me, I want peace. We all want peace, but can we define what peace is? I was only one year [old] when this thing started. I cannot right now even define what peace is. I don't know what peace

means…. And, of course, if we don't know what peace is, it will just remain a dream which never will come true. (Gulu town, July 2002)

For earlier generations who grew up with peace, young adults argue, societal hope had always been there. Now it is different. Opportunities in life are restricted, as war overshadows the social reality. "In the sixties, there were jobs," a young man asserted. "But today even the elders admit, really, there are no jobs for the youngsters." As the young woman quoted above pointed out, even to comprehend what peace means is not that easy. As her lifelong experience told her, the many military campaigns had not brought peace and security, only increased poverty, and had escalated the spiral of violence.

Developments on the ground

"What the opposition groups in the north and east of the country have in common is not ethnic identity or cultural traditions," the Ugandan historian Omara-Otunnu (1995:230) writes, "but a history of being only peripherally included in the economic structures and processes of the country." The idea of the exclusion of peripheral areas in Uganda is not new in Ugandan politics. On the eve of independence in 1962, the division between central Uganda and its peripheries was a central issue in national politics. Vincent (1999:110) traces this division to colonial times and argues that the northern periphery primarily "provided the labor pool required by the 'modernizing' economic sector in the south." The national imbalance remains today, despite efforts to counter these uneven developments. For example, in the most recent years, many technological innovations and new developments have reached northern Uganda. One notable example is Western Union Money Transfer, now available in Gulu town. Another development is a new private hospital built in Gulu town, financed by concerned, wealthy Acholi in the European diaspora. The hospital is well equipped, and the most advanced services will be offered, such as cardiac, keyhole and cosmetic surgery, assisted reproduction, mammography, endoscopy, computerised tomography (CT) as well as magnetic resonance imaging (MRI). Sports injuries will be treated at a special clinic. There is also a rapidly growing NGO led humanitarian industry in war-torn northern Uganda (Finnström 2006).

These recent developments aside, many young people in the war-torn north with expectations of a better future regarding education and work, expressed an experience of being increasingly betrayed. For them, the hospital stands there as proud evidence of modernity and development in Uganda. However, few young adult informants had consulted the hospital. The initial fee, equivalent to about ten US dollars, was just too high.[2] So the hospital also came to represent young adults' disconnection or humiliating expulsion, and even their abjection, as Ferguson (1999: notably chapter 7) says in an analysis of the industrial downfall and economic crisis in the Zambian Copperbelt. Rather than a lack of future possibilities promised by development and modernisation, Ferguson suggests that most people experienced a loss of, a disconnection from, these very possibilities.[3]

Since the war, rather than only being the expression of ethnic rivalry, reflects a Ugandan national crisis in the context of structural adjustment and increasing global inequalities, young people feel excluded from Ugandan citizenship in their daily lives. From their point of view, being able to benefit from health care and education is a civil right. In a more profound sense, frustrated young people claim, it is a question of democracy in everyday life. If a person lacks the funds to obtain health or educational services from private sponsors, this must not limit the citizen's right to obtain them through Uganda's public sector.

Although the Ugandan government admits that the northern region is one of the poorest regions in the country, where 63 per cent of the population is living below the poverty line compared to the national average figure of 38 per cent (*The New Vision*, 16 February 2005), my discussion of young adults' discontent and their experience of abjection is not based on statistics about unevenly or evenly distributed development measures in the aftermath of the various structural adjustment policies (for this see SAPRIN 2001:28). But it is, as indicated, based on their lived experience. The war is, of course, an obstacle to many development schemes in the north, and some development agencies have relocated their projects to other areas of Uganda. In 1997, for example, a feasibility study by the Uganda National Water and Sewerage Corporation proposed Gulu town as suitable for a water supply expansion project, but the German financial institutions turned the proposal down and instead requested the Ugandan authorities to locate

---

2. During additional fieldwork in 2005, I found out that by then the fee had been heavily subsidized.

3. By introducing the terms "disconnection" and "abjection" to the anthropology of modernity and development, Ferguson aims to recapture the experience of his Copperbelt informants. Their stories of unemployment and economic decline articulate the sense that the promises of modernisation had been betrayed, that people were now expelled, or discarded, from the developments of the rest of the world, notably the West (see also De Boeck and Honwana 2005:7f.).

an alternative area for the project. The reason given was insecurity in northern Uganda. The Ugandan independent daily, *The Monitor* (19 December 1997), reported the episode. Typically, as readers of the newspaper noted, a German delegation visited Kampala and Jinja, in central Uganda, but did not bother to visit Gulu town to assess the possibilities on location. "There is not much to say," one of the readers, a young man, told me; "the article speaks for itself." In his view, this was a most common feature of development in Uganda. "The field assessments are done in Kampala," and possible projects are all "cancelled from Kampala," he concluded.

The media of conflict

Wars are partly what the media make them, Allen and Seaton (1999:3) note in the introduction to an excellent volume on the media of conflict. In the media, the consensual declaration is that the LRM/A rebels are fighting for power so they can rule the country on the basis of the biblical Ten Commandments. For example, one media report claims that "The LRA, a group whose beliefs are rooted in Christian fundamentalist doctrines and traditional religions, has been fighting President Yoweri Museveni's government since 1987, with the aim of establishing its own rule based on the biblical Ten Commandments" (UN/IRIN online news, 20 November 2002; reiterated in UN/IRIN 25 March and 8 April 2005; see also *The Monitor* 16, 18 and 27 April 2005; *The New Vision* 22 March and 7 January 2005). The easily accessible Internet sites of BBC and CNN have frequently reproduced the mantra on the Ten Commandments as the sole driving motive of the LRM/A (see, for example, BBC online 22 October 2004; 4 and 5 March; 3 July; 11 August; 22, 30 and 31 October; 25 November 2002; and CNN online 14 and 15 September 2002). This simplistic and one-sided claim has also been recurrent in the reporting of various human rights organisations, Amnesty International (1997:6), for example, or Women's Commission for Refugee Women and Children (2001:82). Some academics embrace this claim too (e.g. Cheney 2005:23). The typical conclusion is that the war in northern Uganda has its roots in ethnic mistrust in Uganda and in the "religious and spiritual beliefs of the Acholi people" (Women's Commission for Refugee Women and Children 2001:81). In another human rights report it is noted that rebel leader Joseph Kony, himself a son of Acholiland, "drew from Acholi religious beliefs and incorporated Christian traditions and rituals into his movement" (African Rights 2000:4).

Behrend (1999:28ff.), an anthropologist, has shown that Alice Lakwena and her Holy Spirit Movement, a predecessor to Joseph Kony's Lord's Resistance Movement/Army, offered a kind of purification from the deeds committed in the recent past in central Uganda, something that was attractive to many soldiers of the fallen government, and to marginalised youth too. Ward (1995), a church historian, suggests that northern Uganda faced a crisis in religious leadership and a collapse of institutional church life which opened up the space for recruitment of young people into rebel ranks. Less contextual accounts are blunter in their simplistic promotion of religious and cultural causes. In producing a character like Alice Lakwena, and later Joseph Kony, it is thus often suggested, opposition in northern Uganda was now at "its most bizarre" (Woodward 1991:181).

Of course, these humanitarian reports and anthropologically informed interpretations are correct in noting that the conflict has taken on a religious dimension. Allen (1991:370) and Ehrenreich (1998:84), however, have warned against the prevailing heart-of-darkness representation of the LRM/A and the war in northern Uganda. The conclusion drawn from this representation, Ehrenreich notes with frustration, is only too familiar to the western public and thus blatantly seductive. The western media consumer will conclude that "the conflict is bizarre, but Africa is simply Like That" (Ehrenreich 1998:84). The focus on the alleged Christian fundamentalism joined with Acholi religious beliefs, together with the focus on the LRM/A as a movement of child abductees, has effectively silenced young adults' alternative conclusions. Former child rebels, and even young adults with clear political opinions, are listened to only if they feature in roles *supportive* of the official discourse (Durham 2000:114). Their agency, in trauma healing and reintegration processes, is restricted to the non-political victim format, and alternative, more complex versions of the socio-political reality are filtered away (see also Ross 2005). Yet, if we make the effort to spend some time with these young people, listening carefully to what they have to say when they confide in us, without editing their stories to better fit into the official discourse, we will find that their political "agency often arises out of the way in which they are capable of crossing and recontextualizing the boundaries between seemingly contradictory elements" (De Boeck and Honwana 2005:10).

For example, young adult informants differentiated between two categories – or, better, dimensions – of armed resistance, the initial and politically motivated insurgency groups and the spiritually motivated groups that emerged slightly later, like Alice Lakwena's Holy Spirit Forces. The first dimension of the resistance they called "the army of the earth" (*mony me ngom*) and the second "the army of the heaven" (*mony me polo*). But from 1997 to 2002, when I was doing fieldwork for this chapter, young informants, who were teenagers at the time when Alice Lakwena was leading the insurgency, maintained that their age-mates joined Alice Lakwena, and later on Joseph Kony, because, as one young man claimed, they were there as a "means of fighting" when there was "no one else to join." Omara-Otunnu's conclusion is similar. "Lakwena was merely a vehicle through which social discontent in the north of Uganda found expression," he writes. "She was able to gain tenacious followers who were prepared to risk their lives against all odds because a cross-section of marginalised inhabitants recognised her as a symbol of both their plight and their aspirations" (Omara-Otunnu 1992:458).

Obviously, if we want to see beyond the heart-of-darkness discourse, the voices of young people are important in understanding how the war in northern Uganda connects to a wider national context. A young unmarried male teacher gave the example of Tito Okello, an army general who held state power during a brief period before Museveni seized power in 1986. In a public speech in Gulu town in 1993, Okello had "talked bitterly" about the LRM/A rebels, although in the mid-1980s he had encouraged young people to join the armed struggle against Museveni. This angered young people. Disappointed with senior politicians and the older generation, the young teacher regarded Okello as a sad but typical example of "the veranda elders." He remembered that the aging Okello blamed young army officers for the violence during the war in central Uganda in the 1980s. "Now, don't you think that the elders also made mistakes?" the teacher concluded. Another young man, then a secondary school and aspiring university student, agreed:

> I think Tito's case is one of the ugliest cases I have ever noted. It is one of the most common historical blunders that most of these African leaders make under the pretext of being elders and aged. There is that over-assumption, that an elder knows everything. An elder just knows everything, and whatever he will say, he is final. Whatever becomes a mistake, be it coincidental or a planned mistake, the elders are the very first to blame the young generation about the result which was negative. And that has been some part of politics of Uganda. If you look at the politics from Obote's coming to Tito, the youths were mainly used as objects to destabilise political space. For example, there was the formation of youth wingers, like the UPC [Uganda People's Congress of Milton Obote] youth wing. So, the youths at that time also took things for granted. Still, that was the result of what the elders educated them about. You see? So

they would misbehave. But the misbehaviour of these youths during Tito and Obote's time is a result of the leaders themselves, the elders themselves. It was a failure, and the elders are the very first to say, 'Ah, it is your failure.' They never see who cultivated this failure. This has been the major mistake in Ugandan politics. The youths are used, highly used, and because they are poor, they are inadequate, they don't have the resources, so they are easily manipulated.... Elders capture power all the time, and they make use of youth in many ways, but all the time not for positive aspects; all the time for something that causes friction in society, social friction in society. (Gulu town, May 2000)

"And this one even caused ethnic conflicts," he concluded, again with reference to Okello's military takeover in 1985. "But it was his failure. What can you do with youth who are hungry and poor?" Even if most young people do not rebel against authority but rather aim at *appropriating* authority, they adapt with a critical mind, maintaining their cultural and political agency (Bucholtz 2002:533f.).

War on terror and the war of propaganda

In December 2001, the global war against terrorism reached Uganda as the US government included the LRM/A as well as the Allied Democratic Forces in western Uganda on its list of terrorist groups with which no negotiations, so it is stated, will under any circumstances be initiated. The Ugandan government immediately welcomed the rhetoric of no dialogue. "We in Uganda know very well the grievous harm that can be caused to society by terrorists, having suffered for many years at the hands of Kony and the Allied Democratic Forces, terrorists supported by Sudan," president Museveni said (as quoted in UN/IRIN online news 12 September 2001; see also *The Monitor* 15, 19 and 23 October 2001; *The New Vision* 10 October 2001).

The Ugandan army promotes itself as the rational and modern party in the conflict. Again the words of the Ugandan president, who is also commander-in-chief of the army, are significant. With reference to Alice Lakwena and her Holy Spirit Mobile Forces, the predecessors of the LRM/A, Museveni has described the rebels in northern Uganda as nothing but criminals and murderers, or at best, victims of primitive and primordial sentiments and perverted local religious traditions. "The poor Lakwena girl was being manipulated by criminals who would intoxicate soldiers on marijuana," and supporters of previous regimes were "intoxicating poor peasants with mysticism and incredible lies," Museveni (1992:115) writes.

It can be noted that in contrast to many rebel movements in West Africa, for example, the LRM/A rebels are strictly opposed not only to the use of tobacco, but also to alcohol and marijuana. They frequently loot soft drinks but most often smash beer bottles. Yet, from Museveni's perspective, they are drugged, and "the Lakwena peasants" used "mysticism instead of science" in their effort to fight his "modern army" (Museveni 1992:116). References to primitive superstition and alleged drug abuse are powerful in the effort to deny any political dimension to the conflict. Instead, "obscurantism," "witchcraft" and "backwardness" (Museveni 1992:173) are said to block modernisation and development in Uganda. Nowadays Museveni uses these latter epithets to describe the LRM/A, and his view of Alice Lakwena seems to have changed somewhat. In declaring the LRM/A a brutal movement without popular support, he sometimes contrasts it to Alice Lakwena's acknowledged popularity (Heike Behrend, personal communication).

President Museveni and representatives of the Ugandan government have now and then agreed to engage in a dialogue with the rebels. More profoundly over the years, however, they have claimed that the LRM/A military campaign is being conducted in the absence of any political agenda, and they conclude that it is impossible to engage in dialogue with people without some kind of agenda. With such a denial of any political dimension to the conflict, and a focus instead on the rebels' incomprehensible religious practices and gross abuses of basic human rights, peace talks have often been dismissed on moral grounds (notably Parliament of Uganda 1997). In a similar way, one report to the United Nations concludes that the LRM/A "lacks any clearly formulated political objective" (Weeks 2002:13), yet another report that "the LRA has no coherent political or other objectives" (Women's Commission for Refugee Women and Children 2001:82). Instead it is concluded that the rebels blindly follow their leader, Joseph Kony, who "has created an aura for himself and his organisation of deliberate irrationality and obscurantism" (Weeks 2002:9).

As already indicated, the religious dimension of the rebellion in northern Uganda has attracted more interest than the political dimension, which may be related to the rebels' destructive violence. To most Ugandans and outside observers, this violence, sometimes motivated in religious and moralistic terms, is spectacular in its brutality. Allen (1991) and Behrend (notably 1999) have delineated the religious and cosmological aspects of the rebel movements in northern Uganda. However, their focus has been on Alice Lakwena's Holy Spirit Movement, active in the second half of the

1980s, and only peripherally about the succeeding insurgency movement. They outline rebel practices as a rather coherent system of beliefs aimed at establishing a new moral order. Yet the wider national, political and socio-economic dimensions of the conflict remain marginal to these analyses. My aim below is therefore to discuss these latter dimensions. During the years of evolving conflict in northern Uganda, the political and socio-economical dimensions have developed as increasingly central issues of debate and contest in Uganda, not only in the war-torn north but also nationally.

"Meaningful rebels"?

The rebels evidently feed on an increasing local discontent with neoliberal developments in Uganda, notably structural adjustment and other development measures demanded by the donor community. Today the programmes of structural adjustment and cost sharing have reached almost every sector of Ugandan society, particularly health and education. Young men and women, especially, often aired their experience of being denied Ugandan citizenship. "Accountable democracy," or "participatory democracy," to reproduce commonly heard catchwords of the international development rhetoric, is defined by a government's ability to make certain services available to its citizens, like clean water, food, health care and education. This is obviously not the case in northern Uganda. In frustration, many young people desperately seek economic assistance. One teenage man wrote in a letter to me, "My father who was struggling for sponsoring my fees was killed by the rebel force. That is why I got stuck on the way." The writer concludes that he can only see one alternative to the education he was forced to drop out from. "I will be compelled to join the rebel force to fight the Uganda People's Defence Forces [and the] government." The lived experience that many young informants communicated is that the war-torn north is a neglected periphery, while the Kampala and other central regions were said to be booming. Young adults feel marginalised in their poverty, to use Englund's (2002:173f.) perceptive claim in his analysis of the political and economic dimensions of social life in the post-war Mozambique-Malawi borderland.

The frustration of young adults must be taken seriously. In their view, they are denied many of the most mundane and everyday aspects of citizenship that most people in the West take for granted. To evoke Ferguson's (1999) argument again, they feel "disconnected" from Uganda's wider developments, even future developments. One issue often emphasised by young people in northern Uganda was the importance of including the northern region in Uganda's development and national future. Integration, not secession, was the issue at stake.

As mentioned, there is a great discrepancy between the LRM/A's written manifestos and the group's violent military tactics. In print, the rebels' programme is in accord with the political sentiments commonly communicated by informants. At the same time, people's practical knowledge of the rebels' violent activities on the ground points towards another, more complex, situation. In short, the rebels do little to follow their own written endorsement of respect for human rights. In the words of an 18-year-old female student, "I do not support the rebels, nor am I supporting the government. I am just in a dilemma. I would like to support the rebels, but they are killing my people."

It is not relevant to analyse such seemingly perplexing questions in terms of logical inconsistency, or as irrational and uninformed, which would indicate an inability among young adults to grasp the complexity of war. Instead I suggest that the young woman's statement is typical of young people's lived realities in northern Uganda, just as seemingly contradictory standpoints are common in every human setting where young people try to establish themselves as adults. Only a contextual approach can disclose the complexities of meanings in use. From an anthropological perspective, it is mistaken to conclude that a person cannot be young in one context, and an adult in another, claim one position in the first context, to shift in another as social relations are continuously produced, reproduced and contested (Bucholtz 2002:526ff.).

Young people often try to comprehend the discrepancy between the rebels' stated agenda and their violent military strategies on the ground. Sometimes these young people put forward very frank conclusions. In 2000, a 25-year-old unmarried man, a teacher by profession, concluded out of frustration that terrorist attacks, sometimes even against their own people, can be legitimate when no other options are open, when the political climate has stifled any oppositional effort, "when you can do nothing." He had never been a rebel himself, neither did he seriously think about joining them on the battlefield, but he still held that in an increasingly hostile political environment, "the rebels are becoming more meaningful." Elaborating upon what he saw as a new phase in the war, in which "the army of the heaven" (*mony me polo*) was giving way to "the army of the earth" (*mony me ngom*), he continued that "they are becoming more meaningful in the sense that they have been able to publish a manifesto, which they used not to have." In 2002, the language of young people had changed even more. Now and then I encountered young men, especially, who talked about the rebels in terms of "freedom fighters." In the words of one such young man, "These people are called terrorists. The world knows them as terrorists." But as long as they are labelled terrorists, the man suggested, the Ugandan government, with the approval of the outside world, will continue to deal harshly with any person who tries to initiate peace dialogues with the rebels. "Which means," the young man went on to say, "as long as they are terrorists in the bush, the people of Acholiland can continue to suffer.... Maybe the world sees them as a terrorist organisation, for real, which they do not still see [themselves]. These are freedom fighters!" Another young man added, with reference to a blanket amnesty offered by the Ugandan government to the rebels, "To me, this amnesty, even if the president accepted it coactively, does not apply to rebels. Amnesty only applies to gangsters, robbers, or those kinds of bandits. But to a rebel who has a constitutional right to liberate his country – because these [rebels] call themselves liberators, they want to liberate the country – they don't see that they have done anything wrong." The discussion went on and a third young man broke in, "I think they have been very wise to know that the amnesty thing was bogus...."

Perhaps these statements are strange to readers who have in mind the atrocities the rebels have committed. Yet, it must be concluded that the young informants who aired these opinions did so from the experience of living with war throughout their childhood and youth. They had little trust in the government's measures to end the war, which they saw as efforts to downplay the armed conflict as merely a northern issue, peripheral to the rest of the country, and, as mentioned, a humanitarian rather than political crisis. In contrast to such strategies of the official discourse and the heart-of-darkness rhetoric, they wanted the political issue at stake to be addressed nationally. Again, to quote one of the young men, "Because the [conflict] is not about northern Uganda. It is about the whole country. Of course, we are taking the upper hand. We are the ones suffering. But it is a national issue that deserves such an address."

Young people in the conflict area revealed discrepancies in their own efforts to understand the violent reality they face in everyday life. In one context, therefore, they would strongly condemn the atrocities committed by the rebels as well as the Ugandan army, and of course, young people too sometimes conformed to the official discourse. More often, however, in contexts that were more private they would argue against the official discourse, for example, in describing the rebels in terms of freedom fighters. In other words, the official approach of belittling the political manifestos of the LRM/A rebels, which has blocked their access to the official political arena, has created frustration not only among the rebels themselves, but also among non-combatant young adults in northern Uganda.

By making this comparison, my intention is to nuance the equally frequent claim that the manifestos of the LRM/A, on the Internet or elsewhere, are inauthentic or diaspora creations and therefore "bear virtually no relation to anything actually happening in northern Uganda" (Ehrenreich 1998:99f, n. 14). This conclusion adheres to the official discourse on the war in northern Uganda. Yet authenticity is not about where a piece of paper has been written, but rather where it is disseminated and discussed, and where its meaning is mediated and reformulated. It is evident that the LRM/A manifestos circulate on the ground in northern Uganda, where I encountered them at first hand. I have also documented that a number of Acholi who are known critics of the government and therefore suspected of having copies, perish in Ugandan prisons. Again the official discourse of denial is violently in play; not only is it denied that the LRM/A has manifestos but, furthermore, that people who voice the contrary are frequently imprisoned. A growing number of people are being arrested on charges of treason or suspected terrorism but are still denied court trials. Locked in army prisons or detention centres commonly known as "safe houses," they disappear from the public arena. This fact gives a very real, lived dimension to the manifestos.

"What we are not…": The LRM/A's agenda

During fieldwork in 1997, I came across an LRM/A political manifesto dated 4 April 1996. Ten political objectives are put forward in the one-page document, notably the immediate restoration of multiparty democracy as well as the introduction of constitutional federalism. In late 1999, I came across another political manifesto, again shown to me in Gulu town. This undated manifesto repeats many of the issues put forward in the previous manifestos. It is an eighteen-page pamphlet of criticism about the practices of Museveni's no-party rule, the so-called Movement, which is held to be a one-party state. Among other things, multiparty politics are again promoted, and Uganda's armed involvement in the Congo is questioned. The manifesto furthermore acknowledges that structural adjustment programmes are necessary but questions how they are being implemented in

Uganda, arguing that people on the grassroots level seem to suffer most, especially in peripheral areas in the north and the east. In both manifestos, the LRM/A promotes human rights. Young people felt sceptical about the rebels' claim to any human rights, however, because of the many abductions and atrocities still committed by rebels.

Kayunga writes that it was only in the process of the evolving conflict that insurgents in northern Uganda were forced to frame their ambitions in terms of a struggle for multiparty politics and democracy, "if only," as he maintains, "to win international sympathy and support" (Kayunga 2000:112). It is important to add, however, that this support must also be won locally and nationally, not only internationally, and it is not analytically satisfactory to reduce the political manifestos of rebel groups in Uganda to addressing external forces only. This Kayunga also acknowledges. "As the LRA lost popularity especially after 1991," he writes, "it began to embrace multiparty propaganda" (Kayunga 2000:115).

It is a notable fact that representatives of the LRM/A often find it necessary to write against the official discourse. For example, the organisation denies that it is motivated by any fundamentalist Christian ideologies. One of the pro–LRM/A Internet homepages, under the heading "What we are not…," stated that the LRM/A is not a religious movement or a Christian fundamentalist group, or a terrorist group for that matter. The opposite was propagated on the now defunct site:

> The name 'LORD'S' was adopted by members of the Rural Population who decided to pray for divine intervention in order to prevent the countless pogroms and massacres of the peasant population by the National Resistance Army now known as Ugandan Peoples Liberation Army [sic, Uganda People's Defence Forces] headed by Major General Yoweri Kaguta Museveni. Thus the name is a representation of the people's Plight and Agony. (Downloaded 15 September 1999)

In the more recent manifesto circulated on the ground in northern Uganda, a note signed by the LRM/A leader Joseph Kony is a preamble to the political issues raised. Again the effort to deny the fundamentalist label is central. "There have been miss informations [sic] about this Movement, its name, objectives, policies and even its entire membership including leadership," Kony writes. The movement is for all Ugandans, he goes on to claim, and the term "Lord" is explained as a simple thanks to the "Heavenly Father" who has made it possible for the movement to resist Museveni's army, which nevertheless "is always armed from tooth to nail" (Lord's Resistance Movement/Army n.d.:5). The rebel leader continues the preface:

> While a big percentage of the Movement's members are ordinary and Practising CHRISTIANS, I would like to strongly deny that these members are or in any way have the intention of becoming Christian Fundamentalists. (Lord's Resistance Movement/Army n.d.:5)

As mentioned, most external observers agree with the Ugandan authorities in questioning the authenticity of LRM/A Internet sites and printed manifestos. When I enquired among government representatives in northern Uganda, there was a solid denial of the existence of any LRM/A manifesto, both in the present and the past. The only official representative of the government apparatus who told me that the rebels had a manifesto was, perhaps illustratively, a local government council *youth* representative. The manifesto had been shown to him at a district meeting with various government representatives. He had also been given the opportunity to listen to a tape with the rebel leader speaking. "The manifesto looks very good," he told me as he recalled the meeting. However, as he added, "But all in all, what matters is what is seen on the ground," indicating that the rebels' violent practices pointed in another, opposite direction.

Today the Kampala region is booming and expanding rapidly. As Leopold (1999:219) notes, for many years Uganda has been widely regarded, among both academics and influential organisations like the International Monetary Fund, as a success story of reconstruction, structural adjustment and economic liberalisation. As indicated by young adults' discontent in the war-torn north, however, peripheral regions are lagging behind, and they said that their area benefits only partially from the development, privatisation and alleged prosperity of the country. Indeed, donor agencies, private enterprises and other financial institutions are reluctant to invest in the northern region because of armed conflict and recurrent periods of insecurity. I therefore suggest that many young adults shared an experience of mistrust, created by war and uneven development, with the LRM/A rebels. The criticism is outlined in the rebel manifesto:

> LRM/A recognize the importance of the World Bank and IMF Structural Adjustment Programs. However, we also recognize that these programs have concentrated on achieving low inflation and deregulating markets to the exclusion of other considerations. The resulting deflationary pressures have undermined prospects for economic recovery, compounding inequalities, undermining the position of women, and failing to protect poor people's access to health and

education services. They have contributed to high levels of unemployment and the erosion of social welfare provisions for the poor. Meanwhile market deregulation have brought few benefits for those excluded from markets by virtue of their poverty and lack of productive resources. (Lord's Resistance Movement/Army n.d.:11)

The Ugandan government is said to be selling out the country and its human and natural resources. Of course, the claim is not unique to the LRM/A rebels. For example, Tangri and Mwenda (2001:132f.) show that the extensive privatisation programmes initiated in Uganda during the 1990s, more often than not infested with corruption, have "promoted the creation of a tiny wealthy class" rather than following the objectives to "broadening the basis of ownership." Even more vulnerable to such developments, of course, are young people who live with war, when little can be done with private means to improve prospects for the future. With such developments in mind, it is notable that the LRM/A manifesto is a critical stance against "the New World Order" as described by the sociologist Zygmunt Bauman (1998:55–76). He does not refer to Uganda in his book. But interestingly enough, Bauman quotes rebels in Chiapas, Mexico (1998:66) when he tries to put his finger on the frustrations in the so-called peripheries regarding today's "process of a world-wide *restratification*" (Bauman 1998:70), which seems to benefit only the very few. The LRM/A's manifestos pinpoint the issues relevant to young people in northern Uganda, I argue, which in fact does give them a certain degree of authenticity.

Encountering Osama Bin Laden in Uganda

In December 2001, as mentioned above, the US-led global war against terrorism reached Uganda. The U.S. government included the LRM/A on its list of global terrorist groups. The Ugandan government immediately welcomed this rhetoric of no dialogue. The LRM/A rebels, for their part, perhaps frustrated with yet another effort to silence their political agenda, occasionally reciprocated the rhetoric of the global war against terrorism. As the rebels were manoeuvring their way to Gulu town in mid-2002, a suspected rebel arrived in the middle of the day in a neighbourhood on the north side of the town, allegedly to survey the area. Typically, as they are obliged to, some people reported their suspicions about the rebel presence to the local army unit, but the military withdrew, leaving the matter to the police. The police did nothing. The suspected rebel disappeared, but his rebel unit came back in the middle of the night. They broke into houses, arrested people, and looted food and clothes. They remained for several hours and they went about their careful work undisturbed. One local government functionary who tried to escape was shot dead. Eventually the rebels decided to pull out, still without having encountered any Ugandan military response. As is common, some local people were forced to carry the plunder towards the rebel hideouts. As they withdrew from town, the rebels asked their abductees if they knew who they were, and why they had come. "You are the rebels, the LRA, I guess," one young abducted man answered. "Yes, we are. We are strong. And we are Osama Bin Laden. We will come back within a few weeks. Remember that!" he was told repeatedly before he and his fellow abductees were released so that they would not be able to disclose the exact position of the rebel hideout. They walked back to town, where I recorded the story the following day.

In the official discourse, it is often claimed that today's rebels in Uganda have been trained in camps of Osama Bin Laden and the al-Qaeda network (for example, Global Witness 2003:13). This is also the firm conviction of President Museveni (see, for example, *The Monitor* 23 October 2001). Regardless of whether or not this is the case, the LRM/A field unit above reciprocated the rhetoric of no dialogue. Simultaneously, many informants were convinced that the rebel leader Joseph Kony, after years of having been told that he is a terrorist, something that he evidently is, has now decided to be one. As one young non-combatant man put it, when he imagined Joseph Kony's way of reasoning, "They say that I am a terrorist. Well, let it be so and let me then give them terrorism." Perhaps such a self-confession to terrorism, as suggested by the young man who gave voice to the rebel leader, can be interpreted as an effort to recover political agency, otherwise denied in the official discourse.

After the September 11 attacks on the United States, one can only conclude that the official and dominant discourse has turned more black and white than ever before. Back in Sweden, I heard conservative and liberal party leaders echoing US President George W. Bush's militant stand after the attacks, "Either you are with us, or you are with the terrorists." When I pressed the conservative party on this issue, presenting the example of Uganda, a party secretary returned my questions with a clarification. It is a matter of being for or against terrorism, I was informed. He also commented upon the issue of poverty reduction, something he did not regard as particularly important in the effort to counter terrorism. The September 11 terrorists were well educated and relatively well off financially, and thus not recruited from the marginalised poor, he concluded. But the politicians' black-and-white rhetoric, in fact common in today's global politics, with its two possible alternatives, narrows young people's ability to manoeuvre their way in life. Societal hope is shrinking (Hage 2003).

If we turn our eyes away from the most spectacular terrorist deeds of today, and instead focus on small-scale dirty wars like the one fought in northern Uganda, it becomes evident that the assertion that Osama Bin Laden is a rich but evil individual is not analytically satisfactory. The liberalist and modernist celebration of "the individual self as the locus of consciousness and experience," Englund (2002:183f.) holds, "fails precisely because *it renders relations invisible* – from personal relationships to transnational and global relations." In other words, instead of the all too common obsession with single individuals like Osama Bin Laden, Saddam Hussein or even LRM/A's Joseph Kony and their alleged wickedness, their individualities or personal biographies, we need to pay attention to the power relations and structural circumstances that promote such persons' positions. Sometimes these relations boil down to the issue of redistribution of global wealth. Above I note that many of the most modern services offered in Gulu town these days, for example, those of the brand new private hospital that wealthy individuals could take advantage of, have less relevance for most young marginalised people than the LRM/A manifestos do. To put it bluntly, rather than being satisfied with the fact that cosmetic surgery can be done today in Gulu town too, most young adults would vote for the LRM/A's (n.d.:15) promise to provide "free basic primary health care for all." This is not to say that these young adults actively support the LRM/A, or that the LRM/A is an organisation they think is capable of realising its promises. But they experience, again as taken up by the LRM/A (n.d.:11), that "[t]he population at the grassroots are hardly feeling the economic achievements of the Museveni regime."

This may be a provocative parallel to draw; yet, it is essential if we are to deepen our understanding with regard to the kind of lived political milieu that has now kept the LRM/A rebels motivated for more than one and a half decades. It is thus not surprising that the logic of war alienates people in the war-torn region from the state apparatus and the central government. To put it simply, the more violence the rebels commit against the non-combatant population, the more the government will be blamed by those same exposed people for its failure to protect and provide for its citizens. A growing number of young people feel that the war increasingly excludes them from the various modern developments in Uganda; in other words, that their right to exercise citizenship is denied them, and that they are excluded and disconnected from the Ugandan nation and its economic, legal and educational services. To young adults living in the war-torn and marginalised north, then, manifestos like those of the LRM/A are increasingly attractive, while the official discourse and the media's heart-of-darkness rhetoric only add to their frustrations. In the words of the unmarried teacher quoted above, "As citizens we shall not accept that injustices continue. If we continue to point out the wrongs yet there is no change, then we shall look for other options. The present rebellion can be used." Either you are with us, or you are with the terrorists, as George W. Bush said.

A note in conclusion

By relating the written manifestos of the LRM/A to the viewpoints of young adult informants, in this chapter I suggest an alternative to the reductionist heart-of-darkness representation of the LRM/A in media and propaganda. At the same time, I have aimed at "re-politicizing war," to use a phrase of Allen and Seaton (1999:4). They describe the opposite, the de-politicizing of war: "Ethnic mythologizing by protagonists and by journalists is precisely a means of taking the politics and the history out of wars, and reducing them to fantastic emanations" (Allen & Seaton 1999:4). Protagonists and journalists often reach for the easy way out, so to speak, and ethnicity has become the shorthand that masks other, more complex, developments. The frequent reference in the official heart-of-darkness discourse to the rebels' religious practices and human rights violations, feeds on the reductionist conclusion. And the global war on terror rhetoric bears little relation to perceptions of the LRM/A amongst non-combatant young adults in northern Uganda. If we take the time to listen to young people's stories, not simply as voices *supportive* of those powerful stakeholders who define official discourses (Durham 2000:114), but also when their voices exemplify the capacity to *question, cross, recontextualise and transform* the very discourses so often taken for granted (De Boeck and Honwana 2005:10), then we will most certainly find that young people's stories, only too often sidestepped or reshaped in the public realm, are of a political dignity which can deepen our understanding of contemporary African societies in emerging global realities. Merleau-Ponty writes:

> What we call disorder and ruin, others who are younger live as the natural order of things; and perhaps with ingenuity they are going to master it precisely because they no longer seek their bearings where we took ours. (Merleau-Ponty 1964:23)

References

African Rights, 2000, *Northern Uganda: Justice in conflict*. London: African Rights.

Allen, T., 1991, "Understanding Alice: Uganda's Holy Spirit Movement in Context", *Africa*. 61(3):370–399.

Allen, T. and J. Seaton (eds), 1999, "Introduction", *The media of conflict: War reporting and representations of ethnic violence*. London and New York: Zed Books.

Amnesty International, 1997, "'Breaking God's Commands': The destruction of childhood by the Lord's Resistance Army", *Amnesty International Country Report*, AFR 59/01/97. (PDF version downloaded 10 Sept. 2002). Available online: http://www.web.amnesty.org/ai.nsf/index/AFR590011997, E-mail: amnestyis@amnesty.org.

Aretxaga, B., 1997, *Shattering silence: Women, nationalism, and political subjectivity in Northern Ireland*. Princeton, NJ: Princeton University Press.

Århem, K. (ed.), 1994, "Antropologins mening: En introduktion (The meaning of anthropology: An introduction)", *Den antropologiska erfarenheten (The anthropological experience)*. Stockholm: Carlsson Bokförlag.

Bauman, Z., 1998, *Globalization: The human consequences*. Cambridge: Polity Press.

Behrend, H., 1999, *Alice Lakwena & the holy spirits: War in northern Uganda, 1985–97*. Oxford, Kampala, Nairobi and Athens: James Currey/Fountain Publishers/E.A.E.P./Ohio University Press.

Bucholtz, M., 2002, "Youth and cultural practice", *Annual Review of Anthropology*, 31:525–52.

Cheney, K.E., 2005, "'Our children have only known war': Children's experiences and the uses of childhood in northern Uganda", *Children's Geographies*, 3(1):23–45.

De Boeck, F. and A. Honwana (eds), 2005, "Children and youth in Africa: Agency, identity, and place", in F. De Boeck and A. Honwana (eds), *Makers and breakers: Children and youth in postcolonial Africa*. Oxford: James Currey.

Dolan, C., 2002, "Which children count? The politics of children's rights in northern Uganda", in Okello Lucima (ed.), *Protracted conflict, elusive peace: Initiatives to end the violence in northern Uganda*. London: Conciliation Resources & Kacoke Madit. Also available online: http://www.c-r.org, E-mail: conres@c-r.org.

Durham, D., 2000, "Youth and the Social Imagination in Africa: Introduction to Parts 1 and 2", *Anthropological Quarterly*, 73(3):113–20.

Ehrenreich, R., 1998, "The stories we must tell: Ugandan children and the atrocities of the Lord's Resistance Army", *Africa Today*, 45(1):79–102.

Englund, H., 2002, *From war to peace on the Mozambique–Malawi borderland*. Edinburgh: Edinburgh University Press.

Ferguson, J., 1999, *Expectations of modernity: Myths and meanings of urban life on the Zambian Copperbelt*. Berkeley: University of California Press.

Finnström, S., 2003, *Living with bad surroundings: War and existential uncertainty in Acholiland, northern Uganda*. Uppsala: Acta Universitatis Upsaliensis/Uppsala Studies in Cultural Anthropology, vol. 35 (PhD Thesis).

—, 2006, "Survival in war-torn Uganda", *Anthropological Today*, 22(2):12–15.

Global Witness, 2003, *For a few dollars more: How al Qaeda moved into the diamond trade*. London: Global Witness. Also available online: www.globalwitness.org, E-mail: mail@globalwitness.org.

Hage, G., 2003, *Against paranoid nationalism: Searching for hope in a shrinking society*. London: Pluto Press.

Human Rights Watch, 1997, *The scars of death: Children abducted by the Lord's Resistance Army in Uganda*. New York: Human Rights Watch.

Jackson, M., 2002, *The politics of storytelling: Violence, transgression, and intersubjectivity*. Copenhagen: Museum Tusculanum Press, University of Copenhagen.

—, 2004, *In Sierra Leone*. Durham: Duke University Press.

—, 2005. *Existential anthropology: Events, exigencies, and effects*. Oxford: Berghahn Books.

Joxe, A., 2002, *Empire of disorder*. Los Angeles: Semiotext(e).

Kapferer, B., 1998, Preface to the paperback reissue of *Legends of people, myths of state: Violence, intolerance, and political culture in Sri Lanka and Australia*. Washington: Smithsonian Institution Press.

Kayunga, S.S., 2000, "The impact of armed opposition on the Movement system in Uganda" in J. Mugaju and J. Oloka-Onyango (eds), *No-party democracy in Uganda: Myths and realities*. Kampala: Fountain Publishers.

Leopold, M., 1999, "'The war in the north': Ethnicity in Ugandan press explanations of conflict, 1996–97", in T. Allen and J. Seaton (eds), *The media of conflict: War reporting and representations of ethnic violence*. London: Zed Books.

Lord's Resistance Movement/Army, n.d., *Lord's Resistance Movement/Army (LRM/A) Manifesto*.

Merleau-Ponty, M., 1964, *Signs*. Evanston, Il:: Northwestern University Press.

Museveni, Y.K., 1992, *What is Africa's problem?* Kampala: NRM Publications.

Mwenda, A.M. and R.Tangri, 2005, "Patronage politics, donor reforms, and regime consolidation in Uganda", *African Affairs*. 104(416):449–467.

Nordstrom, C., 1997, *A different kind of war story*. Philadelphia: University of Pennsylvania Press.

Omara-Otunnu, A., 1992, "The struggle for democracy in Uganda", *The Journal of Modern African Studies*, 30(3):443–463.

—, 1995, "The dynamics of conflict in Uganda", in Oliver Furley (ed.), *Conflict in Africa*. London and New York: I.B. Tauris Publishers.

The Parliament of Uganda, 1997, *Report of the committee on defence and internal affairs on the war in northern Uganda*. Kampala: The Parliament of Uganda.

Ross, F.C., 2005, "Women and the politics of identity: Voices in the South African Truth and Reconciliation Commission", in Vigdis Broch-Due (ed.), *Violence and belonging: The quest for identity in post-colonial Africa*. London and New York: Routledge.

SAPRIN, 2001, Uganda country report: A synthesis of the four SAPRI studies (PDF version downloaded 22 April 2003). Washington: SAPRIN (Structural

Adjustment Participatory Review Initiative Network). Available online: www. saprin.org, E-mail: secretariat@saprin.org.

Shaw, R., 2002, *Memories of the slave trade: Ritual and historical imagination in Sierra Leone*. Chicago: University of Chicago Press.

Tangri, R. and A. Mwenda. 2001, "Corruption and cronyism in Uganda's privatization in the 1990s", *African Affairs*, 100(398):117–133.

Vincent, J., 1999, "War in Uganda: North and south", in S.P. Reyna and R.E. Downs (eds), *Deadly developments: Capitalism, states and war*. Amsterdam: Gordon & Breach Publishers.

Ward, K., 1995, "The Church of Uganda amidst conflict: The interplay between church and politics in Uganda since 1962", in H. Bernt Hansen and M. Twaddle (eds), *Religion and politics in East Africa: The period since independence*. London, Nairobi, Kampala and Athens: James Currey/E.A.E.P/Fountain Publishers/Ohio University Press.

Weeks, W., 2002, Pushing the envelope: Moving beyond 'protected villages' in northern Uganda, (PDF version downloaded 6 September 2002). New York: Report submitted to the United Nations office for the coordination of humanitarian affairs. Available online: http://www.idpproject.org, E-mail: idpsurvey@nrc.ch.

Women's Commission for Refugee Women and Children, 2001, Against all odds: Surviving the war on adolescents. Promoting the protection and capacity of Ugandan and Sudanese adolescents in northern Uganda. Participatory research study with adolescents in northern Uganda May – July 2001 (PDF version downloaded 10 September 2002). Available online: http://www. womenscommission.org, E-mail: webmaster@womenscommission.org.

Woodward, P., 1991, "Uganda and southern Sudan 1986–9: New regimes and peripheral politics", in H. Bernt Hansen and M. Twaddle (eds), *Changing Uganda: The dilemmas of structural adjustment and revolutionary change*. London, Kampala, Athens & Nairobi: James Currey/Fountain Press/Ohio University Press/Heinemann Kenya.

CHAPTER 8

The Serendipity of Rebellious Politics
Inclusion and exclusion in a Togolese town

Nadia Lovell

"Youth" is often associated with processes of exclusion, marginalisation, violence and social modes of behaviour perceived as threatening to the (adult) social order. When analysed in a political light, these modes of behaviour are imbued with an intentionality that overtly challenges the socio-political order and the power of political elites. I argue that the various paths used by young people to channel their ambitions, frustrations and activities often take on a haphazard character, and are not always expressed in openly politicised language. Exclusion, inclusion and dissent are therefore not monolithic categories, but are played upon —sometimes through one's own choice, sometimes through force of circumstance —in ways that enable the protagonists to walk various paths towards socially accepted adulthood. The case studies presented in this chapter illustrate the randomness of the process and the need for more refined tools of analysis. Of course, the notion of civil society and its political impact is not new (see for instance Mamdani 1996; Bayart et al. 1997; or the work of Scheper-Hughes and Lock 1987 and 1990, on the various levels of politicisation of bodily action), nor is the use of religion as the embodiment of political subversion. The manner in which political activism is expressed, and how it intersects with the sociality of young people, constitute the focal points of this chapter.

It is generally agreed that the political activism that characterised the early 1990s in many parts of Africa – including among other countries the Congo, Togo, Benin, Sierra Leone, the Democratic Republic of Congo (then Zaire) – sprang from strong dissent against the hegemony of political establishments which had been in power for too long. Post-independence states had been created in order to free their populations from the yoke of colonialism and oppression, only to find themselves accused of similar abuses of power a few decades later. The promises delivered at the dawn of independence – promises of freedom, democracy, 'development' and 'modernity' – failed to materialise, or became differently perceived and problematised, as several African nation states became characterised by their inefficiency, corruption and disregard of human rights.[1] This discontent, paired with frustration at the overly bureaucratised structure of public institutions, led to burgeoning democratic movements which became more vocal over time, leading in some cases to a relatively peaceful transition to democratic rule (such as was the case in Benin and Zambia) or to violent conflict (former Zaire, the Congo) and to the dissolution of many post-independent state structures. However, burgeoning democratic movements have experienced difficulties in sustaining their original momentum. In the case of Togo, violent upheaval resulted in many bloody deaths, and promises of reform, which have yet to materialise. After initial instability, a *modus vivendi* had been established between the opposition and the president. Eyadéma remained in power until his death in 2005, in spite of years of intermittent dissent.[2]

Yet beyond the discontent expressed against power-holders whose rule is considered too authoritarian and despotic lay other factors which can be analysed from a more structural perspective, and that can be linked to age factors and questions of life-cycle. Many of Africa's postcolonial states are ruled by a gerontocracy, while the vast majority of their populations are below the age of 25. The renewal of the political sphere which is promised with regular intervals by political power-holders tends to replicate gerontocratic ideals, and often leads to the perpetuation of the same age structures as are already in place (for a more detailed discussion, see Chabal and Daloz 1999; Ellis 1996). Thus the transition of governments and the process of democratisation still centre on the empowerment of political establishments whose resources are both symbolic (age) and factual (economic).

---

1. This is not to say that problems of corruption and bureaucratic inefficiency can be attributed solely to the infrastructure of African states. Anyone even vaguely familiar with the political scene in Africa is well aware of the international dimensions of this problem. The waves of protests that swept over many parts of the African continent in the 1990s were as much concerned with reforming the national political scene, as they were with expressing discontent towards international governments and their meddling in African domestic politics. The role of European and American elites in sustaining despotic regimes cannot be underestimated. For more details, see for instance Smith and Glaser 1992, 1997, Bayart et al. 1997.

2. He was succeded by his son, Faure Gnassingbe, after a constitutional coup led, in part, by the country's loyal army.

As Chabal and Daloz (ibid.) postulate, the symbolic capital conferred by age is not only attributed to a general deference to old age: longevity also allows for the accumulation of financial resources and human capital in the form of followers.

It is in this context that youth movements and the political activities of young people need to be understood. It has for instance been pointed out that many youths resort to violence in the expression of political dissent (El-Kenz 1996; Cruise O'Brien 1996; Bayart 1992). Indeed violence may well be one viable response in the face of what is perceived as the intractability of immutable structures, particularly when such violence is channelled through military coups led by young military personnel. Yet much of the discontent which erupted in the 1990s in various places in Africa found its source among populations which were not originally bent on the use of violence, and which strongly opposed the intervention of their countries' armies. This goes to show that the pool of dissent is multifaceted, and that the dissatisfaction felt by the young may find different modes of expression. Street violence may be seen as one response, violence perpetrated by the army as another. Both may find their source in a similar frustration when faced with the same rigid and unreformed political institutions.

Political activism, dissent and the unbridled use of violence have often been characterised as a prerogative of the young. Indeed the very category of youth is itself often recognised through its purported potential to use violence. The definition suffers from circularity, and this dilemma highlights the difficulty of delineating what constitutes the 'young'. The United Nations officially defines 'youth' as including all individuals between the ages of fifteen and twenty-four. Adhering to such a classification would make matters simple, but hardly reflects the complexities inherent in the social relationships that sustain the existence of such a category. All individuals between the ages of fifteen and twenty-four may easily be included in an identifable age-group, yet whether this qualifies them all to be treated, socially, as youths remains open to discussion. Inversely, an elderly man in West Africa may be buried without any funerary rites or celebrations since he never fathered any children. He is therefore not deemed a proper adult by his peers, and is denied an afterlife as well as an appropriate sending-off ceremony. His old age confers upon him certain rights in earthly life, such as the respect of children and economic security, but provides no further privileges in terms of authority or status. Having no children makes him still a youth. Thus a person may be categorised as a youth well beyond the age of twenty-four if individual achievements have failed to seal his/her social status. 'Youth' is therefore best treated as a floating category, one whose boundaries fluctuate and depend both on individual predicaments and on social and political influencing factors (Bayart 1992; Bayart et al. 1997; Argenti 2001, 2005; Argenti and de Waal 2002; Toulabor 1992a).

If being more than twenty-four years of age did qualify an individual as reaching adulthood, one could then easily surmise that the use of violence would dwindle over time among members of the senior group.[3] Yet the fact that dissent and violence are being used to such an extent in many post-independence conflicts, and include groups whose age ranges from childhood to adulthood,[4] may indicate the difficulty in achieving a socially accepted adulthood through other means. The lack of employment opportunities highlights a cycle of exclusion often deemed difficult to break. While exclusion, dissent and, sometimes, violence, may originally be intended only as temporary strategies for the construction of a socially acceptable identity, they may become perennial attributes where only limited opportunities exist for an established sense of adulthood. However, viewing youth and violence as such inextricably linked categories too easily leads to pathologising the condition of young people. Indeed further trouble brews ahead if one considers that the condition of youth is often associated with irresponsible sexuality, unemployment, the use and abuse of drugs, unsettled modes of life, the spread of diseases and many other negative plights. If seen in this light as pathology, the young need to find ways of surviving this condition. They are deprived of a sense of agency in their own predicament, are victimised in the process, and find themselves stripped of being proper contributors in the shaping of society.

Classical anthropological studies have described the transition from childhood to adulthood as characterised by often traumatic and life-changing events (La Fontaine 1985; Richards 1956; Turner 1969). The use of abduction, seclusion, physical punishment, regular beatings and other forms of structural violence are commonplace in the context of what are most often described as initiation rituals. Yet initiation rituals often only

---

3. Indeed the category of the warrior, in classical ethnography, has often been described as concomitant with that of youth. Thus the *moran* among the Maasai and Samburu is characterised by his youth (Sommer 1993); and becoming a warrior and using violence are seen as inherent components in the passage to adulthood (cf. Heald's ethnography of the Gisu, 1999). The Kabye warrior is also represented as the archetypal youth, strong, stubborn and ready to fight (Piot 1999; Verdier 1982). Political power, by contrast, is described as being in the hands of the older, senior men who have thus reached adulthood, and who do not take up arms.

4. If one considers only actual age.

demarcate the first phase in what has been described as a long process of becoming. Thus the abduction which marks the Ndembu's classical initiation rites, and which spatially separates a boy from his homestead and socially removes him from his experiences of childhood, has to be complemented with other acts in order to contribute to the achievement of adulthood. The process of becoming is, in this way, never fully completed. Only the passage of time, and the fulfillment of one's life cycle with its concomitant responsibilities, fully contribute to the process. Initiation and other rituals are therefore best treated only as markers. For instance, the Kabye's initiation of young males is expected to take ten to twelve years, and the initial act of abduction demarcates only the very beginning of this process (Piot 1999). Likewise among the Samburu, where the abduction of young boys signals only the first step towards their becoming warriors (Spencer 1965 1990). The altered status of initiates has been documented in many parts of Africa. Significantly, this shift in status is often accompanied by altered social relationships and, while initiation lasts, a more permissive social code in the youths' behaviour towards adults and elders. Maasai warriors are often irreverent in their treatment of senior men, whom they should normally obey and towards whom they should show deference. Vodhun[5] initiates can insult other adults in their community without sanction during the performance of initiation rituals. Rather than treat these episodes as simply part of an anti-structure (in Turner's sense), they can be seen as a preparation towards the endorsing of ever-increasing responsibilities in the path towards adulthood.

However meaningful these approaches might be, they remain incomplete, primarily because they tend to treat 'youth' as a residual category, as an incomplete agent whose actions have to be directed and orchestrated by adults (senior men and women) in order to achieve proper and complete personhood and walk the proper path towards an already established and fully accepted social identity. Thus youth itself has become, like the rituals that characterise it, a category betwixt and between, marginal to the workings of society. The study of youths has appeared to serve the purpose of confirming the validity of the current social order, thereby taking on a de-

---

5. Vodhun constitutes the major religion of southern Togo, Benin and southwestern Ghana. Although commonly associated in the Western imagination with black magic and superstition, its cosmology and practice are similar to most religious forms, in Africa and elsewhere. The term vodhun is commonly used in Ewe, Fon and Anlo to describe a god specifically, or the religious complex as a whole (see Lovell 2002).

cidedly functional and static bias. Through ritual, the transformation of the young into adults thus serves to reaffirm and reproduce the current social order, and whatever protests are built into liminality itself hardly jeopardise the overall fabric of society. Youths have been particularly subjected to an academic scrutiny where their social, political and economic contribution to social structures has become muted, submerged in a dominant discourse that prioritises the world of adults. As De Boeck and Honwana express it "leurs actions sont le plus souvent reléguées à un champs sous-culturel à peine perceptible et aux effets marginaux" (2000:8). I would argue, however, that this forgetfulness towards the young as a proper subject of investigation, and their marginalisation in methodology and analysis, does not only affect the study of youths in Africa, as De Boeck and Honwana postulate (ibid:8) but is far more generalised. Indeed this state of affairs may reflect the predicament of the observer, rather than a particular neglect directed at youths in Africa or elsewhere. After all, the categories of childhood, adolescence ('youth'), and adulthood are historical products of the modern society configured in Europe since the Enlightenment. Youth itself is therefore created through modernity,[6] through a classification which separates and segregates. Seen in linear terms, the development of a proper sense of personhood can only be achieved through the passage of time, and through an organised and ordered transition from one category to the next. The power of analysis is, therefore, only given to the last category as a repository for fully-fledged knowledge and "rationality".[7]

Youth, in this modern sense, may today be an extant category, but its historical antecedents need to be made obvious. Its transnational applicability may mostly remain unquestioned today especially when its impact on colonial and post-colonial policies is taken into account. However, this "modern" category of youth, often reinforced through the allocation of a specific date of birth, school registration and attendance, membership of

---

6. I use the term "modernity" in a wide sense here, referring to post-Enlightenment developments in Europe, but also to the impact of this concept on areas outside of Europe. Modernity needs to be seen as a European historical concept, which has had consequences on the classification of various population groups since the Enlightenment. For instance, most Francophone nations in Sub-Saharan Africa house a Ministry of Youth and Sports (Le Ministère de la Jeunesse et des Sports), created to promote the leisure activities of the young in their respective countries.

7. In addition, personhood and rationality are also highly gendered attributes. Women's intellectual abilities have often been placed on a par with those of children. The Enlightenment and its focus on the family contributed to entrenching these classifications.

school clubs, access to higher education for a few and so on, intersects with the category of youth as it has been socially carved out in the local context, through, for instance, ritual initiation and the adherence to age groups. As we shall see, it is at the intersection between local forms of defining childhood and youth as social categories, and the wider applicability of these categories within the context of "modern" politics, that such constructs gain meaning today.

The question of agency is of the essence here. If local rituals of initiation confer upon the new members of an age group obligations and responsibilities they lacked before the process had taken place, then young people are only treated as recipients that need to be filled, and whose agency in the process is very limited. Similarly, the notion of the agency of children and youths in political (and violent) contexts has come to the fore in recent studies of child soldiers in areas of armed conflict (see Utas 2003 and Honwana 2000, 2005).

If young people are to be given full agency, the impact of their actions, choices and strategies has to be seen as an integral part of the social fabric rather as action conducive only, in linear fashion, to adulthood as it has preliminarily been defined. Neither category can be fixed in time and place. What young people do, they do for a reason. Some of the motivation may indeed involve replicating an older generation's social structure, doing things for 'tradition' or for pleasing one's seniors, such as partaking in initiation rituals that have been reformed for the purpose. Other things may be done in protest, in direct opposition or conflict with an older generation. Yet there is plenty of room, between adherence and objection, for motivations that go beyond already established routes.

It has been argued that the shifting contexts of social organisation in Africa have contributed to a redefinition of initiation rituals and a reconfiguration of their contents (see Argenti 1998, 2002, 2005; Cole 1998; Piot 1999), while maintaining a sense of continuity with the past. Thus initiation rites have not disappeared with the advent of urban life, schooling and salaried work, but they have, rather, taken on new forms in order to fulfil the purpose of marking important events in the life cycle. As we shall see in the case studies presented below, these transformations, however crucial to the insertion of the individual into the various communities that surround them, fail in the end to provide the necessary anchorage which could have avoided the rupture of the social fabric. This is particularly true in the first case study presented in this chapter. Thus while the African context proves to be highly adaptable to the shifting predicaments of post-independence politics, there is no doubt that a sense of disruption is also present.[8]

Marginality has been described as a typical and temporary feature of initiation rituals in classical anthropological studies, often associated with the liminal position of initiates, and leading to a change in status which confers new and enhanced rights on the protagonists. The power of 'traditional' rituals has however dwindled, although schooling, traineeships or military service may in many cases have replaced initiation rituals as markers of identity and status passage. Yet as the opportunities to acquire jobs and participate actively in the social and political scenes have decreased in the post-independence era, marginality has become a permanent fixture in the life of many young people. Contemporary analysts postulate that the bleak political outlook for many African states resides in their failure to assimilate the young into active economic, cultural and social roles (Mbembe 1985, Chabal and Daloz 1999, Bayart et al. 1997). Thus the disempowerment felt by many young actors on the African continent emerges not from the transformation of past social institutions into forms better adapted to current social and political requirements,[9] but rather from the fact that the purpose of such social institutions itself becomes questionable, and the outcome of participation in the performance of such activities uncertain or even obsolete. Hence the difficulties faced by the young lie in the political failure to reinsert these young individuals into a working community characterised by orderly social relationships. However, as marginality becomes the norm, new forms of agency also emerge.

I now turn briefly to a case study, which illustrates the potential mechanisms underpinning processes of exclusion and inclusion, with the ancillary protests and frustrations commonly associated with youth as a category. The haphazard nature of political activism is also clearly demonstrated here. The often-unforeseen consequences of unpredictable and unintentionally political actions[10] may eventually be constitutive of different kinds of adulthood. Exclusion and inclusion are therefore not given monolithic forms, but are played upon – sometimes through one's own choice, some-

---

8. Whether this is a purely African predicament remains to be debated.

9. Durkheim referred to the loss of past meaning as 'anomie'. Rather than treat changing meanings in terms of loss, the notion of transformation may prove more useful. Thus obtaining an education may replace certain initiation rituals, or military service be equated with formerly becoming a hunter.

10. Or of actions often perceived as insignificantly threatening to the political order.

times through force of circumstance – in ways that enable the protagonists to walk various paths.

Innocent youth or political activist?
A boy's trajectory to unrequested fame[11]

Gabriel[12] is a young, successful, university student in the Department of Philosophy of a West African university. He has just started his second year of a Bachelor's degree, is well acquainted with the social and cultural scene of the capital city, writes short stories and novels in his spare time... He is a highly sociable young man and counts among his circle of friends, a large number of other students like himself and a few mostly French or French-speaking expatriates. He spends his evenings talking late into the night about literature, politics, and cultural events in the city and beyond. He has never been abroad. Education and a perfect command of the *lingua franca* are his tickets to a better life. His mother is a widow and he is, like many of his peers, part of an upcoming generation for whom education is seen as a fundamental means of achieving a better future than that accorded to their parents. Indeed schooling is still considered by the older generation as a viable avenue, although it is becoming obvious to most that the opportunities previously afforded to the educated are becoming increasingly constrained. More than sixty per cent of the young attend at least high school. Problems of employment usually set in later.[13]

---

11. The bulk of the material for this case study was collected at the height of political dissent in Togo in 1990 and 1991. Despite the fictional tone I use here, the case study describes real-life events experienced by one single protagonist, who is also a close friend. I am grateful to the anonymous reader of a previous version of my chapter for pointing out that the heuristic style I have used may lead the reader to believe that the story is made up of composite characters, whose stories have been amalgamated for academic purposes. This is not the case. The protagonist is a single individual. His anonymity is protected in the text out of respect for his privacy. Although he is now safe in his country of adoption, he has not flouted his status as a political refugee, and the details of his arrival in Europe are unknown to most of his readership. In a similar vein, information about his flight has, to my knowledge, remained relatively sketchy in Togo. Preserving his anonymity seems a matter of decency.

12. Not his real name.

13. See Marie-France Lange's (1999) detailed ethnography of schools and schooling in Togo. She includes discussions on 'déscolarisation', the problem of disaffected educated youths and why the educational system has failed in many instances to achieve its goals.

His short stories and novels take on a decidedly more political tone as his experience of university life grows. His lecturers have not been paid for months and, their loyalty to their students notwithstanding, find the economic and political situation increasingly frustrating. Eventually, after months of negotiations with their government, and after many broken promises of a forthcoming resolution, the lecturers decide to go on strike. Their students support them, inciting to student strikes to be held simultaneously. They distribute pamphlets in the streets of the capital, complaining about the lack of opportunities available to those who have completed their studies (their teachers, obviously) but also of the bleak outlook facing the 'déscolarisés', the generation of young people either unable to complete school or those who manage to become educated yet face a future where there are, basically, no jobs to be had. Rumours spread among the students that government infiltrators are also distributing such leaflets, in order to identify "trouble-makers" and student leaders. The crackdown on activists is almost immediate, and relentless. Government troops are sent in, shoot a large number of students and other sympathisers, mostly young men and women living in the city's most deprived areas. Many of the bodies are dumped in the sea.

The country's experience of post-independence is similar to that of many of its neighbours. Public institutions are perceived to have failed their populations in providing the opportunities promised after decolonisation. The political elite is considered too corrupt to be able to deliver anything but empty promises and, on a wider scale, international interests contribute to sustaining the political career of a president whose human rights credentials leave much to be desired. 'Education leads us nowhere' one of my friends tells me. Yet the hope remains.

A short novel entitled 'The Snooping' is sent by Gabriel as an entry to the biennial literary competition organised by Radio France Internationale in order to promote the work of Francophone authors in the French equivalent of the British Commonwealth. The theme of the novel is political: the denouncement of dissidents by ordinary citizens, the creation of undercover security networks which infiltrate everything from youth groups to family structures, attracting private individuals through the promise of quick money and the backing of the political establishment. Based on shifting loyalties, a murky sense of morality and, above all, resignation in the face of a political system which has relinquished all responsibility for the well being of its citizens, such tactics become commonplace and offer informers alternative livelihoods as collaborators with the regime. What

Gabriel describes is the futility of this situation: trust has long disappeared from the relationships between close friends and family members. Snooping itself provides nothing but short-term rewards and the possibility of a quick buck. Above all, most people living in urban centres are acutely aware of this issue. Suspicion reigns. Torture and the violation of human rights likewise.

Much to his surprise, Gabriel wins the first prize, sees his work widely publicised in the international media, and is involved in its setting up as a theatre play in his own country, under the aegis of international backers. As he expresses it: *J'ai écrit ça comme un exercice. Jamais je n'aurais cru que ça pouvait aller si loin*.[14] At this stage, he lands in the political spotlight of the country's authorities. No longer a faceless youth studying at university or staging protests in the streets, he is deemed a dangerous political agitator mobilising public opinion for subversive purposes. Of equal concern to the authorities is the international attention attracted by his work, which puts national politics in the spotlight. The fictional character of his novel fools no one. Gabriel is eventually arrested, taken hostage by the security police. He 'disappears' for a few weeks, is eventually found by a few friends, wandering lost in a derelict area of the city. He has been battered, tortured, starved for many days, stripped naked, electrocuted and put under pressure to denounce his peers. All will be well, he is told, if he agrees to 'cooperate' with the regime. He is told that his talents can be useful to the state. Redemption and a secure future are promised him if he agrees to provide the authorities with names, those of the youths who agitate on the university campus, and create networks of dissent which only lead to political devastation (and here, Gabriel's fiction and reality become increasingly intertwined). It is these activities, he has been told, which bring the country to its knees, and leave it in the grip of unrest and violence. Gabriel is eventually smuggled out of the country, and becomes a test case for Amnesty International in the country where he seeks political asylum. He is among the very first refugees to arrive, and is originally met with incredulity by its authorities. His home country has long been considered one of the most stable in Africa, and has since its independence enjoyed strong and intimate economic ties with many European democracies.

***

In the early 1990s, Togo was deemed by most international (that is European) observers as a stable West African power. Its president, Eyadéma, had

---

14. This was a writing exercise. I never thought it would get this far.

been in power since 1967, and had stabilised the country's finances through the establishment of a tax-free zone which attracted foreign investment and transformed the port of Lomé into one of the most prosperous business ventures in this part of the continent. The authoritarian and despotic nature of Eyadéma's rule was therefore often overlooked by his European counterparts. A tacit understanding between the ruling powers and international actors was put in place: the latter turned a blind eye to human rights abuses and to the lack of economic opportunities available outside the capital in exchange for favourable tax laws and placement opportunities. The fact that large numbers of the population were marginalised through the implementation of economic policies favouring the president's own ethnic group, the Kabye, contributed to growing discontent in many parts of the country, and particularly in the south, where the Ewe have felt penalised for their continued support to the Olympio and Grunitsky dynastic families most vehemently opposed to Eyadéma's rule. While neighbouring Benin experienced unrest, political dissent, violent demonstrations, and economic standstill, Togo managed to remain unperturbed by the wave of demands for greater democratisation that affected many African countries.

The status quo could only last so long. What many had previously described as the placidity and indifference of the Togolese to the political arena suddenly exploded into violent protests, demonstrations and run-ins with the police and military forces. What originally started as student protests in 1990 quickly spread to many sectors of society affected by the economic downturn of Togo after the fall in price of its main exports, phosphates and cotton. The political developments in neighbouring Benin, where the beginning of a democratisation process was taking place, made the opposition increasingly bold and vocal. Despite the violent response of the military, who were ordered to shoot at protesters, dissent continued for many months.

The scene became bloody: the lagoon in the centre of the capital became filled with corpses and blood, the market in the capital (one of the largest in West Africa), was closed, and universities were drained of both students and staff. Work places were deserted, and civil servants were not paid. Bodies were dumped in the sea, hands and feet cuffed, and floated ashore in Ghana. Many people were arrested, tortured, some were released and others killed. The situation in the street can be described as nothing but one of fear. Yet as many neighbouring countries underwent similar experiences, pressure was building on the Togolese government to set up a national commission for the establishment of democratic rule, and to put in place a transitional government to supervise this changeover. This is where Eyadéma demonstrated his skill as a political survivor.[15] Most of the opposition was swallowed into the government, thus restraining the impact of constitutional reforms. Lawyers and other activists lobbying for a renewal of the political arena were neutralised through their inclusion in government, thus leaving oppositional politics in an acephalous condition. Popular protests and violence have flared up at regular intervals since, often culminating in scenes similar to those described above, yet the opposition has remained in check, incapable of regaining its original impetus. Although the situation is now less inflamed, the European Union maintained its economic embargo against Togo until November 2004. Democratic reforms are not imminent.

***

At the level of the individual body politic, the situation need not be as dramatic for most youths as it has been for Gabriel, nor is the outlook as bleak everywhere. Gabriel's case highlights in condensed form some of the issues facing many postcolonial African states, and the vicissitudes of its young population. Yet political activism also involves the positive participation of actors who genuinely seek to highlight their own predicament, contribute to public debates, and inform the political scene while seeking to promote the interests of their age group. The situation of many African countries is often depicted in overly bleak and dramatic terms. While it is important to highlight the difficulties facing the populations of African countries whose political situation does indeed leave much to be desired, a more nuanced focus on the positive outcomes of non-violent political participation is also necessary (as is illustrated by Havard 2001, for instance).

It is to be expected that political activism, both positive engagement leading to the setting-up of collaborative networks with government and civil organisations, and negative engagement in the form of dissidence and subversive activities, occurs at individual and organised levels. Although this area of research is relatively new, it has so far focused almost exclusively on youth violence and marginality (Abbink 2001; El Kenz 1996; Mbembe 1985; Utas 2003), dissent and subversion (Toulabor 1992b).

Furthermore, political activism can be expressed in other ways that also require investigation. The interface between political activities and religion should not be neglected, as religious institutions can provide a springboard

---

15. This is not unusual on the political scene in West and Central Africa. Many opposition figures have thus been restrained through similar political play.

for political action within the postcolonial state. The upsurge of renewal movements such as independent Christian churches or Islamism (for lack of a better term), for instance, can be seen as some of the structures channelling political activism (van Dijk 1998). They provide a rupture with the past, and a distancing from state institutions that have failed to deliver on their promises (Meyer 1998; Mullings 1984; see also Hours (1985) on the state and health care). The fact that religion represents political action, and provides a window of opportunity for the expression of political subversion and activism, has been highlighted elsewhere (see for instance Comaroff 1985; Taussig 1987, 1993) but this aspect of religion has seldom been analytically explored in light of the predicament of young people (but see Argenti 1998, 2005).

The connection between religious activity/activism and the state in Togo is multifaceted. Up until the mid-1990s, Togo adhered rather strictly to a policy of authenticity that favoured local religious movements, at least in theory. Modelled on Mobutu's policy of authenticity in then Zaire, this stance was aimed at promoting local 'traditions' by guaranteeing their right to existence in the post-colony (a badly needed act, considering their exposed status under colonial rule and the concomitant anti-witchcraft legislation). However, this stance also acted to legitimate the state in its capacity as a truly African symbol. The creation of nation-states may have been imposed by colonial powers, and have been sustained in the post-independence era through national governments, but the adherence to Africanity provided a means of securing the authority of the nation-state in the modern era. In Togo, unlike the situation in Zaire, independent churches had barely gained any ground before the 1990s. The Assembly of God had a few churches scattered here and there, but these hardly posed a threat either to the state, to the established Catholic Church, or to 'traditional' religious groups. Nevertheless, religious activity did, in many instances, provide an avenue for the expression of political feelings. The extent to which these could be considered political actions is a matter for further investigation. However, their insertion into the body politic of the country is unquestionable.

The path of religion

A young man, let us call him Koffi, is a student in one of the schools in the capital. He is in his last year, a few months away from his Baccalaureate exams, which he expects to pass without difficulty. He speaks fluent French, his family is, by many standards, relatively well off, although there are no precedents of academic achievement among his relatives. Koffi's confidence in his own ability to perform well in his exams is coupled with an anxiety towards what lies beyond the end of his schooling. Hordes of educated young men and women remain unemployed, unable to find jobs to suit their qualifications. Those with enough means may set up their own business, many become pedlars more through force of circumstance than by choice.

Koffi arrives one day at the shrine of one of the most powerful healers in the south-east region. He is in a state of extreme agitation. He hits out at anyone who tries to approach him, uses the most obscene, aggressive and threatening abuse. Two male relatives walk by his side and try to control his movements. He is, quite simply, in a rage. Most passers-by compassionately get out of the way. Koffi has suddenly fallen ill, he describes his own state as one of madness, saying that others in his vicinity wish to harm him and see him fail his exams. He is acutely aware that his illness most probably signals the end of his studies. The exams are to take place in a few weeks, and in his madness, he interjects with great clarity and presence of mind that he will be unable to return to the capital and to his studies before the exams take place.

For the next few weeks, Koffi remains at the healer's house. He is originally chained to the ground and heavily sedated through the use of local drugs in order for his agitation to subside and his aggression towards others and himself to decline. His effusive ramblings continue for a long time, but become less aggressive as the drugs take effect. Still uttered in perfect French (a language which most around him in the healer's homestead and village could not understand) and interspersed with Ewe, he accuses individuals in his family of having harmed him. He also interjects insults at teachers and politicians who have made his situation impossible. Only the rich are given a chance in the country, only those with connections, and so it goes on.

Whereas such open criticism of civil servants and government representatives would, in other circumstances, have been unacceptable and possibly have led to his arrest, reporting him to the authorities in the current situation was unthinkable for most. His madness made him speak in tongues, and those parts of the conversation that were actually understood by those around him were treated in the same way; as statements uttered under the influence of powers beyond his control. Lucid political commentaries were thus neutralised and condoned by illness.

Koffi gradually felt better, although his heavy sedation continued for several months. He was eventually instructed by his healer to install a shrine on behalf of a vodhun. The deity would offer protection against harmful thoughts (his own) and nefarious actions (those of others upon him) for a lifetime. His connection to the cosmological realm would ensure security, prosperity and, not least, the possibility of becoming an apprentice healer. In due course, this may translate into a potential income as a professional practitioner.

***

The two case studies presented here may appear disparate. To what extent can they be used as exemplars of what has occurred on the political scene in Togo in recent years? The individual predicaments of our two informants may be contextualised differently.

Koffi's story is replicated far and wide in many communities in the south and southeast of Togo, where vodhun religion has provided a strong framework for dissent since colonial times. A large number of adepts are thus 'recuperated' from schools, called upon by the gods to adhere to their shrines. Modernity is thus constantly challenged by religious institutions representing 'authenticity' and purity from outside interference (see also Moran 1988, 1990). However, as I have argued elsewhere (Lovell 2002), this challenge invokes tradition in a highly politicised fashion, and questions in no uncertain terms the predicament of young men and women in the context of the modern state. The gendered aspects therefore are among what is most prominently commented upon, as modernity often has a tendency to polarise gender differences, thus increasing the economic opportunities available to men at the expense of women who have, for a very long time, been predominant in (what is referred to as) the informal market. Bringing young men and women back to the vodhun acts as a powerful reminder of this gender dimension. Women are amongst the most powerful protagonists in this sphere, and men have to acknowledge the duality of creation when being called upon to erect a shrine. Thus Koffi's story is very similar to that of many young men and women in the region, and it is not unusual to witness the arrival of youths of both genders facing similar situations as the one described here. Second-hand information is also common.

Gabriel's story may appear more unique: most youths similarly and unwittingly engaged in politics remain untouched by the level of scrutiny afforded to his case. Many are able to oppose the regime without coming to the authorities' attention. And while political activism in Togo has been largely bridled by the political establishment (and the continued covert activities of informers), 'coming of age' and coping have largely lost their marginality as more young people join the ranks of the officially unemployed. Marginality becomes accepted as prolonged periods of exclusion that gain a momentum of their own. 'La débrouille'[16] becomes a way of life in the city, where seedy life-styles mix with dreams and hopes that the 'informal' market will open up possibilities not available in the orderly and insitutionalised sphere of formal employment. Some do indeed succeed. Yet the predicament of the 'déscolarisés' and the unemployed remains a problem for those in power, who have proved unable to renew the economic, political and social spheres. This would have appeared, a few years ago, to provide the only viable solution to a population in uproar and the political elite, in its efforts to uphold its privileges, is well aware of the double bind this creates. It seems, however, that the notion of politics has to be reconfigured, as the quiet understanding of most urban youths today is that things are happening elsewhere. The 'Politique par le Bas' (Bayart 1992) has particular resonance in this context.

Gabriel's and Koffi's political trajectories spring from similar impulses, and emerge from similar circumstances. Both demonstrate prowess in their academic performance, both are intellectually gifted to the extent of becoming noticed for their achievements, propelling them into the social limelight. Both are subjected to particular scrutiny. Koffi experiences the jealousy and ill-will of his peers and relatives, Gabriel is told in no uncertain terms to put his talent to better use and ally himself with the powers in place. Both are also from relatively simple[17] urban backgrounds. They have no family connections to back them up, few networks to allow for their political activism to be channelled into a future job in government. Both are, according to those around them, gifted and endowed with exceptional academic talent. Yet both perceive that they face a bleak future within the collapsed structure of the state (see Toulabor 1992a on the "conjonctures" in Lomé).

The motivations which lead Koffi and Grabriel to become involved in political activism have a common ground, namely discontent with an overly oppressive political regime, although their responses appear, at least at a superficial level, to be quite disparate. Yet both have to be seen as powerful

16. To cope, to manage. The French term connotes creativity, opportunism and resignation at the same time.

17. Referring to their social situation.

forms of dialogical engagement, and both speak to similar audiences at the various levels of local, national and international politics (see Shaw (2002) on the embodiment of political power in traditional practice). Dichotomising the experiences of these two main actors may lead to analytical conclusions where the realms of politics and religion are separately assessed, and it would indeed be a mistake to treat Koffi's religious activity as a surrogate for political engagement, while viewing Gabriel's overt antagonism as the 'real thing': an action which openly antagonises the political authority of current leaders and which leads to intimidation, threats and, eventually, to exile abroad. It is important to point out, however, that this modernistic and dichotomising view on dissent is adhered to by the regime when attempting to identify political dissidents. The government itself appears to believe that there is real —and unreal? — activism, rational response in the form of demonstrations and the writing of oppositional pamphlets, and irrational performance in the form of healing rituals and acts of possession.[18] Indeed the government seldom clamps down on religious cults, even though many of them offer their space as a sanctuary to the politically malcontented. The military actions taken against political dissidents (as opposed to vodhun adepts, for instance) only reinforce the dichotomy. One action is interpreted as an overt challenge to the authority of the state, while the other remains not only unthreatening but is seen as conformist in light of the authenticity policy implemented by the authorities. The ironic twist comes in the final act of Gabriel's exile. While his literary production denounces the 'recuperation' of dissidents by the political establishment in his home country, his exile abroad announces his own 'recuperation' by the international community; a community which condones only recognised forms of political activism.[19] Koffi would hardly qualify as an asylum seeker in this context. Yet both actors denounce, through the use of different idioms, the abuses of power and the political oppression affected by the regime and its ruling elite.

The framework needs to be broadened. Unlike many other similar contexts in Africa, the Togolese political scene has remained, by and large,

---

18. See Taussig (1997) for an inspiring parallel.

19. A fact which Gabriel openly recognises. Indeed his trajectory from an unknown student to an internationally acclaimed author is fraught with open frustration at being caught in-between various political discourses. Human rights groups claim him as a protégé, the Togolese government wishes to use his services, and the international community which supports his authorship relishes his condemnation of the political elite in his home country.

almost entirely secular, and the official stance is one of tolerance towards all religious manifestations. There is no declared official religion, although Catholicism is widely acknowledged as being the most influential denomination in the south of the country and in many central regions. Most blatantly, the restrictive stance taken by Eyadéma Senior towards the establishment of independent churches on Togolese territory, a direct result of his policy of authenticity, has resulted in their weak presence in Togo. Independent churches have elsewhere often acted as channels for the expression of political dissent, particularly among the young, who have invested these religious movements with political activism and demands for renewal of the socio-economic fields (as well as Africanity, see Mullings 1984). Political activism in Togo has, until recently, not been channelled through such new religious ideologies. Vodhun has provided the most obvious religious context for recuperation and muted defiance (see also Lovell 2002).

Can one interpret this kind of religious engagement in such blatantly functional terms? Is the diagnosis of Koffi's madness nothing but the re-interpretation of symptoms from one politically charged context to another, pacified and made harmless through the use of religious idioms and paraphernalia? In other words, is political oppression so simply neutralised?

Not necessarily. There is no doubt that vodhun, as one of many local/national religious traditions, provides some kind of Geertzian meaning through its historical anchorage and its subtle responses to colonial politics, the advent of 'modernity' and the experience of post-independence. Yet the performance of healing in Togo is also highly politicised: established 'traditional' healers are acutely aware of the power of recuperation inherent in their practices, and know that they express a condensed, muted, yet powerful response to untenable political conditions. The role of traditional healers in the expression of political dissent has been highlighted in several studies on healing in Africa (Comaroff (1985) on healing and colonial politics; Lan (1985) on healing and violence in post-colonial Zimbabwe, and Comaroff and Comaroff (1993) on religion and politics in a broader context) and elsewhere (Kapferer (1991) on the sometimes ludic character of subversion; Taussig (1987, 1993) on the historical dimensions of healing and politics). The fact that religion acts as a conduit for political activism leads to a reformulation of how the political sphere is constituted.

If analysed simply as a muted and subversive response to oppressive political authority, religious activism would too easily fall prey to old Marxist interpretations, which consider it mainly as a surrogate or vicarious activity awaiting real political engagement.[20] In order to evade a purely functional interpretation, one has to shift the focus to the wider arena of power politics. Without overtly condemning the regime, without ever becoming in the least explicitly politically active, healers and their clients are aware that religious activities provide a sanctuary for healing the wounds of 'modernity' and those inflicted by post-independence politics, while simultaneously extending the power of vodhun. Local actors thus turn the president's politics of authenticity, lauded as an effort to celebrate Africanity, into a powerful and ludic commentary on the distribution of power in society. Religion is thus far from being simply a performance of 'tradition' commandeered by the state to be displayed on special occasions. It becomes a pivot in turning authenticity on its head. Power shifts from being in the hands of governmental officials to becoming located in the diffuse realm of religion, where adherents know their reasons and motivations for practicing vodhun, something which often by-passes many a civil servant.[21]

Epilogue

Although 'youths' as a category feature in many scholarly endeavours, the research conducted so far has remained relatively unproblematised not least since the category of youth can hardly be recognised in terms of absolute age. Rather, youth is to do with one's activities, one's demeanour and composure, one's status as a non-adult (not necessarily a child), and one's insertion into recognised power structures. In addition, the debate on youth has remained singularly ungendered. Women, and young women in particular, have often been left outside the realm of politics.

Several aspects could be developed further here: participation in political life is by no means an all male affair. In 1991, the female traders of Lomé went on strike. In effect most of the economic activities in the south

---

20. Cargo cults and prophetic movements have been subjected to similar analysis, and been described as pseudo-political activities (cf. Lucy Mair 1958, 1970; Peter Worsley 1987). Such a subordination of religion to politics is only possible if a rigid classification of these fields is upheld.

21. A number of other works on African vodhun have avoided its political dimension. See the structuralist accounts of Augé (1988), Maupoil (1981), Rivière (1981), de Surgy (1981, 1988), and Preston Blier's psychological essays on vodhun and art in Benin (1995). These provide valuable insights into the metaphysical aspects of vodhun as a religious complex of force in West Africa, but do not extend to include details of how vodhun is incorporated into the daily lives of the actors involved at socio-political levels. Vodhun religion can be seen as intellectual and philosophical theology, but it also informs political practice.

of the country are in the hands of women, who control the market in the capital and also the flow of goods to other parts of the country. Trade is thus almost exclusively a female affair. The market remained closed for several weeks bringing the capital, and large parts of the country, to a complete standstill. There was no food to be bought no cloth to be traded. The women protested at the government's harsh treatment of dissidents.[22] The gender aspect is thus made obvious, as is the issue of age in this context. Yet in spite of women's obvious participation in political action, their role has often been analysed in terms of 'tradition'. In other words, while men are actively protesting against the politics of the postcolonial state, women's involvement is often interpreted, in analytical and theoretical discourse, in terms of its value for preserving the status quo, or representing purity and innocence (see for instance Ogden 1996; Leclerc-Madlala 1997). Thus the activities of young women in the modern state, when it has come under academic scrutiny, have either been cast in light of women's tradition-bearing moral beings in the face of a changing world, providing men and children with security when modernity fails to deliver (thus focusing on the nurturing role of women, while casting this nurturing role entirely in opposition to modernity), or they have been cast as prostitutes and sexual workers when endorsing a modern way of life (thus focusing on women's footloose sexuality when in contact with modernity).

It is at times difficult to discern whether such epistemological polarities result from ethnographic observations or tainted analysis. Nevertheless, new perspectives are needed in order to include women in research on political activism and, in addition, to theorise their contributions in ways which move away from traditionalising discourses or overly sexualising ones. Only through the exploration of the interdependence between men and women can an understanding of each gender's social predicament be achieved.

As for Gabriel, he obtained a permanent residence visa three years after his arrival in Europe, and has not been back 'home' for the past thirteen years. In Europe, he originally joined the ranks of the uninvited, anonymous, homeless and jobless refugees, the endless stream of migrants whose identity is defined mostly in terms of ethnicity and marginality. But that,

---

22. A similar situation has been described in Kenya, where older women protesting against the government's politics under Arap Moi went to the market place and bared their buttocks to the police officers charged with maintaining order during a demonstration. Such a gesture is said to embarrass the viewer rather than the perpetrator, and was a common sign of dissent in colonial times.

as they say, is another story, and another theoretical debate altogether. Nevertheless, things turned out well for him in the end: he continued to write, and is now, after several years of struggling for recognition, widely acclaimed as one of the major Francophone African authors in his country of adoption.

References

Argenti, N., 1998, "Air Youth: Performance, Violence and the State in Cameroon", *The Journal of the Royal Anthropological Institute*, 4(4):753–82.

—, 2001, "Kesum-body and the places of the gods: The politics of children's masking and second-world realities in Oku (Cameroon)", *Journal of the Royal Anthropological Institute*, 7(1):67–94.

—, 2002, "People of the chisel: apprenticeship, youth, and elites in Oku (Cameroon)", *American ethnologist*, 29(3):497–533.

—, 2005, "Dancing in the Borderlands: The Forbidden Masquerades of Women and Children in Oku", in F. De Boeck and A. Honwana (eds), *Makers and Breakers of Society: Children and Youth as Emerging Categories in Postcolonial Africa*. Oxford: James Currey, and Chicago: The University of Chicago Press.

Argenti, N. and A. de Waal, 2002, *Young Africa: Realising the Rights of Children and Youth,* Trenton, NJ: Africa World Press.

Augé, M., 1988, *Le Dieu Objet.* Paris: Editions Flammarion.

Bayart, J.-F., 1992, "La Revanche des Sociétés Africaines". in J.-F. Bayart, A. Mbembe, and C. Toulabor (eds), *Le Politique par le Bas en Afrique Noire*. Paris: Karthala.

Bayart, J.-F., S. Ellis and B. Hibou, 1997, *La Criminalisation de l'Etat en Afrique*. Brussels: Espace International.

Chabal, P. and J.-P. Daloz, 1999, *Africa Works: Disorder as Political Instrument*. The International African Institute, in collaboration with Oxford: James Currey, and Bloomington and Indianapolis: Indiana University Press,.

Cole, J., 1998, "The Work of Memory in Madagascar", *American Ethnologist,* 25:610–633.

Comaroff, J., 1985, *Body of Power, Spirit of Resistance: The Culture and History of a South African People.* Chicago: Chicago University Press.

Comaroff, J. and J. Comaroff, 1993, "Introduction", in J. Comaroff and J. Comaroff (eds), *Modernity and Its Malcontents: Ritual and Power in Postcolonial Africa*. Chicago and London: The University of Chicago Press.

Cruise O'Brien, D.B., 1996, "A Lost Generation? Youth Identity and State Decay in West Africa", in R. Werbner and T. Ranger (eds), *Postcolonial Identities in Africa*. London and New Jersey: Zed Books.

De Boeck, F. and A. Honwana, 2000, "Faire et Defaire la Societe: Enfants, Jeunes et Politique en Afrique", *Politique Africaine*, Special Issue no. 80, Enfants, Jeunes et Politique.

—, (eds), 2004, *Makers and Breakers: Children and Youth in Postcolonial Africa*. Academic Literature. Oxford: James Currey.

Dijk van, R., 1998, "Pentecostalism, Cultural Memory and the State: Contested Representations of Time in Postcolonial Malawi", in R. Werbner (ed.), *Memory and the Postcolony*. London and New Jersey: Zed Books.

El-Kenz, A., 1996, "Youth and Violence", in S. Ellis (ed.), *Africa Now: People, Policies, Institutions*. The Hague: Ministry of Foreign Affairs, in collaboration with London: James Currey, and Portsmouth (NH): Heinemann.

Ellis, S., 1996, "Introduction", in S. Ellis (ed.), *Africa Now: People, Policies, Institutions*. The Hague: DGIS, London: James Currey, and Portsmouth (New Hampshire): Heinemann.

Havard, J.-F., 2001, "Ethos 'Bul Faale' et Nouvelles Figures de la Réussite au Sénégal", *Politique Africaine*, no. 82:63–77.

Heald, S., 1999, *Manhood and Morality: Sex, Violence and Ritual in Gisu Society*. London and New York: Routledge.

Honwana, A., 2000, "Innocents et Coupables: Les Enfants-Soldats comme Acteurs Tactiques", *Politique Africaine*, vol. 80:58–79.

—, 2005, *Child Soldiers in Africa*. Philadelphia: Academic Literature, Pennsylvania University Press.

Hours, B., 1985, *L'Etat Sorcier. Santé Publique et Société au Cameroun*. Paris: L'Harmattan.

Kapferer, B., 1991, *A Celebration of Demons: Exorcism and the Aesthetics of Healing in Sri-Lanka*. Providence: Berg, and Washington: Smithsonian Institution Press.

La Fontaine, J., 1985, *Initiation. Ritual Drama and Secret Knowledge across the World*. New York: Penguin Books.

Lan, D., 1985, *Guns and Rain: Guerillas and Spirit Mediums in Zimbabwe*. London: James Currey.

Lange, M.-F., 1999, *L'Ecole au Togo. Processus de Scolarisation et Institution de l'Ecole en Afrique*. Paris: Editions Karthala.

Leclerc-Madlala, S., 1997, "Infect One, Infect All: Zulu Youth Response to the AIDS Epidemic in South Africa", *Medical anthropology*, 17(4):363–80.

Lovell, N., 2002, *Cord of Blood: Possession and the Making of Voodoo*. London and Sterling (Virginia): Pluto Press.

Mair, L., 1970, "Cargo cults today. Letter with comments on R. Forster's article 'The cargo cults today'", *New Society*, 433.

—, 1958–59, "Independent Religious Movements in Three Continents", *Comparative Studies in Society and History*.

Mamdani, M., 1996, *Citizen and Subject: Contemporary Africa and the Legacy of Late Colonialism*. Princeton NJ: Princeton University Press.

Maupoil, B., 1981, *La Géomancie à l'Ancienne Côte des Esclaves*. Paris: Institut d'Ethnologie.

Mbembe, A., 1985, *Les Jeunes et l'Ordre Politique en Afrique Noire*. Paris: L'Harmattan.

Meyer, B., 1998, "'Make a Complete Break with the Past': Memory and Postcolonial Modernity in Ghanaian Pentecostal Discourse", in R. Werbner (ed.), *Memory and the Postcolony*. London and New Jersey: Zed Books.

Moran, M., 1988, "Women and "civilization": the intersection of gender and prestige in southeastern Liberia", *Canadian Journal of African Studies*, xxii(3):491–501.

—, 1990, Civilized women: gender and prestige in southeastern Liberia. Ithaca, NY: Cornell University Press.

Mullings, L., 1984, *Therapy, Ideology, and Social Change: Mental Healing in Urban Ghana*, Comparative Studies of Health Systems and Medical Care. Berkeley: University of California Press.

Ogden, J.A., 1996, "Producing' Respect: The 'Proper' Woman in Postcolonial Kampala", in R. Werbner and T. Ranger (eds), *Postcolonial Identities in Africa*. London and New Jersey: Zed Books.

Piot, C., 1999, *Remotely Global: Village Modernity in West Africa*. Chicago and London: The University of Chicago Press.

Preston Blier, S., 1995, *African Vodun: Art, Psychology and Power*. Chicago and London: The University of Chicago Press.

Richards, A., 1956, *Chisungu: A Girl's Initiation Ceremony among the Bemba of Zambia*. London and New York: Tavistock Publications.

Rivière, C., 1981, *Anthropologie Religieuse des Evé du Togo*. Paris: Les Nouvelles Editions Africaines.

Scheper-Hughes, N. and M. Lock, 1987, "The Mindful Body: a Prolegomenon to Future Work in Medical Anthropology", *Medical Anthropology Quarterly*, 1:6–41.

—, 1990, "A Critical Interpretive Approach in Medical Anthropology: Rituals and Routines of Discipline and Dissent", in T.M. Johnson and C.F. Sargent (eds.), *Medical Anthropology: Contemporary Theory and Method*. New York: Prager Publishers.

Shaw, R., 2002, *Memories of the Slave Trade: Ritual and the Historical Imagination in Sierra Leone*. Chicago: The University of Chicago Press.

Smith, S. and Glaser, A., 1992, *Ces Messieurs Afrique, vol. 1*. Paris: Calmann-Lévy.

—, 1997, *Ces Messieurs Afrique, vol. 2*. Paris, Calmann-Lévy.

Sommer, A., 1993. "Tradition and modernization in Africa today. Modern morans: Samburu warriors at the Kenyan coast", *Acta ethnographica Hungarica*, 38(1/3):331–40.

Spencer, P., 1965, *The Samburu: a Study of Gerontocracy in a Nomadic Tribe*. Berkeley: University of California Press.

—, 1990, *Anthropology and the Riddle of the Sphynx: Paradoxes of Change in the Life-Course*. London and New York: Routledge.

de Surgy, A., 1981, *Géomancie et le Culte d'Afa chez les Evhé*. Paris: Publications Orientalistes de France.

—, 1988, *Le Système Religieux des Evhé*. Paris: Editions l'Harmattan.

Taussig, M., 1987, *Shamanism, Colonialism and the Wild Man: a Study in Terror and Healing*. Chicago and London: The University of Chicago Press.

—, 1993, *Mimesis and Alterity: a Particular History of the Senses*. New York and London: Routledge.

—, 1997, *The Magic of the State*. New York and London: Routledge.

Toulabor, C., 1992a, "L'Enonciation du Pouvoir et de la Richesse chez les Jeunes "Conjoncturés" de Lomé, Togo", in J.-F. Bayart, A. Mbembe, and C. Toulabor (eds), *Le Politique par le Bas en Afrique Noire*. Paris: Karthala.

—, 1992b, "Jeu de Mots, Jeu de Vilains: Lexique de la Derision Politique au Togo", in J.-F. Bayart, A. Mbembe, and C. Toulabor (eds), *Le Politique par le Bas en Afrique Noire*. Paris: Karthala.

Turner, V., 1969, *The Ritual Process: Structure and Anti-Structure*. New York: Cornell University Press.

Utas, M. 2003, *Sweet Battlefields: Essays on Youth and the Liberian Civil War*, PhD Thesis. Uppsala: Dissertations in Cultural Anthropology (DiCa), Department of Cultural Anthropology and Ethnology, Uppsala University.

Verdier, R., 1982, *Le Pays Kabiyé: Cité des Dieux, Cité des Hommes*. Paris: Karthala.

Worsley, P., 1987, *The Trumpet Shall Sound*. New York: Schocken Publisher.

AFTERWORD

Afterword

Michael A. Whyte

We are in rural Uganda, an afternoon in 2002. A very small child – a baby of some four months – has been ill with a cough and fever. He is the first born and his parents have purchased medicine from the shops as well as trying grandmother's own herbal remedies. Now they have called a ritual specialist, a diviner with curative ability, who is trying to communicate with a spirit agent by encouraging the agent to possess the child's mother. In order to help her work along, the diviner is regularly given sips of locally distilled "hard stuff". People from nearby homes – mostly married women and children – have gathered to watch and to contribute advice. The scene is informal and relaxed. Respiratory illness kills small children in this part of Uganda, yet the baby is not too ill at the moment and there is no immediate crisis. The possession trance that the diviner is trying to induce is the first – and crucial – step in a cure; she seeks to communicate with a possible cause – a spirit twin who has gone unrecognized until now and is jealous and demanding.

Jasi, a young women from the larger family, stands apart, looking. She has lived in town for some years, where she completed most of her secondary schooling before dropping out. She attends a computer class for boarders at a nearby convent school, trying one more time to acquire skills and certificates useful in the "modern" world. I join her, and we watch proceedings that are at once entertainment and – for the distressed parents at the centre – deadly earnest. Jasi is a quiet one, not usually very easy to talk with. But suddenly she turns to me and says, with unaccustomed bitterness: "I hate these spirits – I don't want them in my life." Slowly we begin to talk. Do I believe such ceremonies can help a child? Jasi does not. "No", she adds, "I will *not* believe." She tells me about her computer course and her teachers, and how she prefers that world with its rules and certainties.

We are joined by Ronald, a young man of Jasi's age, a relative of Jasi's sister-in-law. Ronald and Jasi are both secondary school products, modern youth. We listen to Jasi, who is by now becoming more distressed by the ceremony and the impending approach of spirits. She repeats that she does not want them, that *she* chooses school and studies. Ronald, who works in the shop of his brother-in-law and is saving up to enter a teacher training college, watches with the detached interest of a young, unmarried man who cannot imagine that this particular scene could ever involve his life world. But Jasi turns back and forth, her body engaging and disengaging with the singing women and the chanting diviner.

Suddenly, the young mother rolls to the ground, shaking. The spirit twin has arrived. The diviner speaks with it, eliciting demands. Calm returns and the young mother collects herself and returns to her normal world. The diviner is tired and irritated by hours spent inducing a trance – and somewhat the worse for drink, she makes a list of requirements for the rest of the ceremony, to be held the next day. The spectators disperse and those from our home join us, bubbling with enthusiasm for a good show. We are swept up in a project of calling an absent sister who works far away and, luckily, we find a place where there is a mobile telephone network. Everyone, even Jasi, clamours to describe the ritual, laughing and commenting loudly about the wonders of modern life: using a mobile phone to describe the last stages of a possession ritual to an absent kinswoman.

* * *

Navigating Youth, Generating Adulthood: Social Becoming in an African Context has provided us with compelling ethnographic portraits from contemporary Africa. Beverly Grier has argued recently that children and youth, too long invisible in Africanist scholarship, must now be recognized as "actors who are not only shaped by their circumstances but who also help shape them" (2004). Social becoming and the concept of navigation resonate well with this goal. In what follows I unpack my simple story and connect Jasi and Ronald with some of the other young people and social situations in this book. I use Jasi and Ronald to suggest three analytical areas where the notion of "social becoming" is important to our understanding of African youth – and also for our appreciation of Africa today.

Youth, gender and navigation: Different compasses?

In normal parlance (and certainly in East Africa) "youth" refers to boys and young men from puberty until perhaps thirty years of age – and to girls from puberty to about 18 or 19. These "youth" have long been objects of attention from churches, educational establishments, donor programmes and even governments. Youth clubs, youth-in-the-community activities, young farmers' associations, church youth choirs, sports clubs and tournaments, youth wings of political associations.... these are just a few examples. Some programmes are specifically gender segregated and many are predominately or overwhelmingly devoted to boys. Girls seem to be in short supply in modern programmes open to both sexes where they may be considered to be a special category: "female youth". "Traditionally" girls have also been relatively scarce. The problem is categorical rather than demographic: female youth is – and has long been – scarce because girls become mothers and wives – and thus women – many years before their brothers and male cousins manage to marry and establish themselves as men. "Female youth" become women when they marry or, in many societies, when they deliver children; male youth become men when they are settled and accepted by the generation of *patres familiae* who are also their competition in the market for marriageable girls. Seku, from Guinea Bissau, complains that "Fathers want to be in control of their sons." He bemoans his prolonged youth and his continuing dependence: "I want to be a man of respect, a complete man, complete... I want to have my own house, children, a wife" (Vigh, this volume, chapter 1). Girls in the meantime become mothers and even wives.

Navigating youth is gendered youth – and at least in Africa it is preponderantly male. Jasi as a twenty-something young woman, unmarried and with no children, at home and making a fresh start with schooling is still what schooled Ugandans call "female youth" – but only just. Although the same age as Ronald, she is rapidly becoming old. Most of her generation are married, or at least "settled" away from their natal homes, yet Jasi is still home, still a "daughter".

Ronald, on the other hand, is a clearly recognized "youth" – a status that he entered at puberty and where he will remain for some years, until marriage, paternity and a degree of domestic independence are established. Navigating male youth is here a matter of "detachability". Ronald – like many of the young man is this volume – has temporarily "detached" himself from his own local home and is here looking for a pathway to adulthood ("hoping to find something" is his phrase). This is normal and even expected. Later, in some years and if all goes well, he will re-attach himself, returning home to build a house where he may live with wife and children. Here at least Ronald is lucky. In rural Uganda, there still tends to be paternal land, a place to be, a place to return to.

In patrilineal and largely patrilocal Uganda, female youth become women, wives and mothers in other homes. Or at least they should. Jasi, hanging on to female youth and natal home, is in an anomalous position – and shows us that navigation can also involve immobility! Boehm's Lesotho, provides another example of "immobile" young women, at home because they can find neither a husband nor a well-paying job.

In my vignette, Ronald and Jasi are caught in an ethnographic instant. Ronald's *youth* stretches out ahead of him, a life-space for manoeuvre and planning. Marriage, paternity, responsibility are very much part of a future that is still some years away and the events of the afternoon are simply "interesting." Jasi's female youth is drawing to a close and with it her own space for manoeuvre. School, computers, Christianity shape a world that – for the moment – allows her to explore other social selves. The spirits that she "does not want in her life" may nonetheless catch her. Ronald is navigating towards a future that may be difficult to achieve but is at least "on the chart" – a known harbour. Jasi, like many young women, is caught up in a journey both fraught and commonplace. As a girl, a sister, a youth she has been able to mobilize support from family and even from some of her institutional connections. As a woman, things will be more difficult. Motherhood will involve Jasi with the responsibilities of parenthood, perhaps single parenthood; marriage will mean a husband and a mother-in-law, domesticity, children, being detached from her home and re-attached to a social world whose new limitations are at once compelling and distressing.

While female youth, strictly conceived, still contrasts with youth, the navigations of young women have clearly changed. In this volume, Christian Boehm (chapter 5) draws on material from Lesotho and connects the several navigations of a modern family: husband and wife, sons and daughters. Without the anchor of a job in the mines, the financial independence that marriage requires is less easily achieved, with clear consequences for young men and women. And even within established families, husbands and fathers have been retired or made redundant, forcing a reshaping of intra-family responsibility. Daughters have become wage earners – and mothers – yet still remain at home, unable to find a husband, unwilling to accept a casual union. Clearly, young Basotho women are navigating as never before, but while their compass north was once a mineworker, today multiple orientations are being explored.

Navigating Youth, Generating Adulthood shows us that the time when "female youth" could be perceived as a kind of social glue re-connecting male youth to development cycles, household responsibility and geronto-cratic order has passed. Africa is changing – in the spirit of the book, youth are changing Africa – and even though young and detached men make more of a show, I suspect that it is the navigation of young women that is at the roots of much that can be called "new social becoming." Their roles – and their interactions with husbands, brothers and fathers – need to be better understood. Traditionally young women have been even less able to move from categorical significance to collective action than their brothers, but despite small wars and the political use of sexual violence, things here may also be changing. I am left with two questions:

1. Christine Obbo has written about the ways in which navigating women were quietly exploring alternatives to marriage, and in so doing reshaping gender systems in Uganda Obbo (Obbo 1980). Some thirty years on, I wonder if the strategies of young women are still so threatening to patriarchal order?

2. More and more young men seem unable to find the economic security needed for marriage. It is clear that, for their "fathers" and "grandfathers", promoting the progression of their offspring from youth to culturally accepted manhood is no longer always possible. Is it perhaps the case that patriarchal norms and structures are being transformed, that re-attaching the next generation of males no longer has the same social priority?

Christianity and the spirits: Scylla and Charibdis on the road to adulthood

In their introduction, Christiansen, Utas and Vigh point out that youth has become a focus for donors, NGOs and humanitarian organizations and that, increasingly, this attention is phrased in terms of the discourse of entitlement. "Youth" – the quotation marks remind us that here we are dealing with a discourse, see The Anti-Politics Machine (Ferguson 1990), are defined chronologically and their entitlements are phrased in universalist, developmental terms: the right to education, physical security, economic opportunity. The pattern is clearly taken from more established discourses about "the rights of the child." The new "Youth" discourse, backed by programmes and money, seeks to assist a category that donor activity has itself created.[1]

The studies in this volume all demonstrate that another youth can be discovered, one that is connected with, yet not subsumed by the Northern, humanitarian discourse. These youth are the navigators, and their strategies and actions, their different practices, both shape and reflect diverse and specific social conditions. They are caught up in webs of kinship obligation (from which they sometimes seek to flee). Tronde Waage's street children (chapter 2), living by their wits, continue to create social systems that are too precariously rooted to persist; Ruth Prince's Luo youth (chapter 4) sing with nostalgia, but also with irony, of the confusion of values and actions that is killing the land and its people. Personalized and parochial values expressed through kin and neighbourhood interaction, through participation in life crisis rituals, provide a framework for action. Experience with the pragmatics of everyday life however will itself vary greatly; the poor, orphans, perhaps also many girls and young women, may have few social skills to draw upon. Almost by definition, youth will lack social and cultural and economic capital.

Youth navigations are – at least initially – local journeys, embedded in the specific. But the specific is not simply a matter of an "African" tradition. The discourses – and even some of the institutions – that make up "civil society" and reflect the entitlements it promises, are also there at the beginning of the journey. For many decades, African young people have grown up within institutions – schools, churches and mosques – that promote global and universal values. They have been treated by biomedicine, they have cheered national football teams, some – like Sverker Finnström's Acoli youth (chapter 7), have participated in international humanitarian actions. Young people these days, like their elders, live also in a *local* world shaped by global and universalist values, by experiences gained in schools and churches and workplaces. Navigating the pathway to adulthood means making use of local charts *and* GPS. However, and this is what I wish to emphasize here, navigation is not simply arriving, by any route. If we are to avoid, as we certainly should, reducing youth to "economic youth" then we must also make room for values, style, individual preferences. Hamadou,

---

1. This donor interest may be recent, but "youth" have long been of interest in economic and political development contexts. Youth clubs such as 4H, the Scouting movement, the YMCA/YWCA and other church fellowships, and of course organized sports, all reflect the Northern interest in "youth" that dates back to the beginning of the post-colonial era, if not before.

in Trond Waage's account from Cameroon, has left the school he could not manage and now sits at home, with dignity, associating as much as possible with learned, respected men (chapter 2).

Scylla and Charibdis, we remember, are the monsters that lay in wait for mariners navigating the Straits of Messina. Avoiding one, as Ulysses discovered to his cost, can lead you too close to the other. Successful navigation takes account of both, avoiding the perils of each. Hamadou, a young man at home, continues to navigate between local, parochial values and a localized, yet universalist, world of learning. For Jasi, a young woman in a patrilineal society, sitting at home "with dignity" is more difficult. When she tells me that she hates the "things of spirits" I interpret this in parochial-universalist terms: it is not the spirits as such that she hates, but rather the uncertain, complex and contingent domestic world in which they can exist. Female youth like Jasi may well feel that they must take greater care to avoid the Scylla of domesticity and choosing computer courses and Christianity may amount to rejecting a set of choices, symbolized by the "things of spirits", that lead on to a life-world where a woman's entitlement is never secure. Jasi's problem, shared with many of her fellow youth, is that her universalist qualifications are almost certainly not enough to keep her afloat and Scylla always threatens. (For the young mother who became possessed, the ceremony we watched is of course an expression of agency and responsibility in the face of possibly life-threatening illness. Scylla is not always a monster.)

Navigating Youth, Generating Adulthood is about journeys made through a space made up of competing claims and value systems. The space itself is generally examined from the point of view of a youthful actor who is caught, enmeshed in *dubriagem*, unable to move on to adult life. Certainly there are contradictions in this space, not least Vigh's description (chapter 1) of the continuum from the personalistic claims of kinship through patrimonialism to warlordism (and, one might add, the universalistic, the "rational," pretensions of organizations). Attention in this volume is generally fixed on the young agents as *acting subjects*, a choice that proves to be ethnographically strategic in many respects. These young people are moving, acting and making choices – and sometimes, as Jasi's outburst shows us, the choices are hard. Vigh, citing de Certeau, reminds us that navigation is "centred both on the near and the far" (chapter 1). It is important not to reduce the agency of youth to a mere response to immediate social contradictions – a matter of continuous coping strategies. It is also useful to explore from time to time "the near and the far", the meanings and values that navigation between a particular Scylla or Charibdis expresses.

A donor focus on youth is problematic in another sense. In the chapters in this volume, navigating youth are regularly placed within a larger network of social roles and relationships. We meet youth in same-generation relationships and contexts, with mates and school-mates. But we also meet youth interacting with proximate generations and other authority figures – fathers and mothers, teachers and even employers. A gendered and a generational space is marked out because, put simply, much of the business of youth is shown to be carried out in relation to adults. Navigating youth is also youth positioned in respect to specific adults and the "rights of youth" need to be understood in relation to the understandings and indeed the navigations of adults

This is an important, and at times overlooked observation, and one that can usefully be pursued. A case in point is provided by a Ugandan anthropologist, looking critically at the results of the first programme cycle of Universal Primary Education in her country. She sees the failures of many children in the system as, at least in part, the failures of parents – and of a child-focused system to reach parents. "You must learn to be the parent of an educated child" she argues. "You do not give the child to the school and go your way." Yet this is what seems to be happening. Youth (and children) become national resources, NGOs and advocates demand entitlements, and too few look carefully at the range of generational inter-relationships that must be articulated to manage a transition to socially and economically meaningful adulthood.

Navigation, intimacy and (e)scape

Johannes Fabian has famously argued that "... relations between the West and its Other, between anthropology and its object, were conceived not only as difference but as distance in space *and* time." (1983:147 italics in original) He continues:

> "What are opposed, in conflict, in fact, ...are not the same societies at different stages of development, but different societies facing each other at the same time." (1983:155)

This picture of different facing different at a point in time is important. Fabian himself introduces the concept of "coevalness", insisting that those whom we study are not our *past* but rather our *now*, part of our temporal world, just as we are part of theirs. The point is especially relevant for studies of young people in Africa, where Northern agendas and discourses, as we have seen, risk introducing an unreflected element of social evolution. Differences in values, in practices, in opportunities are subtly – and blatantly – transformed into difference in time: the rights of the child are *not yet* generally accepted, universal entitlements will be recognized *in future*... They are different because they are *"at a different stage of development"*.

The implicit denial of coevalness is one of Fabian's enduring insights. It pervades (perhaps "naturally"?) much development discourse (*we*, the North, have nothing to do with the political, economic even ecological conditions in which *their societies* find themselves). It is also easily – and perhaps paradoxically – to be found in that part of NGO and donor discourse where humanitarian imperatives weigh heaviest. The absolute right to demand, to command obedience to a particular definition of rights-based entitlements – as Alex de Waal argued in *Famine Crimes* (1997) – is inherently undemocratic, a framework for not hearing the contemporary Other. When Northern discourses on youth are framed in universalistic terms the policy that is promoted risks paying scant regard to social and cultural difference.

The contributors to *Navigating Youth, Generating Adulthood* have chosen another route. The dilemmas of real people that this book takes up involve us intimately in the connections "between the West and its Other" that structure navigation and engender adulthood. In their introduction, Christiansen, Utas and Vigh (see Introduction) argue the need to understand African youth both conceptually – as a scape – and also as movements – escapes. The chapters themselves make an additional point: exploring the ways in which *scapes* and *escapes* are linked to the intimacy of the local and to the acts and policies of the dominant North.

This sort of linkage has, of course, a prehistory. In the 1950s and 1960s, Max Gluckman and his colleagues (in particular Clyde Mitchell and A. L. Epstein) engaged in an important debate about migration and cultural tradition that is worth revisiting (Gluckman 1961). Opposing those who argued that many of the institutions created by urban migrants were attempts to preserve tribal practices, they argued that the "Tribesmen" of rural Northern Rhodesia, when entering the city or the workplace, become "Townsmen." They operate, navigate, within an urban or industrial space, a social field with new rules. Should they return home, they return to a set of relationships that define them – re-define them – in "tribal" terms. Individuals navigate, make choices, and pursue strategies and interests in relation to the social fields (Gluckman spoke of "sociological relations") in which they find themselves. As actors, they must be studied and understood in space and in time – where they are and also when they are.

Intimacy – which is not a particularly Manchester concept – is nonetheless relevant here. Town immigrants (like migrating children and youth) live and navigate in an intimate present, peopled with friends and enemies, kin and strangers and "urban tribesmen." The particular temporal dimensions of these specific intimate life worlds became the stuff of extended case methodology for the Manchester School, revealing new ways to conceive of social structures. This agenda, with its evident colonial connections, is no longer wholly appropriate, but their critique of a "tribalistic" anthropology still rings true (Gluckman 1961). The parallel with navigating youth lies elsewhere, not in new models of social structures but in techniques for linking the specific agendas of (positioned) social actors with the specific places and contexts where actors find themselves. The mine compound or the textile factory, the room in a courtyard in an urban slum, the verandah where street children sleep – these intimate settings are the spaces and the times where social action is meaningful.

Fabian uses unrecognized coevalness to develop a critique of anthropological practice and western scholarship; Gluckman and his colleagues are also concerned with unrecognized use coevalness to develop a more specific analytical position about social situations in time and space. They argued for an anthropology focused in the present, the immediate now, and to some extent they succeeded in achieving their goal, in focusing attention on the intimate *present* rather than the tribal *past*. The notion of "social becoming," it seems to me, can be traced back to this enterprise.

A final point. Gluckman's oft-cited dictum that "...the starting point of our analysis of tribalism in towns is not that it is manifested by tribesmen, but that it is manifested by townsmen" (1961) can still inspire good ethnography. But there are issues. *Navigating Youth, Generating Adulthood* lays much emphasis on agency and social and physical movement. The Introduction states: "As the different chapters of this book will illuminate, young people are thus on the lookout for both social paths and social escapes." In other words, young people look to the future, they imagine new possibilities and new places. Their lived worlds are not simply the town, the now of a job on the street or a career as a political novelist (see Lovell, chapter 8). A focus on actors and navigators would seem to demand that we look further than the immediate social field or the encompassing "sociological relations" deployed by Gluckman. If we believe in navigation, then actors do choose, do remove themselves from some sociological situations – and sometimes they even attempt to transform situations radically (or at least to support those who claim to be able to do so). Agency and navigation all demand memory and a sense of biography. Memory and hope are key elements of agency. And if this is so, then the tribesman who goes to town and comes home again, seen as an agent, has the history of the journey, has experience to draw on.

The Manchester argument was against an image of Africa caught up with the tribal past, a world of essentially tribalized identities. Thorsen's contribution gets to the heart of the oversimplification inherent in this debate (chapter 3). Her migrating children have tribal identifications and cultural expectations of appropriate behaviour. But they move with biographies and autobiographies, hopes for future identities in imagined adult worlds. At work they may behave like workers (a point that Grier also makes) putting aside earlier and now inappropriate social behaviour, yet they very clearly do not passively accept their conditions of labour. Their navigations are directed by visions of self that were not realized in their immediate social worlds – but were nonetheless shaped in those worlds.

Navigation, as we have seen in the ethnographies that make up *Navigating Youth, Generating Adulthood,* surely begins from a here and now which must be recognized from the outset. But navigation is also about changing narratives, rooted in a sense of the past as well as a search for a future. "Social becoming," as a corollary of navigation, expresses nicely processes that are played out in real time and, simultaneously, in the imaginations of young people.

References

Fabian, J., 1983, *Time and the Other: How Anthropology Makes Its Object.* New York: Columbia University Press.

Ferguson, J., 1990, *The Anti-Politics Machine: "Development," Depoliticization, and Bureaucratic Power in Lesotho.* Cambridge: Cambridge University Press.

Gluckman, M., 1961, "Anthropological problems arising from the African industrial revolution", in A. Southall, *Social Change in Modern Africa*, pp 67–82. London, New York: Oxford University Press.

Grier, B., 2004, "Child labor and Africanist scholarship: A critical overview", *African Studies Review*, 47(2):1–25.

Obbo, C., 1980, *African women: Their struggle for economic independence.* London, Zed Press.

de Waal, A., 1997, *Famine crimes: Politics and the disaster relief industry in Africa.* Oxford: African Rights & the International African Institute in association with Oxford: James Currey and Indiana University Press.

Contributors

Christian Boehm holds a Ph.D. in social anthropology from the University of Copenhagen in Denmark. He conducted applied research within the fields of migrant labour and agrarian change in Lesotho between 1998 and 2002. He is currently working for the Danish Refugee Council within the context of humanitarian aid in East Africa.

Catrine Christiansen is a research fellow at the University of Copenhagen. Her current research addresses links between religion, HIV/AIDS, and youth in Uganda. She has worked and published on issues of faith, development, sociality, childcare and health. She was as a researcher at the Nordic Africa Institute 2002–2005.

Jónina Einarsdóttir is Associate Professor in anthropology at the University of Iceland. Her main research fields are anthropology of children, medical anthropology and development studies. Einarsdóttir has fieldwork experience from Guinea-Bissau (1993-98) on which she based her book Tired of Weeping. Mother Love, Child Death and Poverty (2004).

Sverker Finnström received a Ph.D. in anthropology from the University of Uppsala with the thesis Living with Bad Surroundings: War and Existential Uncertainty in Acholiland, Northern Uganda (2003). He has published widely in international peer-reviewed journals. His current research focuses on the state and the nation as imagined and experienced by young Ugandans in the diaspora and 'at home'.

Nadia Lovell received her Ph.D. from the School of Oriental and African Studies, the University of London. Her research focuses on issues of gender, religion, ethnicity and power. She has conducted research in Togo and Ghana among the Ewe people and more recently in Cuba. She has published Locality and Belonging (1998) and Cord of Blood (2002).

Ruth Prince received her Ph.D. in anthropology from the University of Copenhagen, Denmark. She has performed extensive ethnographic research among the Luo people in Western Kenya and published in international peer-reviewed journals on Christianity, tradition, kinship, and social reproduction in the context of HIV/AIDS.

Dorte Thorsen has a doctoral degree from the University of Sussex, UK and is currently a research fellow at the Nordic Africa Institute. She has carried out extensive fieldwork in Burkina Faso on topics such as gender, intra-household economies, rural livelihoods, migration, child and youth identities and methodological questions related to the notion of agency.

Mats Utas is a researcher at the Nordic Africa Institute and senior lecturer at Fourah Bay College, Sierra Leone. He has a Ph.D. in cultural anthropology from the University of Uppsala from 2003 and has since then published numerous journal articles and book chapters on youth, violent conflict, gender and media. He has conducted fieldwork in Ivory Coast, Liberia, and Sierra Leone.

Henrik E. Vigh holds a Ph.D. in anthropology from the University of Copenhagen. Based on research on issues of youth and conflict in both Europe and Africa he developed the concept of social navigation. He is currently researching undocumented West African migrants in Europe and the networks they depend on, develop and in which they are caught up.

Trond Waage is an Associate Professor at the Visual Culture Studies Centre at the University of Tromsø, Norway. He has been working on youth related issues in both Norway and in Cameroon. His Ph.D. dissertation with related films focuses on the social processes within seven youth milieus in urban Cameroon.

Michael Whyte is Associate Professor at the Institute of Anthropology, the University of Copenhagen. He has carried out long-term ethnographic research in eastern Uganda and western Kenya on kinship, language, food security, agricultural and economic change and HIV/AIDS. His publications include *Children's children: Time and relatedness in eastern Africa* (2004).

Index